Literacy Theory in the Age of the Internet

Literacy Theory in the Age of the Internet

Edited by Todd Taylor and Irene Ward

COLUMBIA UNIVERSITY PRESS NEW YORK

Columbia University Press
Publishers Since 1893
New York   Chichester, West Sussex
Copyright © 1998 Columbia University Press

Library of Congress Cataloging-in-Publication Data
Literacy theory in the age of the Internet / edited by Todd Taylor and
    Irene Ward.
        p.   cm.
    Includes bibliographical references and index.
    ISBN 0–231–11330–7 (case : alk. paper). — ISBN 0–231–11331–5
(paper)
        1. Computers and literacy—United States. 2. English language—
Rhetoric—Computer-assisted instruction. 3. Internet (Computer
network) in education—United States. 4. Language arts—United
States—Computer-assisted instruction. 5. Educational innovations—
United States. I. Taylor, Todd W. II. Ward, Irene, 1950–   .
    LC149.5.L49   1998
    302.2'244—dc21
                                                                98–21549

Casebound editions of Columbia University Press books
are printed on permanent and durable acid-free paper.
Designed by Chang Jae Lee
Printed in the United States of America
c 10 9 8 7 6 5 4 3 2 1
p 10 9 8 7 6 5 4 3 2 1

To Max and Erin

Contents

Foreword/Forward (Into Electracy)

Gregory Ulmer

The syntax of the title of this book binds together three terms—literacy, theory, the Internet—whose unstable relationships are explored in the essays that follow. The collection as a whole may serve as a benchmark for measuring the shifts and movements within the disciplines devoted to writing. My purpose in this foreword is to sketch some of the historical and theoretical contexts for the issues addressed in the essays, with the caveat that my frame is not necessarily acceptable to all the authors gathered here. Rather, I offer it as an explanation for why I admire this book. Thomas Kuhn demonstrated how paradigms form around certain key problems and their prototypical solutions. One of the paradigm-forming problematics of our moment concerns our response to the new electronic technologies developing within our civilization. With the advent of the Internet these technologies have achieved a critical mass, one of whose effects is the exposure of the relativity of literacy. The material condition of the problematic is simply this: the computer is in the classroom, and we are asked to teach students how to write with it. What is to be done?

The question is posed from within the current moment. We ask ourselves, each one of us individually—the authors in this volume and many others besides—how we should help our students learn to live and thrive in this postindustrial information age. The tone of the question may vary, similar on one end of the scale to that of scientists dealing with ozone depletion, scenarios for avoiding collisions with asteroids, and other catastrophes, to the other end, where the tone resembles that of poor folks hoping to win the lottery. Yet though we ask the question individually, we look to our disciplines, our various fields of expertise, to find an answer.

Yes, I am using *we* and offering a vision of the circumstances given to us in order to provide a frame for the choices and commitments made by these professionals. The circumstances relate to the point where our disciplines are anchored in the institution of education. We know that "discipline" refers to an institution in its own right, distinct from "school." Hence the conflicts over research and teaching that mark the frontier where the two institutions attempt to coexist uneasily, like cattlemen and sheepherders on the prairies of old. "English" as a discipline is a recent phenomenon, and an absurd one at that, whose delimitations are to the full range of language what "Poland" is to the history of Europe (and think of the way the borders of Poland have fluctuated over the centuries).

Nonetheless, this Poland of writing is a large country with a glorious ancestry traceable to ancient Greece and providing a desirable buffer between high school and practical majors in the sciences and professions. As a service course in general education, English is a nearly universal requirement. Remove this requirement, and the state collapses. Or does it? Our colleagues in the other divisions of knowledge have been supportive of requirements in English and the humanities. Until recently this support was due largely to assumptions about humanism. Our colleagues honored the contribution of humanism to the Enlightenment traditions that made science thinkable. Whatever went on behind the closed doors of the literature major, general education in writing was believed to prepare students in three broadly defined areas: (1) *specialized learning*—the language of instruction in every field depends on the ability to write, meaning the ability to transform information into knowledge using the practices of literacy (library research, analytical thinking, outlining, paragraphing, argumentation, the essay genre); (2) *citizenship*—a free society depends on critical thinking and rhetorical skill to recognize the difference between a true and a false argument, whether in politics or all manner of propaganda produced in whatever form or medium; (3) *self-knowledge*—the humanistic credo argues that the unexamined life is not worth living and that mastery of written language of the sort found in literature is the highest expression of what it is to be human: that which paves the high road to self-knowledge.

But what happens to these responsibilities in the era of electronic media? Given the positivistic and utilitarian tendencies of our society, it is not surprising that other divisions of knowledge have always felt some ambivalence toward us. The current version of this ambivalence may be seen in the simultaneous recognition in the sciences that the humanities are no longer humanist (and this is a reason to abandon us) and that the time has come to bring general education in writing into the era of advanced computing (the need for general education in computing arises from the same reasons motivating general education in aid of literacy). Who should teach this computeracy if not "English"?

The present volume is addressed to this particular moment and condition, for in bringing together literacy, theory, and the Internet a number of disparate issues come into focus. We ask what is to be done and in looking for answers we behave as any discipline behaves: we apply our methods and theories to the problem at hand. Our domain in its modern configuration acquired a theoretical dimension only in the past three decades. Theory introduced into arts and letters the movements of cultural studies, the postcolonial, identity politics, multiculturalism. When considered outside the contexts of literacy and technology, the debates of the culture wars make little sense to colleagues and to the general population (or, worse, are held against us as a kind of Jacobin "political correctness"). When reviewed within the history of writing (grammatology), however, the story is different.

What is this different story? It depends on which theories one chooses to work with, given that facts are always relative to theories. Jay Bolter among others has argued that poststructuralist theory is to the Internet what cognitive science has been to artificial intelligence: there is a synergistic fit between the theory and the technology in both cases. Any theory may be applied to the problematic of literacy, but poststructuralism has the most to offer. That claim, however, is now falsifiable in the laboratory of quotidian computing. Here is the challenge to our discipline: the society as a whole, and education in particular, have committed to a new apparatus. We look to our theories for the design of experiments, to create practices for all the needs of storage and retrieval of an information society. The pressure to act comes from the society and is ignored at our own risk. One choice is business as usual (the computer as an extremely efficient way to do the work of literacy, just as the alphabet was an extremely efficient way to memorize an epic). Alternatively, if poststructuralism is incapable of generating effective new practices, it will be consigned to the archives of history along with many other fads and fallacies.

The different story poses questions about the connection between identity politics or multiculturalism and the electronic apparatus. *Apparatus* in this sense refers to the social machine organizing language use in a civilization. We became self-conscious about the nature of the language apparatus only recently (the best introduction to this discovery is Eric Havelock's *The Muse Learns to Write*). Havelock and other grammatologists argued that we rediscovered the shift from orality to literacy precisely because we are moving out of literacy. The shift under way in our own moment thus becomes intelligible through this commonplace analogy with previous changes of technology. A closer examination of this analogy, however, shows that a language apparatus includes more than just the technology (such as the alphabet to record speech, or the camera to record visual images). It also includes the invention of a new institution with methods for using the new technology. Plato founded the first school and produced the first discourse on method to be used to explore the full possibilities of the apparatus. The implication, if we are to be true heirs of this foundation, is that we must pose to ourselves the same question posed by the classical Greeks. The analogy suggests that our purpose should not be to continue the practices invented specifically in the context of alphabetic literacy, but to find what is specific to the new recording instruments, to develop our own equivalents of the Academy, philosophy, and method.

Moreover, there is one more dimension to the apparatus. Grammatology also shows that the formation of identity in terms of "selfhood" is specific to the experience of literacy. The feeling of being a "self"—the ghost experienced inside for the first time instead of outside as a visitation from a god—and the behaviors that resulted from this feeling are as much a part of the invention of writing as the equipment and the institution. Now we know what the debates over identity politics are about, coming from our newly acquired theories. The "ghost" is leaving "me" again, mutating, certainly not into a god but neither any longer is it a self. We are fully within areas of controversy now. Literacy? Is it a humanistic concept whose persistence beyond its proper apparatus produces nothing but paradoxes and contradictions? To speak of computer literacy or media literacy may be an attempt to remain within the apparatus of alphabetic writing that has organized the Western tradition for nearly the past three millennia. To what extent is using the computer to teach argumentative writing of a piece with a politics that raises humanistic selfhood to a universal and eternal value? What about the feminist charge that just when women and other groups subordinated within patriarchy claimed the status of full selfhood, the (male) theorists abandoned it as a value?

A new name such as *electracy* helps to distinguish this epochal possibility that what is at stake is not only different equipment but also different institutional practices and different subject formations from those we now inhabit. This much the theory shows us, even if theory is not "cause," not determinism, but a guide for action. Poststructuralist theory of grammatology shows us the scale and scope of our problematic. It is not a matter of taste: whether one does or does not honor and love the achievements of literature, the greatness of our nation, the rights of individuals. It is not a matter of whether these qualities are in flux, but to what degree we have any influence in shaping the outcome.

Whatever approach one takes, the imperative is that the questions be posed holistically, taking into account not only the theory of the apparatus but also the three justifications for general education in writing: the pragmatics of specialized method, citizenship, and identity. If we isolate any one of these dimensions on either side (theory and practice), the debates are reduced to nonsense: there is no way to tell whose arguments might provide the best guides for living. In specialized knowledge we feel the utilitarian pressures of our colleagues who still want us to teach literate arguments and only literate arguments; in citizenship we feel the nationalist pressures to teach "American" values or Western traditions only; in identity formation we feel ethical pressure to promote selfhood. And why not, in each case, since school is literacy, and these are the features of the literate apparatus? At the same time, our theory (i.e., the one specific to the humanities disciplines) shows us a history in which these sacred properties of literacy are relative to a specific apparatus. What is to be done? It is a time for experiment and invention. *Literacy Theory in the Age of the Internet* is a good introduction to how we might take up this challenge.

Introduction

Todd Taylor and Irene Ward

Have networked, computerized environments and the Internet changed literacy and the teaching of literacy? Yes and no. Regardless of whether we can accurately talk in terms of a significant change, we can say that *something* changed, some people are using new writing tools in new environments. In the 1990s the number of Internet users began to double or triple annually; current levels are estimated at thirty to forty million users worldwide (Elmer-DeWitt 9). In June 1993, the World Wide Web comprised a mere 130 sites; by June 1996 there were 252,000; by August 1997 there were 1,269,000 (Zakon). The number of host computers connected to the Internet grew from 159,000 in late 1989 to 9,472,000 in January 1996 to 19,540,000 in July 1997 (Lottor). In January 1989, when Arpanet (the predecessor to the Internet) was being phased out, the NSF backbone (the core of the Internet) was carrying 39 million packets of information monthly; in January 1995, Internet traffic had increased to more than 165 million packets *daily* (Merit). Most important for literacy theory, most of the information suddenly flying back and forth was not just data; it was electronic discourse: digitized written words. Instructional use of email increased in this period from almost nothing to being used in one out of every four or five courses (reported in Deloughry). During the 1996 presidential campaign, Bill Clinton promoted national Internet access in the same breath as he cited the ability to read a book as being an important part of his vision for the schoolchildren of the twenty-first century. URLs popped up seemingly

overnight on print and television advertisements, at first a strange and mysterious code decipherable only by the Internet savvy but soon enough a natural
part of the media landscape.

Change or not, it's safe to say that from 1990 to 1995 *Internet* suddenly became a household word. A word, it's important to point out, with no rough
equivalent or similar connotation to any other word; it isn't as if the Internet replaced something else in the popular vernacular, as when the latest tune re-
places a predecessor at the top of the charts. We are left therefore with the task
of trying to assess and respond to the Internet and other kinds of networked
computerized environments. And for all we know, greater changes may lie in
the future.

Literacy theorists will need some time to reestablish their bearings and re-
situate notions of literacy given the sudden reality of a networked world and
electronic texts. In *The Electronic Word*, Richard Lanham asks, "What does this
new medium do to us and for us? We ask this in a deep way only when the new
medium reveals what profound effects the old one has had on us." He goes on
to predict that electronic text will create "not only new writing space, but a new
educational space as well. Not only the humanities curriculum, but school and
university structures, administrative and physical, are affected at every point"
(xii). Undoubtedly, we will need additional research, both theoretical and empirical, in order to understand these changes more fully. We hope that this collection is a contribution in that direction.

Instead of being frustrated by the disorientation brought on by such
changes, we suggest that teachers and researchers embrace the current uncer-
tainty and theoretical disarray as the most reasonable way to negotiate new notions of literacy as they appear on the horizon. Consequently, if the authors in
this collection seem, at times, distinctly outlandish (from some strange place
with different notions of literacy), it is because they have chosen explicitly to
reimagine literacy from outside conventional thought. Nevertheless, these authors aren't aliens or cyborgs. They don't reside primarily in cyberspace or teach
at Virtual U. They are flesh-and-bone teacher-scholars who, much like everyone
else, are primarily concerned with helping the students that they meet (mostly
face-to-face) improve their capacities for reading, writing, and critical thinking.
They are teachers and writing program directors just like those we hope will
read this book. The result is that this book is also very much about the material realities faced by literacy teachers, especially in terms of the politics of instructional technology.

Literacy Theory in the Age of the Internet is concerned with the politics of technology and education. As a whole, the collection argues that teachers, adminis-

trators, politicians, parents, and students alike should join together to break the repeating cycle of past mistakes in which instructional technology has been used in dubious ways for questionable purposes. Several of the chapters suggest novel ways to solve some of the complex issues that we all face.

Computer technologies currently present significant possibilities for improving education, but too often these have gone unrealized. For instance, many view computer technology as a means to enhance lectures through more sophisticated visual aids and to automate delivery. Such approaches may be valuable in some cases; however, they tend to suppress the potential of computer networks to improve communicative interaction among students, teachers, and even texts, interactions that are fundamental in most contemporary visions of literacy and literacy instruction.

Some of the following chapters explore new kinds of writing and writing situations, while others discuss innovative and progressive approaches to literacy theory, particularly those made possible by networked computers and Internet technologies such as email, MUDs (Multi-User Domains), MOOs (Multi-User Object-Oriented Domains), and the World Wide Web. While the authors in this collection identify a number of political obstacles to the effective application of literacy technologies, probably the most significant barrier we all face has been a perceived technoliteracy crisis. Some who have analyzed the history of writing instruction in the United States have identified the mid-1970s *Newsweek* article "Why Johnny Can't Write" as the most recognizable articulation of a perceived literacy crisis in this country. An almost identical phenomenon can be identified relating to computer literacy. Like the *Newsweek* article, a 1986 report from the Carnegie Commission gives voice to a perceived crisis: "Advancing technology and the changing terms of international trade are remolding the basic structure of international economic competition. We believe [educational systems] must be rebuilt to match drastic changes needed in our economy if we are to prepare our children for productive lives in the 21st century" (qtd. in Barton and Ray 280). In chapter 10, Tim Mayers and Kevin Swafford examine the Carnegie report and the cultural anxiety it reflects. Misapplication of instructional technology can be largely attributed to the crisis-oriented, uncritical rush to place computers in schools in order to keep up, apparently, not only with competing schools but also with competing nations. To date, not enough effort has been invested in making sure that educational institutions are "rebuilt" in ways that support effective pedagogy. Classroom teachers and educational researchers must actively determine what works, which theories should hold sway, and what should be done. More of us need to move ahead of the technology curve.

Our call to action is, of course, a tall order, one that is certainly beyond the scope of any scholarly book. In fact, this call to action does not even begin with *Literacy Theory in the Age of the Internet* but at least as far back as the mid-1980s, in books such as Cynthia Selfe's *Creating a Computer-Supported Writing Facility: A Blueprint for Action* and Gail Hawisher and Cynthia Selfe's edited collection *Critical Perspectives on Computers and Composition Instruction*. The community of online scholars and teachers has since adopted a critical and explicitly antiutopian perspective on instructional technology. We hope that this collection will reinforce and extend what these leaders have been saying for over a decade.

Unfortunately, such reinforcements seem more necessary now than ever. Political pressures to computerize are anything but subsiding. Public fascination with online technologies has reached a fever pitch, and, at the same time, educational budgets are shrinking, meaning that administrators will be more tempted to solve the problem of more students and less money by looking to automate the delivery of educational services instead of improving them. Shrinking budgets also mean that less time and money is available to train teachers in the theories and skills necessary to make them effective in ever-changing electronic environments, and, unfortunately, lack of teacher training is already at the top of the list of reasons why technology is often misapplied. Undoubtedly, difficult decisions need to be made and will be made; perhaps this collection will help make those decisions more informed than in the past.

It seems that volumes of scholarship such as that contained in *Literacy Theory in the Age of the Internet* will be required to address all the issues involved. The specific motivation to produce this collection has been to encourage those who teach writing at all levels to intervene in recently invented spaces such as the Internet, email, synchronous chat programs (*Daedalus*, MOOs, MUDs, IRCs, etc.), and the World Wide Web so that teachers and students will determine the possibilities for these potentially groundbreaking and dialogic sites instead of having others do so for them. Teachers and scholars can, of course, answer this call to action and work to shape these spaces through a variety of means. Refusing to take a back seat in local decision-making forums on instructional technology is, in many ways, a more important activity than reading a scholarly collection, but we hope that books such as ours can provide crucial support for such decisions.

Toward the goal of providing such support, this collection might have taken a number of forms. But in order to match the forward-looking enterprise of shaping the future of online education, we chose to develop a collection of speculative chapters authored by some of the freshest and most progressive voices in the field of literacy studies. The reader will find in this book a foreword and eleven chapters that challenge mainstream perceptions of literacy, technology, and education. Many of these chapters assume a broad theoretical perspective, yet most retain a focus on pedagogical and practical concerns.

The collection is divided into three thematic divisions, each of which examines an important dimension of literacy theory after the Internet. The four chapters in part 1, Literacy in the Information Age, explore notions of literacy in response to changes brought on by globally networked economies in which information has become a primary commodity. Lester Faigley's landmark 1996 CCCC chair's address, "Literacy After the Revolution," is reprinted in this section as a call to retheorize literacy in response to the advent of the Internet and information-based economies. Johndan Johnson-Eilola's "Negative Spaces" uses hypertext and the World Wide Web as an example of the ways that popular pedagogical practices such as collaboration have failed to embrace genuinely new notions of literacy that challenge current-traditional approaches. William Covino mines William Gibson's *Neuromancer* to examine emerging myths of the power of technology-based literacy and the possible impact of such myths on the teaching of rhetoric and writing. "Writing in the Hivemind," by Don Byrd and Derek Owens, relates the story of a group of creative writers who worked together to create a radically collaborative, networked writing community, an experimental environment well beyond the boundaries of conventional collaborative workshops or peer-response sessions.

Part 2, Literacy and the Body Electric, adds to the continuing discussion of one of the most important and controversial issues in contemporary literacy theory: the relationship between material reality and rhetoric, between what we are and what we say or write, an issue that is foregrounded in networked writing environments. Much of this discussion has focused on changing notions of the body and on literacy as an embodied practice, and cybertheory has a great deal to contribute to these discussions. At stake in this seemingly unusual scholarly conversation about the body is an emerging vocabulary and a new set of metaphors for critically discussing new notions of literacy. Just as *empowerment*, *border-crossings*, and *contact zones* were metaphors that gave shape to Freirian literacy theory, *meat*, *body*, and *prosthetic* are important terms that frame more contemporary visions of literacy, especially literacy in response to the Internet. Both Beth Kolko and Raul Sanchez demonstrate how the current debate about the bodilessness of virtual spaces supports limited notions of the power of rhetoric and literacy, arguing that because our notions of the "body" and the "self" are constructed through rhetoric and because rhetoric is clearly present online, networked interchanges cannot, in fact, ever completely suppress the body of the online writer. In chapter 6, Cynthia Haynes offers a kinetic and provocative response to the prosthesis metaphor, likening outdated notions of literacy to a decaying limb and embracing the prosthesis of computer-mediated literacies.

Part 3, Electronic Pedagogies, outlines important practical and theoretical considerations for technologically responsive instruction. In "The Persistence of Authority: Coercing the Student Body," Todd Taylor takes a stark look at the practices of writing teachers in networked classrooms and challenges us to recognize how we continue to wield authority and coerce students despite claims to "student-centered" pedagogies. In chapter 9, "Rhetoric of the 'Contact Zone,'" Terry Craig, Leslie Harris, and Richard Smith challenge simplified and utopian approaches to contact-zone and community-oriented pedagogies by discussing the hostile and dysfunctional interchanges they witnessed in a semester-long MOO conversation among students in three universities separated both geographically and culturally. Tim Mayers and Kevin Swafford first critique the utopianism they find in much research on computer-mediated literacy instruction and then describe a pedagogy through which they encourage students to "read" networked technologies and networked classrooms actively as cultural texts. Patricia Hunter and Charles Moran narrate an exceptionally proactive and resourceful campaign to stretch a $51,000 grant toward improving teacher access to computer technology. The beauty of Hunter and Moran's approach is that they not only motivated local schoolteachers to campaign for additional access but also managed to influence dozens of teachers and hundreds of students while spending a vast majority of their meager grant on teacher training, not equipment, an ideal model for the effective application of instructional technology.

Together these eleven chapters begin to touch on changing approaches to literacy theory that the Internet and other networked technologies seem to be ushering in. But only years of additional experience and research will complete the picture. While all the chapters are united in their attempt to reenvision literacy theory in terms of networked technologies, they approach the issue from different perspectives and through varied methods. As editors, we are pleased that the resulting collection is distinctly polyvocal. Confronted with such a complex and constantly shifting subject as literacy theory in the age of the Internet, we are more comfortable listening to useful noise than to synthetic harmony.

The editors wish to acknowledge the departments of English at the University of North Carolina, Chapel Hill and Kansas State University for their support. From those departments, Erika Lindemann, Darryl Gless, William Andrews, Larry Rodgers, Linda Brigham, Craig Stroupe, and Gregory Eiselein in particular contributed to this volume in numerous ways. At Kansas State, our thanks also goes to Shay Baker and Anita Hallauer for their careful and accurate typing of editing changes. We also want to thank Jennifer Crewe, Anne McCoy, Ron Harris, Mary Ellen Burd, Sarah St. Onge, and the anonymous manuscript reviewers at Columbia University Press for their enormous help developing the manuscript and preparing this book. Special recognition is due Gary Olson for his years of personal and professional guidance. Our family and friends were also essential in bringing this project to life; their names belong here too: Max and Jill Taylor, Sally and Jack Taylor, Marie Branson, Evelyn Ashton-Jones, Julie Drew, Sid Dobrin, Raul Sanchez, and Sarah Kanning.

Works Cited

Barton, Ellen, and Ruth Ray. "Technology and Authority." In *Evolving Perspectives on Computers and Composition Studies: Questions for the 1990s.* Ed. Gail E. Hawisher and Cynthia L. Selfe. Urbana, IL: NCTE, 1991. 279–99.

Elmer-DeWitt, Philip. "Welcome to Cyberspace." *Time,* special issue, spring 1995, 4–11.

Deloughry, Thomas J. "Campus Computer Use Is Increasing, But Not as Fast as in the Previous Year." *The Chronicle of Higher Education,* 22 Nov. 1996, A21–22.

Hawisher, Gail E., and Cynthia L. Selfe, eds. *Critical Perspectives on Computers and Composition Instruction.* New York: Teacher's College Press, 1989.

Lanham, Richard. Preface to *The Electronic Word: Democracy, Technology, and the Arts.* Chicago: University of Chicago Press, 1993.

Lottor, Mark. "Internet Domain Survey. Network Wizards." http://www.nw.com/zone/WWW/report.html (24 Nov. 1997).

Merit Network, Inc. "NSFNET Backbone Statistics." ftp://nic.merit.edu/nsfnet/statistics/history.packets (30 Nov. 1996).

Selfe, Cynthia L. *Creating a Computer-Supported Writing Facility: A Blueprint for Action.* Houghton, MI: Computers and Composition, 1989.

Zakon, Robert H. "Hobbes' Internet Timeline." http://www.isoc.org/zakon/Internet/History/HIT.html#Growth (24 Nov. 1997).

Literacy Theory in the Age of the Internet

Literacy in the Information Age

O N E

I Literacy After the Revolution: 1996 CCCC Chair's Address

Lester Faigley

The condition of living in a highly urbanized, mobile, and transient society allows remarkable sets of circumstances to direct the paths of particular lives, and my life is no exception. When I graduated from high school, I never planned to be an English major, never planned to get a Ph.D., never planned to be a college teacher, and certainly never planned to be chair of the Conference on College Composition and Communication (CCCC). In each case I could narrate a series of minor events that were pivotal in shaping years of my life. I'm sure each of you can think of at least one small event where if a particular person were absent or if you had arrived at a particular location just a few minutes earlier or later, the subsequent course of your life would have been very different.

But if the particular paths that our lives take are strongly influenced by seemingly chance events, the broader tracks show a great deal more regularity. After all, there are more than three thousand of us at this convention. Evidently some common forces brought us here. I only gradually became aware of these forces. Like most other college writing teachers of my generation, I was not trained specifically in rhetoric and composition. I taught writing in graduate school as a teaching assistant, but at the universities where I did my graduate work, there

Faigley, Lester, "Literacy After the Revolution," *CCC* 48 (1997) © 1997 by the National Council of Teachers of English. Reprinted with permission.

was no specialization in rhetoric and composition at that time. Teaching writing was something you did for a living but not something you thought about very much. For those of us who found our way into rhetoric and composition, somewhere along the way we began thinking of teaching writing as more than a drudgery from which we wished deliverance. We understood that likely we would always be teaching writing in some form if we were to have a professional career, but, more pertinently, we recognized that we were teaching something quite valuable for our students' lives.

It is not coincidental that early experiences of teaching basic writers figure so prominently among the past chairs of my generation—Jacqueline Jones Royster, Lillian Bridwell-Bowles, Anne Ruggles Gere, Bill Cook, Don McQuade, Jane Peterson, Andrea Lunsford, David Bartholomae, Miriam Chaplin, Lee Odell, Rosentene Purnell, Jim Hill, and Lynn Quitman Troyka—and among many other of my contemporaries. We came of age when the great social issues of the civil rights movement and the Vietnam War were being debated publicly and when education was widely believed to be the chief means of ending social inequality. Early experiences of teaching basic writers exposed for these teachers the role and power of institutions in maintaining social divisions. But these teachers also found spaces where institutional power could be challenged and where students who had been labeled as deficient could succeed.

That the good classroom could help produce the good society seemed self-evident when I began teaching college writing courses. The students I taught were becoming more diverse, and I believed that composition teachers were better situated than anyone to respond to their needs. We were the faculty who were exploring antiauthoritarian ways of teaching and who were encouraging our students to use literacy to participate in democratic community life, to engage civic issues, and to promote social justice. Even though, like nearly everyone else teaching composition, I was relegated to second-class status as a writing teacher in an English department, I felt that composition was going to do fine in the long run. We were in step with the new mission of colleges and universities to provide education for all who wanted it. History seemed to be on our side.

Now that we are more than halfway through the 1990s and closing quickly on both the end of the millennium and the fiftieth anniversary of CCCC, it no longer seems like we are riding the wave of history; instead we appear to be caught in a riptide that is carrying us away from where we want to go. Part of this frustration is linked to the growth of rhetoric and composition as a discipline. Had not the members of CCCC been so successful in creating an expansive discipline, fostering important research and scholarship, and broadening the ways in which writing is taught, perhaps visions of restoring rhetoric to a central place in the American college curriculum might have remained nostalgic images of the past. At the same time, however, writing teachers who have been at the forefront of initiating change have run up against a multitude of institutional barriers and attitudes that would limit writing instruction to teaching students to replicate the traditional forms of academic and professional discourses. Most disappointing, the discipline's success has not influenced institutions to improve the working conditions of many teachers of writing. A huge percentage of college writing courses are taught by part-time faculty who endure uncertain employment, heavy workloads, poor pay, and nonexistent benefits and often lack support services as meager as a desk and a mailbox.

A decade ago Maxine Hairston, in her CCCC chair's address, blamed the literature faculty for the problems writing teachers face. Now, the situation for writing teachers might seem rosy if the problems could be resolved within English departments, no matter how petty and vicious the politics. Larger forces of change, however, affect how we see ourselves and what we do. These changes are of such magnitude that they have been labeled revolutions, one a technological transformation called the *digital revolution* and the other an economic, social, and political transformation called the *revolution of the rich*. These revolutions have been described as having very different impacts—the digital revolution is said to expand access and the revolution of the rich to contract it—but we may eventually come to see them as different aspects of an even larger scale change.

I want to begin with the revolution of the rich. What no one, including writing teachers, foresaw twenty years ago was the extent to which the creation of wealth would be divorced from labor and redistributed, leaving the United States the most economically polarized of the industrialized nations, with the divide between rich and poor continuing to widen. The most recent Federal Reserve figures available, from 1989, indicate that the wealthiest 1 percent of the population, living in households with a net worth of at least 2.3 million dollars each, own almost 40 percent of the nation's wealth. The top 20 percent of U.S. households, worth $180,000 or more, own nearly all its wealth—more than 80 percent (Bradsher).

Those in the middle have increasingly struggled to maintain their position. The workweek in the United States has increased and leisure time has decreased since 1970. Juliet Schor found that the average working American in 1989 put in 163 more hours a year than twenty years earlier, the equivalent of an extra month of work. Those who work harder for lower real wages and reduced benefits have found life precarious. Business executives take great credit for increasing corporate profits through downsizing, but these profits have come out of the pockets of the workers. During the 1970s and 1980s, corporations succeeded in busting unions and in rolling back government social programs.

But the most important strategy to increase profits has been to seek greater flexibility in hiring workers. Between 1979 and 1995, the *New York Times* estimates, based on Department of Labor statistics, that forty-three million jobs were eliminated in the United States (Uchitelle and Kleinfield). The layoffs in the 1990s read like casualty totals from World War I battles: 123,000 gone from AT&T; 50,000 fired by Sears; 18,800 pink slips at Delta Airlines; 16,800 cut from Eastman Kodak. Four companies out of five in America laid off workers in 1995. These reductions came not at a time of economic depression but during a period when the economy was booming and the stock market was reaching record highs. While unemployment is currently low in the United States and millions of new jobs have been created, there has not been such job instability since the Great Depression and never before have highly paid, highly educated workers been so vulnerable. Only 35 percent of currently laid-off, full-time workers find jobs comparable to the ones they held.

Workers have not shared in the prosperity of the last fifteen years. The median wage in 1994, adjusted for inflation, is nearly 3 percent below what it was in 1979. Household income climbed 10 percent during the same period, but the richest 20 percent received 97 percent of the gain (Uchitelle and Kleinfield). The accumulation of wealth at the top is staggering even when compared to acquisitions of the robber barons of the nineteenth century. On November 29, 1995, Steven Jobs, the cofounder of Apple Computers, made 1.2 billion dollars on paper on the first day of the public issue of his company Pixar Animation Studios, when the stock price jumped from twenty-two to thirty-nine dollars per share. In August 1995 Jim Clark, the cofounder of Netscape, made 1.3 billion dollars when the company went public. These sums are over double the annual gross domestic product of a small nation like Belize (CIA). That's what I call empowerment.

What is different today from the era of monopoly capitalism in the nineteenth and early twentieth centuries is that people in the last century looked to government to regulate the monopolies of industries, railroads, and banks. For example, San Francisco newspaper editor Henry George attacked speculators who reaped huge profits from the rising price of land that they did not improve. He proposed a tax on this "unearned increment" that the government would use to address the misery caused by industrialization. Today no one is calling for taxes to ameliorate poverty created by speculation. Instead government is identified with bureaucracy, inefficiency, and waste. Current defenders of the free market go even further than Andrew Carnegie, who justified laissez-faire economics by appealing to Social Darwinism but nonetheless saw the need for public schools and libraries.

Today the invisible hand of the unregulated market is trusted to do nearly everything, and publicly supported higher education is becoming an institution of the past. Tax dollar support for higher education is being reduced so rapidly that huge tuition and fee increases cannot keep pace. From 1991 to 1995, the California State Legislature slashed the budget of the University of California at Berkeley by seventy million dollars, or 18.8 percent; over the same period, the City University of New York's budget was cut by 200 million dollars, or 20 percent (Honan).

More and more often, politicians unfamiliar with higher education are ordering colleges and universities to make sweeping changes. Seeing colleges and universities as bloated, they want to reengineer higher education on the market-driven principles of downsizing by imposing heavier workloads, eliminating tenure, and converting full-time jobs into "permanent temp" positions. In the corporate world, these changes are called "planned staffing." Arizona Regent John Munger, an opponent of tenure, puts it bluntly: "There's plenty of faculty out there who want to teach and are willing to teach without tenure, and frankly who we might be able to obtain at a cheaper price and with more hiring flexibility" (Mayes). Munger and his allies are already far along in these so-called reforms. According to the Education Department's National Center for Education Statistics, the percentage of part-time faculty in institutions of higher education rose between 1970 to 1991 from 22 to 35 percent, and these jobs are disproportionally held by women.[1] In this respect, writing programs have been pioneers in the new employment structure of higher education.

The revolution of the rich has been facilitated by another related revolution: the digital revolution of electronic communications technologies. In 1949, the year of the first meeting of CCCC, computers were comparable to automobiles in 1899: bulky, slow, expensive, and difficult to use, their utility confined largely to replicating certain functions of mechanical calculators. And just as in 1899 it would have been impossible to predict the influence of automobiles on America's landscape, cities, and cultural practices—right down to eating habits—so too in 1949 it would have been next to impossible to predict the many effects of computers. Even though the transistor had been invented in 1947, the big advances that allowed the rapid increase in computing power and decrease in cost were yet to come, especially the development of the integrated circuit in 1957 and the microprocessor in 1971 (Braun and MacDonald). A throwaway greeting card that sings "Happy Birthday" has more computing processing power than existed in 1951; a home video camera has more power than a 1976 IBM 360, the standard mainframe machine that I used when I was an assistant professor (Huey 37).

Personal computers invaded the academy in large numbers beginning in the early 1980s, and where they were available in composition classrooms, they enhanced process pedagogy by making it easier for students to revise their papers. But as personal computers became enormously more powerful in memory and speed, they began to challenge the unproblematic relationship between familiar pedagogy and new technology. When personal computers became linked to other computers in local-area networks, writing teachers were forced to devise new pedagogies because the traditional lines of authority had to be renegotiated. With the coming of the Internet and the World Wide Web, another major renegotiation of pedagogy and authority is now in progress.

I direct a large college writing program that aims to give every student opportunities to practice the new electronic literacies unless they prefer to be in a traditional classroom. We are committed to teaching the great majority of our writing courses in networked classrooms by 1998. The Division of Rhetoric and Composition and the University of Texas administration believe that college students should be able to use the media of literacy that they will likely use in their later lives. The division also makes it a central goal to encourage students to read and write about significant public issues.

Discourse on significant public issues abounds on the Internet, and giving students the means to participate in these discussions at first seemed like a wish come true. Our instructors quickly explored the potential of connecting students with ongoing worldwide discussions of political and social issues. For example, at the time of the elections in South Africa that brought Nelson Mandela to power, a graduate instructor, Noel Stahle, directed his students to the online newsgroup soc.culture.southafrica, where they were able to obtain firsthand accounts of the elections and to contact people in South Africa. Other instructors have involved students in online discussion groups concerning domestic and international issues.

But as talk radio so vividly demonstrates, providing venues for the discussion of public issues does not necessarily lead to a more informed public, increased civic engagement, or enhanced democracy. The problems our instructors have encountered in introducing students to newsgroups reflect larger debates over the impacts of the Internet. In the wake of the exponential growth of the Internet—from 213 host computers in 1981 to over 9 million in early 1996—and sweeping pronouncements on the scale of John Perry Barlow's that (forget Gutenberg!) the coming of the Internet is the most transformative event in human history since the capture of fire, others have begun asking into what changed state people are being transformed.[2] One of the most strident critics of the Internet, Mark Slouka, sees the appeal of life in virtual worlds as being motivated by the degradation of our physical environment. Slouka blames technology for our present lack of civic engagement, arguing that when our own communities have become unsafe, uncertain, unpleasant, and ugly, we seek artificial ones.

The stampede to get online has prompted much hype and horror about the Internet, but before we pronounce it good or bad for our discipline, we should pause to examine how it developed over several decades and what actually is new about its widespread use.

The Internet has its origins in a cold war project in the 1960s that addressed how the military would maintain communications in the aftermath of a nuclear war, when presumably many if not most lines of communication and most major communications centers would be destroyed. The ingenious solution was to flatten the communications hierarchy, making every node equivalent so that the loss of any one would not collapse the system. Each node would have the capability to originate, pass, and receive individually addressed messages bundled in packets. The routing of messages became relatively unimportant. A message would bounce from host to host like a beach ball batted around in the crowd at a free concert until it finally reached its destination.

In 1969 the Pentagon began connecting researchers at military and university sites on the Arpanet, enabling them to transmit data at high speeds and to access each other's computers. The Arpanet grew rapidly in the 1970s because its utility was obvious and its structure accommodated different kinds of machines, overcoming the problem of incompatibility. Because the demand for high-speed communications was so great when the National Science Foundation took on the expansion of the Internet in 1986, the NSF decided to build a network capable of connecting most of the nation's researchers. By 1990 the Internet had outgrown the community of scientists as corporations and individuals began to take advantage of the Internet's speed and low cost, and by 1993 the growth of the Internet became explosive.

It is not surprising that the Internet became so widely used so quickly: it became available at a time when other new low-cost, high-speed communications technologies—fax machines, cellular telephones, and cable television—were also growing in popularity. But what is surprising is how the Internet came to be used. Soon after the introduction of the original Arpanet in 1969, researchers began to do more than access and transfer data at remote sites. Researchers who had personal accounts soon exploited the net for person-to-person communication that ranged from project collaboration to schmoozing to the first hobby bulletin boards. Just as was the case for older technologies, researchers on the Arpanet quickly discovered new uses that hadn't been imagined by the designers.

A decade later, between 1979 and 1983, programmers wrote the software that led eventually to thousands of newsgroups created on Usenet and other networks.[3] The number of words posted each day on these newsgroups may now exceed the number of words printed each day, a fact that enthusiasts like Barlow celebrate as a step toward overcoming the barriers to communication and that skeptics like Slouka decry as a morass of babel in which reflective thought disappears. Overlooked in these pronouncements is that a significant new medium of literacy has come into existence with the Internet.

In 1982 Thomas Miller and I conducted a survey of 200 college-educated people writing on the job, stratified according to type of employer and type of occupation. We found that everyone in an occupation that requires a college education wrote on the job, with nearly three-fourths of the people sampled claiming to devote 10 percent or more of their work time to writing. Very few, however, reported writing much off the job. For many people who have access to the Internet, that situation has changed. They may be using work time for personal writing, but they are nonetheless writing for purposes other than work. For many people, online newsgroups and chat rooms have become something close to an addiction.

The Internet will soon be as ubiquitous as cable television, as the costs of computers and connections continue to drop. At least ten million people today in the United States are connected either directly to the Internet or to commercial online services. Even more phenomenal has been the growth of the World Wide Web, which in months became a major medium of publishing. By August 1994, just two years after its introduction by the European Nuclear Research Center, Internet traffic on the World Wide Web was greater than the volume of electronic mail. If this growth pattern continues, traffic on the Web will surpass the total world voice communication traffic by 1998 (Rutkowski).

When the NSF backbone was turned off on April 30, 1995, the Internet became privatized, and with the signing into law of the Telecommunications Reform Act in February 1996, the rush is on for the control of cyberspace. So far, the part of the telecommunications bill that has been the most controversial is the Communications Decency Act, a truly benighted piece of legislation that is likely to be struck down in numerous court challenges.[4] The major long-term impacts, however, will come from removing regulations that now govern corporations involved in computing, communications, publishing, and entertainment. The new media megaliths created by the mergers of Time Warner and

CNN, Westinghouse and CBS, and Disney and ABC are only the beginning consolidations of power as the giants buy up the technology to control how we work, how we get information, how we shop, how we relax, and how we communicate with other people.

AT&T, which we used to think of as a telephone company, has been fast out of the starting blocks following the Telecommunications Act to reach out and crush someone—notably Prodigy, CompuServe, and America Online, along with MCI—by offering five hours of free Internet service monthly to all of its eighty million long-distance customers beginning on March 14, 1996. This move points the way of the future because it not only gives AT&T an advantage in its telephone business but greatly expands its share of telecommunication and financial services. Soon AT&T is going to launch its WorldNet Internet service, which will insure credit card transactions for users of its Universal Card, creating a worldwide home shopping network with massive possibilities for cross-marketing with other partners.

As much as I resist AT&T's "you will" advertisements offering scenes of technological determinism, I do not foresee colleges and universities for long remaining unaffected by these developments. AT&T and the other telecommunication giants are committed to putting every household with a computer and disposable income online in the very near future, and soon the majority of students we teach are going to come from these households. Many colleges are already responding by giving students easy high-speed access to the Internet. By December 1996 my university will have installed ethernet connections in every dormitory room, boasting "a port for every pillow." In 1995 student traffic on the Internet at the University of Texas doubled from the spring to the fall semesters.

When students enter one of our networked classrooms, they quickly dispel any assumptions of their teachers that they do little writing on their own. Most use email, and several already have personal home pages on the World Wide Web. While many of these personal home pages are little more than self-advertisements, the students who made them have experience producing and publishing multimedia forms of literacy.

Some have made quite remarkable use of this new literacy. Even though Generation X often gets bashed for its political apathy, many students have used their digital literacy to engage social and political issues. For example, the Web site of an undergraduate student at Swarthmore, Justin Paulson, became an important distribution point for the publications of the Zapatista rebels in the Mexican state of Chiapas. Many thousands of people have connected to Paulson's Web site and have read essays, communiqués, and articles about the Zapatistas. The Web site itself has been much publicized through articles in many magazines and newspapers, including *The Guardian* (U.K.) and *Reforma* (Mexico). In April 1995 the Mexican foreign minister, José Angel Gurría, declared that the uprising in Chiapas is a "Guerra de Tinta y de Internet" (a war of ink and of the Internet). The role of the Internet in the Zapatista movement becomes evident when the Chiapas uprising is contrasted to the Shining Path rebellion in Peru. The Zapatistas have been able to historicize the context of their rebellion and convey the complexity of a peasant society without resorting to ongoing violence.

While I am much encouraged by the creativity and commitment of students like Justin Paulson, their Web sites need to be placed in a larger perspective. Pointing to their work as proof that digital literacy necessarily leads to democratic participation and civic engagement is a variation on the myth that the good classroom will automatically lead to the good society. We as teachers have little control over who gains access to higher education and even less control of access to the Internet. Very simply, the Internet is not the world. Use of the Internet is even more skewed than consumption of the world's energy resources. The United States, where less than 5 percent of the world's population lives, annually consumes nearly 25 percent of its energy resources (*Economist Book*). In January 1995 nearly 98 percent of Internet hosts were located in the United States, Western Europe, Canada, Australia, and Japan. The presence on the Internet of much of Africa, Asia, and Latin America is nonexistent (in Africa there were ninety hosts outside South Africa).

Even within the United States, Internet users are far from being equally distributed across the population. A major Internet publisher, O'Reilly and Associates, conducted a survey of United States residents over eighteen years of age that used random telephone dialing to obtain a statistically representative sample and followed up with interviews of nearly thirty thousand people. This survey, released in October 1995, confirmed findings of other surveys that younger people are the most frequent users of the Internet.[5] Over half the users are between the ages of eighteen and thirty-four (57 percent) and only 4 percent are fifty-five or older. They are also well off financially. Median annual income in 1994 is reported as between $50,000 and $75,000. And they are mostly white. There is no doubt that African-Americans are severely underrepresented because their percentage of ownership of computers is far lower than that of white Americans. A 1989 U.S. Census Bureau report estimated that nearly 27 million whites but only 1.5 million African-Americans used computers at home (Stuart).

The O'Reilly survey found that a third of Internet users are women, a higher percentage than reported by earlier surveys, which estimated that 80 or 90 percent of Internet users were men. Nonetheless, even the O'Reilly figures have the gender skew at two to one. The disparity between men and women on the Internet indicates that factors beyond merely owning a computer with a connection to the Internet and being literate in English determine access. People must have time to keep up with the abundant discourse if they are to be active participants, and the people who have this time are most likely to be young, affluent white men.

Up to now, the debate over the Internet within the humanities has been conducted in terms of the printed book. In *The Gutenberg Elegies*, Sven Birkerts asks, "What is the place of reading . . . in our culture?" (15), and he answers that it is increasingly shrinking, with the attendant effects of the loss of deep thinking, the erosion of language, and the flattening of historical perspective. Birkerts calls on us to resist the tide of electronic media, and his last words in the book are "refuse it." It is disappointing for someone as thoughtful as Birkerts to allow his book to derail by collapsing all electronic media into a single form and then offering an either/or vision of the future. Anyone who has used email knows that it bears little similarity to television beyond light appearing on a screen, and we haven't thrown away pencils, legal pads, or the good books that Birkerts loves to curl up with.

The more misleading either/or that Birkerts posits, however, is that reflective thinking can occur only in acts of reading. I would like to let him in on a little secret that writing teachers know: college students often become more careful, critical, and appreciative readers after a semester in a writing course. I'm learning that little secret again. This semester for the first time I am devoting a significant part of a writing course to graphic design, and I am discovering, after years of attempting to teach students to analyze images, that they learn much more quickly when they create images on their own. Active learners can think reflectively about any human symbolic activity, whatever the medium.

If we return to our annual convention a decade from now and find that the essay is no longer center stage, it will not mean the end of our discipline. I expect that we will be teaching an increasingly fluid, multimedia literacy and that we will be quite happy that attempts in the past failed to drop our fourth C, for *Communication*, a label that David Bartholomae noted in his 1988 chair's address "keeps us from ever completely knowing our subject" (45).

What concerns me much more is whether we as a professional organization can sustain a shared sense of values when in many respects history is not on our side. Benjamin Barber summarizes our condition when he writes that the more hollow values of the Enlightenment: "materialism, solipsism, and radical individualism [have triumphed] over certain of its nobler aspirations: civic virtue, just community, social equality, and the lifting of the economic yoke from what were once known as the laboring classes" (222). These nobler aspirations were developed and spread primarily through the practices of literacy. We know that literacy education has often not lived up to these ideals and has functioned instead to label individuals and groups as deficient, inferior, and unworthy. Nevertheless, these ideals have provided the means of critique for educational practices that uphold illegitimate hierarchies of power.

When I first came to the annual convention in 1977, I needed CCCC for the intellectual community it provided. Over the years I have come to appreciate more the values we share in common. In a culture that is increasingly cynical about the belief that schools should offer equal opportunity to education, we have remained steadfast to the goal of literacy for equality. Even if many of us occupy less powerful positions in less powerful departments, we still have many strengths. We are not tied to narrow disciplinary turf. We can cut across traditional disciplinary boundaries. We can be confident that the need for what we teach will only increase. And as part of a much larger professional organization, we have many possibilities for working with teachers in the schools and with colleagues in the other college organizations of NCTE.

But we also have some hard questions before us. Can we do anything to stop the decline in publicly supported education? Can we promote a literacy that challenges monopolies of knowledge and information? Can we use technology to lessen rather than widen social divisions? The overriding question facing us as a professional organization is, What do you do when the tide seems to be running against you? I don't think there is any big answer, but there are some little ones: You have to look outward. You have to be smarter and more aware. You have to look for opportunities to inform people about what you do. You have to practice what you preach and engage in public discourse. You have to form alliances. You have to be more tolerant of your friends and look for common ground. You have to organize.

Our charge is in the last two sentences from *Rhetorics, Poetics, and Cultures*, the recently published final book from Jim Berlin, who sustained me through his work and his friendship. He writes: "It is time all reading and writing teachers situate their activities within the contexts of the larger profession as well as the contexts of economic and political concerns. We have much to gain working together and much to lose working alone" (180). May Jim Berlin remain present among us.

Notes

1. National Center for Education Statistics 230, 234. The statistics on full-time higher-education faculty count full-time adjuncts; thus the percentage of non-tenure-track faculty is much higher than 35 percent. In 1991 the percentages of full-time women and men faculty were nearly equal, but the percentage of women in part-time positions was more than two-thirds (66.8 percent).

2. This debate is enacted in "What Are We Doing On-Line?"

3. See Salus, chapters 15 and 18.

4. A panel of federal judges ruled the Communications Decency Act unconstitutional in June 1996.

5. A January 1994 survey found that 62 percent of the respondents were under age 35; 73 percent were under age 45 (Quarterman).

Works Cited

Barber, Benjamin R. *Jihad vs. McWorld.* New York: Times Books, 1995.

Bartholomae, David. "Freshman English, Composition, and CCCC." *College Composition and Communication* 40 (1989):38–50.

Berlin, James A. *Rhetorics, Poetics, and Cultures.* Urbana, IL: NCTE, 1996.

Birkerts, Sven. *The Gutenberg Elegies: The Fate of Reading in an Electronic Age.* Boston: Faber, 1994.

Bradsher, Keith. "Gap in Wealth in U.S. Called Widest in West." *New York Times,* 17 Apr. 1995, nat'l. ed., A1+.

Braun, Ernest, and Stuart MacDonald. *Revolution in Miniature: The History and Impact of Semiconductor Electronics Re-explored.* 2nd ed. Cambridge: Cambridge University Press, 1982.

Central Intelligence Agency. *The World Factbook 1995.* Washington, DC: Central Intelligence Agency, 1995.

The Economist Book of Vital World Statistics, 1990. New York: Times Books, 1990.

Faigley, Lester, and Thomas P. Miller. "What We Learn from Writing on the Job." *College English* 44 (1982):557–69.

George, Henry. *Progress and Poverty: An Inquiry Into the Cause of Industrial Depressions and of Increase of Want with Increase of Wealth.* San Francisco: W. M. Hilton, 1879.

Hairston, Maxine C. "Breaking Our Bonds and Reaffirming Our Connections." *College Composition and Communication* 36 (1985):272–82.

Honan, William H. "New Pressures on the University." *New York Times,* 9 Jan. 1994, late ed., sec. 4A, 16.

Huey, John. "Waking Up to the New Economy." *Fortune,* 17 Jun. 1994, 36–46.

Mayes, Kris. "Tenure Debate Worries Faculty." *Phoenix Gazette*, 28 Sep. 1995, final ed., B1.

National Center for Education Statistics. *Digest of Education Statistics 1995*. Washington, DC: U.S. Department of Education, 1995.

O'Reilly and Associates. "Defining the Internet Opportunity." http://www.ora.com/survey (31 Oct. 1995).

Paulson, Justin. "Ya Basta!" http://www.peak.org/7Ejustin/ezln/ezln.html (31 Oct. 1995).

Quarterman, John S. "The Internet Demographic Survey." *Matrix News* 4 (Jan. 1994):2–6.

Rutkowski, Anthony-Michael. "Bottom-Up Information Infrastructure and the Internet." http://info.isoc.org:80/speeches/upitt-foundersday.html (31 Oct. 1995).

Salus, Peter H. *Casting the Net: From ARPANET to Internet and Beyond*. Reading, MA: Addison-Wesley, 1995.

Schor, Juliet B. *The Overworked American: The Unexpected Decline of Leisure*. New York: Basic, 1992.

Slouka, Mark. *War of the Worlds: Cyberspace and the High-Tech Assualt on Reality*. New York: Basic, 1995.

Stuart, Reginald. "High-Tech Redlining." *Utne Reader* 68 (Mar.–Apr. 1995):73.

Uchitelle, Louis, and N. R. Kleinfield. "On the Battlefields of Business, Millions of Casualties" *New York Times*, 3 Mar. 1996, late ed., sec.1, 1.

"What Are We Doing On-Line?" *Harper's Magazine*, Aug. 1995, 35–46.

2 Negative Spaces: From Production to Connection in Composition

Johndan Johnson-Eilola

Writing has always been about making connections: between writer and readers, across time, and through space (Eisenstein; Ong). At another level, writing connects ideas and people. We have come to understand relations operating through footnoting, repetition, vocabulary, parenthetical citation, paraphrase, and commentary (Porter, "Intertextuality"; Devitt; Hilbert; Berkenkotter, Huckin, and Ackerman). At this second level, it is now common to see such intertextual connections as so pervasive that they question the possibility or necessity for subjects to speak in unified, singular voices: we live (and literally are at least partially "composed") at the nexus connecting an apparently infinite number of social and technological forces of varying weights, strengths, and directions.

In many respects, my assertions are nothing new. Composition theorists and practitioners have, for some years, explored the idea of subjectivity as a multiple, dynamic, often contradictory set of forces acting to construct people in their everyday lives, especially in writing and reading texts. Social construction and postmodernism in composition theory and practice go back at least twenty-five years (if not further), although much of these complex and wide-ranging movements remain rooted in outdated notions of what counts as a text in composition practice. Even though theorists regularly apply the term *text* to a variety of cultural artifacts, in the composition classroom *text* remains rooted in relatively concrete, individualist notions of authorship. This often uncriticized viewpoint persists across numerous sites, including classrooms involving collaborative writing or environments such as hypertext. The reasons for this persistence become apparent when we trace the history of social construction and postmodernism, including ideas about authorship, ownership, media, intertextuality, and process theory.

Social construction gained popularity with Kenneth Bruffee's early work in composition. Bruffee argues that writing depends on and contributes to social conversations: "We converse; we internalize conversation as thought; and then by writing, we re-immerse conversation in its external, social medium" (641). Bruffee characterizes writing as internalized conversation, an activity learned through social interaction. One of the problems of education is that students seek to enter new communities (the workplace or the academy) but do not yet have the knowledge necessary to act as "knowledgeable peers" in the community conversation. Collaboration between students can begin to bridge these gaps because "pooling the resources that a group of peers brings with them to the task may make accessible the normal discourse of the new community they together hope to enter" (644). John Trimbur revises Bruffee's model in order to highlight issues of power and dissensus in society. Traditional models of collaborative learning, Trimbur suggests, perpetuate existing structures of unequal power in classrooms, corporations, and factories because they "bolster morale, promote identification with the corporation, legitimize differential access to knowledge and status, and increase productivity" (611). Trimbur proposes a new emphasis on *dissensus* that does not replace consensus but sees it as one way in which power functions to "provide students with exemplary motives to imagine alternative worlds and transformations of social life and labor" (615).

Writing teachers in computer classrooms have added weight to Trimbur's complications of consensus. Lester Faigley, for example, discusses the ways in which writing in networked classrooms often disintegrates community in significant ways: in electronic discussions, students "are forced to confront different ways of constituting meaning from experience and to negotiate those meanings with other students" (185).

But while we have come to value interconnection and dissensus in composition as it acts to construct texts and subjects, we often fail to reconsider the fundamental concept of what counts as a text. We value connection, but only secondarily. We still think of the text as a relatively coherent body of information with determinable bounds produced by an author of one sort or another. (That author may be a group of individuals acting in concert, more or less.) We teach writing as a process, but primarily as a way to map more clearly a final product: the text, the best draft, produced at the end of the writer's struggle to make meaning. We want to point to some*thing*, written by some*one*. Even when

working in hypertext, a medium defined by many as exploding traditional notions of writing and authorship (Bolter; Landow; Slatin), the presence of connections between nodes often acts only to contextualize the positive objects (the
text or graphics located within the nodes). Discussing a hypothetical hypertext
on Joyce's *Ulysses*, Landow points out that if one possessed a hypertext system
in which our putative Joyce article was linked to all the other materials it cited,
it would exist as part of a much larger system, in which the totality might count
more than the individual document; the article would now be woven more
tightly into its context than would a printed counterpart (5). In short, while hypertext suggests new possibilities for connection, most of our current uses
apply links to augment our visions of traditional authorship: writing with individual letters and words made up by the *author* of that text.

None of this is to say that we should abandon the notion of text production. But
what would happen if we disposed, for the moment, with the text and looked primarily at the relations? What would happen if we wrote with fragments?

In this essay, I begin by briefly tracing some of the reasons for our current
definitions of *text* and *writer*. Following this analysis, I highlight some of the opportunities for alternative views of writing based on open hypertexts such as
those possible (but still rare) on the World Wide Web. Such spaces, which follow an associational rather than accumulative or circulating economy (Johnson-
Eilola), are "written" by the mere act of linking together preexisting materials,
something Gregory Ulmer has termed a "heuritics" of multimedia. In his attempts to rethink the concept of invention in a postprint world, Ulmer intends
heuritics as part of the transition from print logics (linear/indexical) to hypermedia logics (associational) (*Heuritics* 36). A primary aspect of heuritics is
chorography, a rethinking of space. The roots of chorography are numerous, including geography (where it describes a method of historicizing spaces) and
Plato via Derrida (where it describes an *inventio* founded on geography).
Chorography operates through "function[s] by means of pattern making, pattern recognition, pattern generation. It is not that memory is no longer thought
of as 'place,' but that the notion itself of spatiality has changed" (36).

Furthermore, although Ulmer explicitly lays out his work in *Heuritics* as applying to hypermedia, heuritic texts develop toward linear, relatively static
works. "Grammatology (in the Stacks of) Hypermedia," for example, is written
as a linear string of quotations from sources as diverse as colonialist narratives,
hypertext theory, and cinema theory. According to Ulmer, the material comes
from a "diverse bibliography of materials relevant to hypermedia" (141). While
the text is insightful—and Ulmer's introduction to the text raises a number of
important concepts—the text itself is still constructed in the format of a line, al-

though the associational qualities of the text are present in the form of inter-textuality and in the actions of the reader linking the material in the text to other, personal responses in the act of reading. The text does not depart physi-cally from book culture and, in essence, remains ineffectual in changing it. It is, in fact, difficult to reconcile Ulmer's linear, print texts with the associational networks of multimedia, except as analogies and examples of the slippages within cultural systems of signs. From Ulmer's work, however, we can borrow a number of useful concepts, especially his emphasis on collage technique, "re-lying on the remotivation of preexisting fragments in a new context for the pro-duction of its own significance" (142).

A Brief History of Product

Writing has historically been viewed as product, something produced as (liter-ally) an afterthought in response either to deeply held and inchoate feelings (ex-pressivism) or to seeing the world truthfully (objectivism). In either case, writ-ing is the result of other activities. The expressivist, subjective paradigm focuses on the activities of feeling truthfully and then expressing those feelings in language. The objectivist paradigm approaches language as a (usually im-perfect) lens for describing external reality. In contrast to these product-orient-ed conceptions of writing, the triumph of the process approach is that it at-tempts to gain access to the previously ignored (and often hidden) activities of writing and reading texts. According to Donald Murray, "Most of us are trained as English teachers by studying the product: writing. Our critical skills are honed by examining literature, which is finished writing; language as it has been used by authors. And then, fully trained in the autopsy, we go out and are assigned to teach our students to write, to make language live" (89).

The process approach reconfigures the teaching of writing so that, rather than practicing medicine based on autopsy, as Murray put it, we understand (and help our students understand) the processes of living. Maxine Hairston, summarizing the influence of Mina Shaughnessy's research on basic writers, insists that "we cannot teach students to write by looking only at what they have written. We must also understand how that product came into being, and why it assumed the form that it did. We have to try to understand what goes on dur-ing the internal act of writing and we have to intervene during the act of writ-ing if we want to affect its outcome" (22).

More recently, process pedagogy has been rethought to focus not only on the production of the text but also the power structures in which that text emerges. Bruce Herzberg, for example, details the experiences of students working as tutors in adult literacy programs at a shelter in Boston. While tutors early on in the project read texts such as Mike Rose's *Lives on the Boundary* and Jonathan Kozol's *Savage Inequalities* and "are indeed distressed by systematic discrimination against poorer people and disenfranchised groups" (312), the same tutors tended to see their own tutees as disadvantaged by personal problems: lack of motivation, alcoholism, mental disease. But over a long period of tutoring, discussing, reading, and writing, Herzberg points out, students learned not only to tutor but also (and perhaps primarily) to "investigate the social and cultural reasons for the existence of illiteracy—the reasons, in other words, that the students needed to perform the valuable service they were engaged in" (316–17). Similarly critical versions of process have been constructed by computer and writing theorists such as Marilyn Cooper and Cynthia L. Selfe, Susan Romano, and Allison Regan, who point out the potential for computer networks to facilitate deeper understanding of process as well as critical social inquiry.

Clearly, our conceptions of writing have shifted dramatically over the last twenty years or so. What is most striking about this shift, however, is that the process paradigm perpetuates the idea that the text is a product, a concrete, relatively bounded object for viewing, even though it develops through a process of critical inquiry and may enact or reflect social changes. Portfolio systems of assessment, for example, perpetuate the idea of text-as-product. Portfolio methods actually refine and strengthen notions of the text as relatively coherent and bounded through a historicization of the concrete activities of writing and revision. Liz Hamp-Lyons and William Condon, for example, describe portfolios as "a more complex, more comprehensive 'snapshot' of the writer's ability" (181). The portfolio acts as a series of analytical measurements showing how a writer's work has progressed from start to finish. Portfolios are surely an improvement over conventional term-paper assignments, to be graded with red pen for problems in structure, development, transitions, style, grammar, and spelling. But, at the same time, the portfolio points only *implicitly* to other voices, to social and political forces that determine the value of the text in the portfolio.

For years, compositionists have thought that moving from product to process offered a more dynamic, humanistic, social approach to composing. Perhaps it does. But as James Berlin correctly pointed out some time ago, the process approach grows out of a cognitivist view of writing, understanding text production as a dynamic process that occurs in a writer's mind. For these reasons, portfolios are constructed as a way to take time-sequenced slices of the development of product over time, toward some tangible, final goal. Always, the goal relates to what the individual writer is able to produce, in *their own words*. Although in many ways we have moved away from an expressivist approach to writing, in other ways, we have barely departed from that school. But if we examine these assumptions against the evolution of the social construction movement, especially as it has been taken up by cultural studies approaches to composition, the social model would have us focus on the creation and negotiation of contexts rather than the production of an "original" text. Unfortunately, however, while current approaches to research-based writing do begin with the process of locating information, as practiced in most classrooms today, these approaches place primary value not on the collection and arrangement of information but on the text the student produces.

It is not surprising therefore that collaborative writing is so difficult: texts are valued when they speak in a single, authentic voice. The field's recent attempts to place some value on dissensus points to the tension here, the recognition that when groups agree on everything they are merely acting, more or less, like a single mind. They are *de*socializing the text in one way or another because either they work so well together that they no longer act as individuals or (perhaps more frequently) a single person writes everything and the group takes credit. Moving to a notion of composition that values arrangement and connection/disjunction is useful for a number of reasons: the skill is more highly valued than single-authored production of a finished text in our emerging digital society because it focuses on problems easily applicable to rapidly expanding information spaces and because it embraces notions of knowledge "production" in cultural rather than cognitivist-individualist ways.

Interdisciplinary Parallels to Connection

Composition theory and pedagogy must overcome a reliance on the idea of writing as *production* and look instead at ways for considering the values inherent in *connection* between texts and fragments. We can begin to see some of the cultural tendencies toward connection rather than production in information systems such as the World Wide Web.

The movement to valuing connection or arrangement over production is not limited to composition; as Jean-François Lyotard points out, this shift is characteristic of an increasingly postmodernist society. Indeed, composition is behind the curve on this transition: connection is already as valuable or more valuable than simple production in a number of areas, including such diverse places as information design, architecture, art, and finance. These other fields show that while composition may still be able to think of writing as the production of text, doing so lowers the status of writing and writers. Artists such as Nam June Paik and architects such as Frank Gehry work through the techniques of collage and quoting, bringing together preexisting materials in important ways (see discussions in Jameson; Soja). Similarly, in the contemporary factory, value has shifted over time from crafting concrete products (automobiles, furniture, whatever) toward the management of information flow (Reich; Drucker). Line workers are still crucial, but they are seen as concrete instances of easily replaceable resources (either through worker turnover or by relocating plants to areas where labor is cheaper).

As social theorists including Robert B. Reich and Edward Soja have pointed out, late capitalism thrives on uneven development across states, nations, and the world. In a global economy, corporations feel no qualms about closing a plant in one area of the country or world when wage demands rise too high and opening a new plant in a low-wage area. As wages in that area rise, the cycle begins anew. As wage demands in the first area fall, corporations move back in. Workers who rely on their skills at manipulating fragments of information do not suffer in the same way during these flood/drought cycles for two primary reasons:

1. The skills of symbol manipulation command higher pay.
2. Symbolic-analytic workers can either work remotely or, related to the first reason, afford to move.

The devaluation of routine production skills can be largely attributed to the rise of automation in our culture. One of the hallmarks of automation is the removal of control from the worker (Hirschhorn; Zuboff). As workers are deskilled, it becomes easier to shift them in and out of functional positions with little training: knowledge has become exteriorized and now functions within the machine rather than in the worker.

This process, in our culture, is unavoidable.

Possibilities for negotiating this phenomenon are constructed by drawing on a number of important discourses that have already begun to rethink ideas about production. In business and industry, for example, theorists and consultants from Peter F. Drucker to Robert B. Reich now insist on a postcapitalist or decentered model in which highly paid workers orchestrate information flows in order to bring together profitable arrangements in market, finance, and production.

The shift from production to connection in massive, dynamic fields marks a parallel shift in identity, from internalized to externalized notions of subjectivity. The beginnings of these shifts are evident in composition's attraction to the ideas of process and intertextuality. But these phenomena fail to realize *connec-*

tion at a postmodernist level because they continue to focus on the production of texts rather than the connection between text fragments, what I termed above "writing with fragments." This process takes relatively radical and influential social theories in composition such as Patricia Bizzell's "contact zones" or Henry Giroux's "border-crossings" and multiplies them a thousandfold.

Bizzell, Giroux, and others have constructed useful approaches to subjectivity and cultural power, but as with most contemporary composition, such approaches are infrequently carried over adequately into conceptions of what counts as a text. On the one hand, contact and border pedagogies rely on an older model of text in which subjectivities work valiantly (if often unsuccessfully) through personal, internal battles negotiating two opposing worldviews; on the other hand, experts working in massive information contexts negotiate differences and connections on a much vaster scale including sometimes thousands of different factors and cultural forces (and millions of potential intersections). We are closer here to Frederic Jameson's cognitive mapping, the juggling of enormous amounts of information that seem to act through an externalization of at least some portions of identity. Cognitive mapping describes the ways that subjects position themselves provisionally and multiply in relation to the world and history. Cognitive maps "enable a situational representation on the part of the individual subject to that vaster and properly unrepresentable totality which is the ensemble of society's structures as a whole" (51). Jameson describes the process working within the contexts of video art such as Nam June Paik's video screens, through which a viewer "is called upon to do the impossible, namely, to see all the screens at once" (31) and John Portman's architecture, including the Los Angeles Westin Bonaventure Hotel, a "space [that] makes it impossible for us to use the language of volume or volumes any longer . . . a constant busyness that gives the feeling that emptiness is here absolutely packed" (43). Subjects no longer battle it out within the recesses of their individual and somewhat fragmented minds, but "out there," in culture.

The Politics of the Link

The problem with this work is that it fails to question late-capitalist assumptions about society. The contradiction within late capitalism is that it values postmodernist fragmentation of identity and localization while still aligning itself with the *grand récit* of individual success stories (e.g., Bill Gates, Marc Andreesen, and even the theorists themselves: Peter Drucker, Tom Peters, etc.). There's no easy escape from this contradiction. As Frederic Jameson points out, postmodernist artists are sometimes respected because they see postmodernist conditions more truthfully, a condition that harkens back to enlightenment; Jameson is himself valued because he sees postmodernist conditions clearly. The lack of debilitating tension in most of these paradoxes is itself a hallmark of postmodernism: the ability to appropriate without shame.

The limitations of this view seem especially dangerous given the other powerful spheres in our culture now valuing the skills of connection as much or more than those of production, from information management and brokering in business, finance, and industry to working on the World Wide Web. Despite suggestions inherent in social construction, postmodernist, and cultural studies movements, we continue to think of writers as people engaged in the production of relatively original texts. A useful but unresolved tension resides in these problems of recognition: areas such as cultural studies are involved in recognizing the ways that individuals negotiate power relationships in social contexts. These investigations often productively affirm the power of individuals to resist social domination (if not to the point of resisting change, but at least by surviving and perhaps retaining a sense of dignity). At the same time, however, the importance granted to individual versus social contexts approaches a return to conservative versions of culture currently used to batter the poor, minorities, and women (and nearly everyone else not already on top): a circular argument in which only the so-called fit survive and those who survive are considered unquestionably more "fit."

This conundrum is not new. It has haunted our work since the onset of social constructionist theory. But the importance of an associational-social viewpoint in composition is critical on at least two fronts. First, it connects individuals with social contexts in ways that can help us recognize tendential forces in society and work to change them in productive ways; for example, improving welfare rather than merely restricting it or abandoning it. On the second front, our own pedagogies have increasingly valued *connection* in theory but not in practice. While we espouse social construction and cultural studies, we continue to position students as lone individuals struggling to bring forth "original" texts. Even in cases where students write papers in peer groups, we set those groups up as little more than hiveminds, the subgroup acting as an enlightenment artist capable of seeing truth better than a single student can.

In addition, framing *connection* as an eminently creative act can help us to reintroduce ethics into spheres that work repressively according to the application of "objective" principles. Take, for example, the ways in which nightly television newscasts arrange their stories. In a first-year composition course I taught in the late 1980s, I asked students to look critically at such shows to ex-

amine how each show constructed "the news." Students were almost uniform-
ly unwilling to see newscasts as ideological because, they said, good newscasts
merely reported what had happened without the distortions of commentary.
Only by stepping back and examining the processes of writing and producing a
newscast did it become apparent to them how difficult it is to be objective: each
show involved the selection of news topics, events, or commentaries from a
nearly infinite number of possibilities; once a topic was selected, each segment's writers and producers had to decide who to interview, what footage to
show, and in what sequence to arrange the material; each segment needed to be
ordered and edited so that it fit neatly into a half-hour format while leaving time
for commercials. Critical processes such as these highlight the importance of
selection and arrangement.

Viewing connection as creative act places emphasis on selection and
arrangement. Traditional ideas of text, to which we still cling, identify writing
with positive objects: this text as distinguished from all others. The relations between texts are taken to indicate both similarity and difference (e.g., in traditional literature reviews authors must both rehearse the similarities between
their writing and others but then also prove that their work is different). But in
a system of writing based on association or connection, writers are ethically responsible not only for the things they write but also for their selection and
arrangement of preexisting things. It is no longer so easy to retreat behind the
impartial shield of objectivism, asserting that one was only reporting facts. Re-
configuring writing as social connection requires a corresponding recognition
of deep responsibility to communities that extends beyond merely asking students to collaborate on producing a text.

The individualist ethic is supported and perpetuated by institutionalized
standards of text that value "original" words over connection. As James Porter
points out, "Despite the considerable emphasis on collaboration and social construction, the field's principle orientation is still the individual student writer
(and also, 'the text'), and the field still favors an individualist ethic (albeit largely an implicit one) over communitarian and other sorts of ethical positions"
(*Rhetorical Ethics* n.p.). Ulmer raises a parallel set of critical and ethical questions concerning the use of databases.

Ulmer's linear texts are explicitly reports on the navigation of information
spaces ("Grammatology" 141). The concept of information as spatial is somewhat problematic but has gained currency through numerous cultural forces,
including the commodification of information in late-capitalist culture, the historical roots of patent law and intellectual property legislation, and contemporary graphical user interfaces that portray the computer screen as terrain.

Ulmer, however, uses the metaphor of terrain to critique colonialist aspects of literacy and writing: "As a politics of writing, chorography rehearses this problematic, polysemous association linking the metaphors of method with a 'frontier' whose diagesis includes colonization and wars of imperialism" (*Heuritics* 166). This perspective makes literacy a condition bound up in gestures that are always potentially colonialist, especially in seeing citation as occupying or taking another's space. This does not automatically make quoting an act of violence (although in some cases quoting does enact violence), but it can help us transform our notions of space from something owned to something that is shared by a community; thus texts become social (ethical) responsibilities. If information must be spatialized (and it seems we are too far gone to avoid that), then we need to push harder toward the realization of information spaces as places where discourse communities can form.

Two Examples: Alliance for Computers and Writing and ERROR 404

In this final section, I describe two examples of works oriented toward the collection and arrangement of previously written information fragments, pointers, summaries, etc.; in other words, texts that are not original in the traditional sense of the term. Both examples reconfigure hypertext in useful ways. Although the WWW has been frequently described as a collaborative hypertext, most sites continue to apply hypertext in fairly conservative ways, as an informal form of public relations (corporate or personal), big databases, global libraries, etc. And most Web sites make only cursory and nonsubstantive use of links by merely connecting to a handful of other sites with related personal interests.

The texts that follow represent attempts to work within and against existing structures while granting importance to the acts of writing. The first text is the World Wide Web home page for the Alliance for Computers and Writing (ACW). The ACW page (fig. 2.1) acts as a clearinghouse for information on computers and writing designed to be used primarily by composition teachers, students, and scholars who use or study computers. The subdiscipline of computers and writing is, as might be expected, growing rapidly, and the Alliance represents members from a wide variety of specializations and institutions.

Because of the staggering amount of information on the WWW and the speed with which that information is changed, expanded, and deleted, ACW founders decided that one of the primary functions of the organization would be to disseminate information to a diverse body of users. Although the ACW site does contain a few traditional essays, most of the site is a collection of references organized to be quickly accessed and easily browsed. A small portion of the ACW index is shown in figure 2.2; it includes a collection of pointers to other sites on the WWW that may be useful to computer and writing teachers and students who are new to the Internet.

The ACW site represents a substantial undertaking in research and revision, primarily on the part of Fred Kemp at Texas Tech University. The site is extremely popular in the field, precisely because it values connection over production. It would be difficult to imagine a single person—or even group of people—writing a traditional essay that could serve the purposes the ACW site does; even if a text could be written that provided an expository overview of the

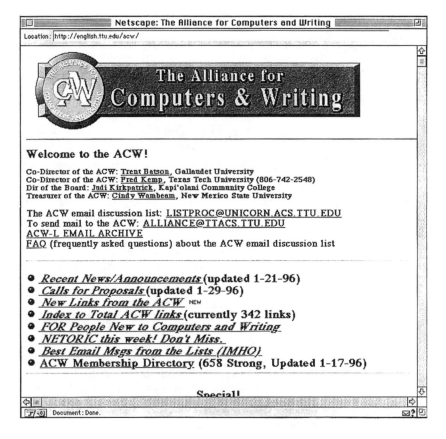

FIGURE 2.1   Alliance for Computers and Writing Home Page

information referenced from the ACW site, it would undoubtedly be more difficult to read and use.

A slightly different approach is taken by a different connection-based site: the ERROR 404 essay. ERROR 404 was collected in the fall of 1995 by a seminar in computers and writing at Purdue University. The seminar, which I facilitated, attempted to address issues of identity, creativity, and argument from a postmodernist perspective—many of the issues developed above—by writing with fragments of other texts.

Consider, for example, the ways that the arrangement of quotes in the thread below, titled "Erotic," critically interrogates the meaning of each of the

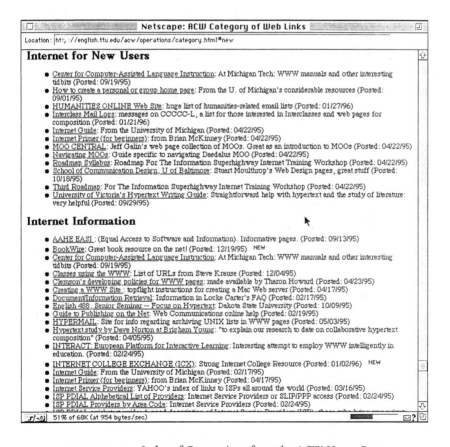

FIGURE 2.2   Index of Connections from the ACW Home Page

texts through contrast and complication (node titles are in brackets above node contents):

[Conley.Seductions.180]
Nowhere are the problematic effects of vr clearer than in the realm of the erotic. . . . Bruce Clark has pointed out that the violation or dissolution of body boundaries is inherently erotic; the same observation has been made by writers as diverse as Ovid, St. Teresa, and the Marquis de Sade.
[imag.teler.5]
Teledildonics lend new dimensions to Ma Bell's slogan: "Reach out and touch someone."
[anon.1]
:-o
Anonymous request for a virtual blow job. 9/15/95.
[Flame.Rape]
To participate, therefore, in this disembodied enactment of life's most body-centered activity is to risk the realization that when it comes to sex, perhaps the body in question is not the physical one at all, but its psychic double, the body-like self representation we carry around in our heads.
Julian Dibbell. A Rape in Cyberspace: or, How an Evil Clown, a Haitian Trickster Spirit, Two Wizards, and a Cast of Dozens Turned a Database into a Society. *FlameWars*, Durham: Duke Press 1994.

The texts here were not written by workshop participants, but the configuration of fragments, I argue, is an important form of writing, a Lyotardian act of creativity that is more reflective of postmodernist theories of culture and value than that available in most versions of contemporary composition. Each of the fragments enters into a dialogue with the others in ways not available to the works in their original, relatively isolated form (the book, the essay, the email message). Indeed, the individual fragments retain much different meanings that are read and rewritten as the reader-writer traverses different threads in the text. The anon.1 node is the first in another thread in ERROR 404: an "alphabet" thread that rearranges the text according to alphabetical order.

On first reading the "alphabet" thread, I saw the emoticon as a somewhat immature prank written into the text. But, reading along the "Erotic" thread offers a markedly different perspective, juxtaposing the anonymous request for sex with fragments on eroticism and disembodiment, telecommunication, and a response to a figurative rape. None of these readings exhausts the fragments, but each perpetually rewrites its meanings. Each is crossed by numerous other threads, and the text is still open for the addition of either fragment or link.

Neither the ACW nor the Error 404 sites succeeds completely in reorganizing "text" in a way that adds enough social importance to the act of linking. (This might always be the case, for if a technology perfectly matches our needs, it is often because our needs have been carefully and complexly orchestrated). The ACW page, for example, like all WWW pages, does not allow readers to become writers (either in the classic sense or in the postmodern sense of reorganizing or connecting). The WWW is, at this writing, still largely tied to individual ownership of pieces of text: individuals point at other individual's or institution's files.

The ERROR 404 text, in its WWW incarnation, suffers from the same difficulties, although the Storyspace version (in which most of the text was linked together by seminar participants) did allow everyone to add connections and new fragments—and even to delete them, although participants avoided this, as far as I can tell. Storyspace, despite its many other benefits, allows individual writers to "sign" nodes that they add but not links, perpetuating once again the idea of the node as primary. Connection and arrangement in ERROR 404 and Storyspace seem more creative than in traditional texts, but these impulses could easily be extended further.

Conclusions/Renegotiations

Over the last twenty-five years we have enriched our work in composition studies by increasing our focus on the social and political roles of writers. We have replaced a concern for static product with a sense of texts as dynamic, social processes. We have introduced discussions of power into our journals and our classrooms, facing head-on the often embittered process of challenging the status quo in order to bring about a more just society. But such renegotiations must also encourage us to think through the implications of those shifts at cultural, disciplinary, and individual levels. On one hand, we insist that writing is social and that texts are not unified, bounded objects; on the other hand, we require our students to write single-voiced texts (even when they write in groups their texts aren't supposed to sound disjointed or as though they were written by committee); we grade those objects by what they contain rather than what they connect. Except for unique circumstances, such as writing annotated bibliographies, we estimate a text's value not according to the information it gathers and arranges but by what the writer *adds*. We need to learn to reverse this approach or at least to correct the imbalance.

None of this is to say composition should abandon the production of text. The dialectical tension between node and link provides us with a way to navigate a path between extremes of enlightenment authorship and postmodernist dispersal of agency and identity into powerless lines of indeterminate intensities. But, like systems of language, positive objects only gain relative values by being related to one another: positive spaces are constituted out of negative ones.

Works Cited

Berkenkotter, Carol, Thomas N. Huckin, and John Ackerman. "Conventions, Conversations, and the Writer: Case Study of a Student in a Rhetoric Ph.D. Program." *Research in the Teaching of English* 50 (1988):9–44.

Berlin, James A. *Rhetoric and Reality: Writing Instruction in American Colleges, 1900–1985*. Carbondale: Southern Illinois University Press, 1987.

Bizzell, Patricia. "'Contact Zones' and English Studies." *College English* 56 (1994):163–69.

Bolter, Jay David. *Writing Space: The Computer, Hypertext, and the History of Writing*. Hillsdale, NJ: Lawrence Erlbaum Associates, 1991.

Bruffee, Kenneth A. "Collaborative Learning: Some Practical Methods." *College English* 34 (1973):634–43.

Cooper, Marilyn M., and Cynthia L. Selfe. "Computer Conferences and Learning: Authority, Resistance, and Internally Persuasive Discourse." *College English* 52 (1990):847–69.

Devitt, Amy J. "Generalizing about Concept: New Conception of an Old Concept." *College Composition and Communication* 44 (1993):573–86.

Drucker, Peter F. "The Coming of the New Organization." *Harvard Business Review* (Jan.–Feb. 1988): 45–53.

Eisenstein, Elizabeth L. *The Printing Press as an Agent of Change: Communications and Cultural Transformations in Early-Modern Europe*. 2 vols. Cambridge: Cambridge University Press, 1979.

Faigley, Lester. *Fragments of Rationality: Postmodernity and the Subject of Composition*. Pittsburgh: University of Pittsburgh Press, 1992.

Giroux, Henry. *Border Crossings: Cultural Workers and the Politics of Education*. New York: Routledge, 1992.

Hairston, Maxine. "Diversity, Ideology, and the Teaching of Writing." *College Composition and Communication* 43 (1992):179–93.

Hamp-Lyons, Liz, and William Condon. "Questioning Assumptions About Portfolio-based Assessment." *College Composition and Communication* 44 (1993):176–90.

Herzberg, Bruce. "Community Service and Critical Teaching." *College Composition and Communication* 45 (1994):307–19.

Hilbert, Betsy. "Elegy for Excursus: The Descent of the Footnote." *College English* 51 (1989):400–404.

Hirschhorn, Larry. *Beyond Mechanization: Work and Technology in a Postindustrial Age*. Cambridge: MIT Press, 1984.

Jameson, Frederic. *Postmodernism; or, The Cultural Logic of Late Capitalism.* Durham, NC: Duke University Press, 1991.

Johnson-Eilola, J. "Accumulation, Circulation, Association: Economies of Text in Online Research Spaces." *IEEE Transactions on Professional Communication* 38 (1995):228–38.

Landow, George P. *Hypertext: The Convergence of Contemporary Critical Theory and Technology.* Baltimore: Johns Hopkins University Press, 1992.

Lyotard, Jean-François. *The Postmodern Condition: A Report on Knowledge.* Trans. Geoff Bennington and Brian Massumi, trans. Minneapolis: University of Minnesota Press, 1984.

Murray, Donald M. "Teach Writing as a Process, not a Product." In *Rhetoric and Composition: A Sourcebook for Teachers and Writers.* Ed. Richard L. Graves. 2nd ed. Upper Montclair, NJ: Boynton/Cook, 1984. 98–92. Reprinted from *The Leaflet,* Nov. 1972: 11–14.

Ong, Walter J. *Orality and Literacy: The Technologizing of the Word.* London: Methuen, 1982.

Porter, James E. "Intertextuality and the Discourse Community." *Rhetoric Review* 5, no. 1 (1986):34–47.

Porter, James E. *Rhetorical Ethics and Internetworked Writing.* Norwood, NJ: Ablex, in press.

Pratt, Mary Louise. *Imperial Eyes: Travel Writing and Transculturation.* London: Routledge, 1992.

Regan, A. "Type Normal like the Rest of Us: Writing, Power, and Homophobia in the Networked Classroom." *Computers and Composition* 10, no. 4 (1993):11–23.

Reich, Robert B. *The Work of Nations.* New York: Vintage, 1992.

Romano, S. "The Egalitarian Narrative. Whose Story? Whose Yardstick?" *Computers and Composition* 10, no. 3 (1994):5–28.

Slatin, John M. "Reading Hypertext: Order and Coherence in a New Medium." *College English* 52 (1990):870–83.

Soja, Edward. *Postmodern Geographies: The Reassertion of Space in Critical Social Theory.* London: Verso, 1989.

Trimbur, John. "Consensus and Difference in Collaborative Learning." *College English* 51 (1989):602–16.

Ulmer, Gregory. "Grammatology (in the Stacks) of Hypermedia: A Simulation." In *Literacy Online: The Promise (and Peril) of Reading and Writing with Computers.* Ed. Myron C. Tuman. Pittsburgh: University of Pittsburgh Press, 1992. 139–58.

——. *Heuritics: The Logic of Invention.* Baltimore: Johns Hopkins University Press, 1994.

——. *Teletheory: Grammatology in the Age of Video.* New York: Routledge, 1989.

Zuboff, Shoshana. *In the Age of the Smart Machine: The Future of Work and Power.* New York: Basic, 1988.

3   Cyberpunk Literacy; or, Piety in the Sky

William A. Covino

To call up a demon you must learn its name. Men dreamed that, once, but now it is real in another way. You know that, Case. Your business is to learn the names of programs, the long formal names, names the owners seek to conceal. True names. . . .
                                                            —William Gibson, *Neuromancer*, 243

And, finally, whether it has essential limits or not, the entire field covered by the cybernetic *program* will be the field of writing. If the theory of cybernetics is by itself to oust all metaphysical concepts—including the concepts of soul, of life, of value, of choice, of memory—which until recently served to separate the machine from man, it must conserve the notion of writing, trace, gramme [written mark], or grapheme, until its own historico-metaphysical character is also exposed.   —Jacques Derrida, *Of Grammatology*, 9

You want you a paradise.   —William Gibson, *Neuromancer*, 81

William Gibson's 1984 *Neuromancer* has been celebrated as the prototype for cyberpunk fiction (McCaffery 130) and has helped to spawn the huge popular media arena of sci-fi technoculture (Bukatman 199). At the same time, Randy Schroeder is correct that "Gibson burns archaic fuels to run a postmodern engine" (162). Despite its often disorienting futuristic descriptions and its portrayal of technological possibilities that remain well beyond the limits of the current practical imagination, *Neuromancer* is also a familiar story, with its hard-boiled, computer cowboy-detective hero Case raiding the bad guys, rescuing the girl, and ending up alone again: the strong, laconic, cool individual holding steady in a crazy world. In short, while *Neuromancer* employs the stylistics of sensory overload associated with postmodern virtualities, it is also a traditional modern masculinist fantasy. Scott Bukatman notes that *Neuromancer* has been "damned as masculinist fantasy for a new era" (199), but he also proposes that "despite its ideological limits, *Neuromancer* remains a consequential bricolage that moves us further from Edenic fantasies of essentialism" (329). This chapter will propose that *Neuromancer* actually *maintains* such essentialist fantasies, specifically, that *Neuromancer* is a traditional story of the fortunes of advanced literacy, continuing a centuries-old nostalgia for cosmological symbolic power and the belief that certain worthy individuals could achieve it.

Ostensibly, *Neuromancer* narrates the future of cyberpunk literacy, with the portrayal of its main character, Case, as a talented cyberpunk who can navigate and invade virtual and material realities from his computer console. Thus the novel maintains advanced technoliteracy—the cyberpunk riding the matrix—as a version of magic; as such, cyberpunk literacy operates as a transci-fiormative and transcendental force associated with the control and manipulation of reality. Popular analogs to *Neuromancer* maintain cyberpunk literacy as such a power: For instance, in the 1995 movie *The Net*, typical of stories that make cyberpunk literacy the focus of a battle between criminals after money and power and good citizens who want to maintain an enterprise zone free of harassment, the control of the international business world is at stake; the agonistics thus take on cosmic significance. So too with the 1983 *Wargames*, in which cyberpunk literacy in the right hands assures nothing less than the deliverance of humankind from nuclear holocaust. Cyberpunk literacy can deliver us from evil and forestall death; it can, in the instant of a keystroke, transci-fiorm one impending version of reality into another.

As I have argued elsewhere, transci-fiormation, transcendence, efficiency, and the expansion of the self are the traditional functions of magic (Covino, *Magic*); the elaboration of these in current sci-fi versions of cyberpunk literacy certainly follows a template offered in *Neuromancer*, which is itself a continuation of the centuries-old Western compulsion to discover a magic procreative language. *Neuromancer* is, essentially, the search for a magic word: Gibson's Case must discover a secret code that, once uttered, will change the shape of the corporate-cosmological matrix, a word that will, actually, de-create and re-create the world. With this quest, Case joins a long tradition of mystics, philosophers, scientists, and "strong, stubborn, creative individual[s]" (Leary 245) for whom uttering "the right word at the right time" (*Neuromancer* 173) becomes an urgent goal. As Allison Coudert explains, the search for an "alphabet of nature," based on the belief that "symbols and sounds could reflect reality and therefore be 'natural' or 'real' rather than conventional" (57) extends through Platonic, Neoplatonic, Hermetic, and Kabbalistic writings and entails the impulse to *create reality through language* (one prominent manifestation of this impulse is the golem, an artificial anthropoid theorized by medieval kabbalists as the product of a precisely formulated recitation of the Hebrew alphabet [Covino, "Grammars" 357–62]). The magico-religious search for a procreative natural language does not disappear with the rise of science; instead, science revaluates language that reflects natural reality as plain, transparent, unambiguous. Such a view, advanced in seventeenth-century England by the Royal Society, insists on a direct correspondence of words to things, "to make faithful *Records*, of all the Works of *Nature*, or *Art*," so that "Mankind may obtain a Dominion over *Things*" (Sprat 61–62). Scientific literacy, then, maintains the impulse to create and subdue reality, and this impulse is reconstituted as magical with the advance of computer technology in this century. Norbert Wiener, the inventor of cybernetics, fears that computer enthusiasts ("gadget worshippers") will mistake the power of machines for magic power and employ it stupidly and destructively. With this view, he predicts to some extent the motives of the Silicon Valley hackers of the 1960s who see technology as a vehicle for mind expansion, and he introduces magic as the metaphor most often used to describe the remarkable powers of cybernetic machines.

Full of allusions to magic, mysticism, and religion, *Neuromancer* continues the search for an ultimate magic literacy. As Coudert explains, that search has always had social harmony as its ostensible goal: our disagreements and divisions—so proponents of nature's alphabet argue—result from the ambiguity of human language. By replacing corrupt human language with the alphabet of God and Nature, we can live in peace and speak Truth. This goal is easily understood as disguised religious or cultural oppression, especially as it has informed reactionary arguments for maintaining an elite class as the norm, as in Francis von Helmont's 1667 *Alphabet of Nature* (see Coudert 56–64), which argues for the universalizing of pure Hebrew; in Thomas Sprat's contemporaneous *History of the Royal Society*, which does the same for plain English; and in the many consequent advocacies of language reform as the cure for social ills, which find their current expression in "English Only" legislation in the United States.

Neuromancer, which has helped define and reflect what postmodern technoliteracy can be, abandons nostalgia for uniformity while maintaining the possibility of transcending the dizzying ambiguities that attend both the real and virtual worlds. Perhaps the most threatening of these ambiguities rests in the difficulty of distinguishing good from bad, true from false, of *authenticating* who people are and what they say. That difficulty is represented by Case's worry about a passing stranger:

> He stepped out of the way to let a dark-suited sarariman by, spotting the Mitsubishi-Genentech logo tattooed across the back of the man's right hand.
>   Was it authentic? If that's for real, he thought, he's in for trouble.   (10)

Is this an M-G thug programmed to detect proscribed goods smugglers like Case or not? In *Neuromancer*, the authenticity of those we encounter is always at issue, because bodies and identities are constantly alterable: Case's associate, Julius Deane, is 135 years old but doesn't look it because every year "genetic surgeons re-set the code of his DNA" (12); Case's boss, Armitage, has been surgically reconstituted, psychologically and physically, and strikes Case as "a con-

servative amalgam of the world's leading media faces" (45); and Riviera, one of
the mission team, is programmed to generate virtual-reality images from his
imagination, thus disguising his own identity and populating the scene with ex-
traordinary visuals nearly impossible to perceive as unreal.

In this world, then, Julius Deane's quip to Case—"Not always that easy to
know who your friends are, is it?" (13)—is quite an understatement. Of course,
Gibson's world is a species of postmodern indeterminacy, populated by Bau-
drillardian simulacra, or Protean magicians, and raises the question, What sort
of literacy is viable when the codes that constitute meaning, in particular the
ethos of individuals, are in flux?

Ethos—understood as the character of the speaker—has long been regarded
as an unstable, potentially deceptive, and substantially indeterminate characteristic, from its presentation in Aristotle's fourth century B.C.E. treatise *On
Rhetoric*. There Aristotle presents ethos as a kind of "proof" or, put another way,
as an element of effective persuasion. For Aristotle, a speaker creates an effective ethos through words that demonstrate *phronesis*, or practical wisdom; *arete*,
or moral virtue; and *eunoia*, or good will toward the audience. All these ethical
virtues entail sincerity and imply a speaker who is telling the truth about himself. But the problem of verifying ethical sincerity seems insoluble: Plato's at-
tacks on rhetoric—in his *Sophist*, *Gorgias*, and *Phaedrus*—stress the likelihood
that most speakers are interested in the *effects*, rather than the *truth* of what they
say and will pretend to have authority and virtue that they do not really possess.
In this century, Wayne Booth reiterates the problem of ethical sincerity by not-
ing that "sincerity is more difficult to check and easier to fake than logicality or
consistency, and its presence does not, after all, guarantee very much about the
speaker's case"; Booth recognizes that no pedagogy yet has taken us very far toward the development of a reliable ethos sensor: "If one mark of an educated
man [sic] is that he can recognize a good person when he sees one, is it not
strange that almost nothing in our enormous program of higher education
deals with the question of how it is done?" (157–58).

Since the advent of the Enlightenment, the most common approach to the
problem of ethical indeterminacy has been to exhort plain style and to insist, as
Bob Dole did during his candidacy for president, that a plain speaker is a sin-
cere speaker. The association of spare and unadorned language with truth and
sincerity is institutionalized by London's Royal Society (see, e.g., Sprat 61–62)
and connected with religious morality: Puritan writer and preacher John Bunyan declared in 1666 that all who would do God's work must abandon "play" in
language and "be plain and simple, and lay down the thing as it was" (15). This
attitude, without the religious emphasis, informs advice on speaking and writ-

ing up to the present in statements such as E. B. White's pithy injunction in *The Elements of Style*: "Omit needless words" (23).

Of course, as Wayne Booth implies, plain style has never guaranteed either clarity or sincerity, the two virtues with which it is most often associated. And in the cyberpunk era where *Neuromancer* is set, even the false promise of plain style is an irrelevance. This is a world in which, as we will see, writing as human communication is associated with the backward poor, and writing as the occult encryption of "the long formal names of programs" that contain corporate secrets represents the only source of power.

Further, the art of determining ethos, which in Aristotelian tradition has been a primarily verbal skill tied to critical engagement with spoken or written arguments, has become—in our age of electronic media and even more so in Gibson's cyberpunk future—a primarily *visual* skill. Case is betrayed by his former lover, Linda Lee, because he fails to "read" that betrayal in her eyes: "There was something in the grey eyes now that he couldn't read, something he'd never seen there before" (10). This eyes-are-the-windows-of-the-soul assumption (which accounts in part for Case's alertness to the "bleached" blue eyes of the dehumanized Armitage, the hidden eyes of Molly and Julius Deane/Wintermute, and the "calm and distant" eyes of the protean Riviera) culminates in Case's felt recognition of his own unique individuality: "It was his own darkness, pulse and blood, the one where he'd always slept, behind his eyes and no other's" (263). Allied to a romantic tradition in which sincerity can be read through the eyes (see, for instance, Matthew Arnold's "The Buried Life"), Gibson is also suggesting that language—disembodied signs and symbols—cannot itself bear a determinate ethos, that one's "character" is the production of one's embodied soul. But at the same time that Gibson mistrusts verbal literacy as an indicator of either virtue or corruption, he offers cyberpunk literacy, which is the art of constant movement and steady navigation within an endless matrix of indeterminate appearances (with an eye on the code that will transcifiorm it all), as perhaps the only mode of effective counterpolitics in a corrupt, completely commodified world.

But in this connection, the most widely perceived trouble with *Neuromancer*, which I noted above, is its maintenance of an essentially male teenage fantasy: "Cyberpunk's idea of a counterpolitics—youthful male heroes with working-class chips on their shoulders and postmodern biochips in their brains—seems to have little to do with the burgeoning power of the great social movements of our day: feminism, ecology, peace, sexual liberation, and civil rights" (Ross 152. Csicsery-Ronay, Hollinger, Nixon, and Suvin also offer worried surveys of cyberpunk).

The cyberpunk hero still has celebrators, though. Timothy Leary defines the cyberpunk in grand terms, as a "strong, stubborn, creative individual who explores [*cyber*, in Leary's etymology, means "pilot"] some future frontier, collects and brings back new information, and offers to guide the gene pool to the next stage" (245). This cyberpunk continues a tradition of legendary rebels, typified by the Greek demigod Prometheus, who defy authority. Cyberpunk types include Christopher Columbus, Mark Twain, Charles Lindbergh, Andy Warhol, Gertrude Stein, and William Gibson, all—for Leary—innovators who disdain "static, verbal abstractions, conformity to dogma, reliance on authority" (258). One would expect such a romantic characterization of the cyberpunk from Leary, who was at the center of the psychedelic sixties, when celebrations of the autonomous self emerged from the antiwar movement, accompanied by the exploration of self-expansion in the form of altered psychological states.

Such altered states—which would constitute for Leary unconventional modes of self-navigation associated with the cyberpunk—were effected through both hallucinogenic drugs and the newest cybernetic prosthesis: the personal computer (Scott Bukatman reports a Silicon Valley hacker who, echoing similar pronouncements by Leary, says that "computers are to the eighties what LSD was to the sixties" [*Terminal Identity* 139]). But technoculture enthusiast Leary's "problem person" in postmodern cybernetic society—"the one who automatically obeys, who never questions authority, who acts to protect his/her official status, who placates and politics rather than thinks independently" (246)—is the same person that Jacques Ellul posits as absolutely essential to a functioning technological society: "properly trained, aware of his responsibility, capable of attention and solidarity, and proof against sabotage or striking" (3). While Leary and Ellul are not in disagreement that a culture of automatons is dismal, Leary welcomes cyberculture as an opportunity for innovative individuals, while Ellul envisions the imminent foreclosure of radical thought.

Leary finds counterparts in hypertext enthusiasts such as Jay Bolter and George Landow, who speak of traveling the hypertext docuverse in grand, visionary terms: "Whereas terms like *death, vanish, loss,* and expressions of depletion and impoverishment color critical theory, the vocabulary of freedom, energy, and empowerment marks writings on hypertextuality. . . . Most poststructuralists write from within the twilight of a wished-for coming day; most writers of hypertext write of many of the same things from within the dawn" (Landow 87).

The evangelical association of technological growth with the transcendence of material conditions (death, disease, pain, loss; what *Neuromancer* calls "meat" things) is typical of technological advocacies; the introduction to the

1995 *Cyborg Handbook* exhorts us to do good works in a new cyborg world: "We live in a world that is changing before our eyes. . . . It may help us to confront these changes if we accept our new status as cyborgs and begin to look at these changes from a cyborgian point of view. . . . In any event, if your grandmother, or anybody you love, is thinking of getting a pacemaker, you can't afford neutrality" (Gray 13). The comically desperate tone here suggests some recognition of the eternity of the cyborg state: cyborgs aren't going to go away, and this is the large measure of their appeal. We are all already cyborgs, to the extent that any of our capabilities and tolerances is mechanically modified; just so, we are all already hypertextual cyberpunks, versions of characters in an IBM commercial, like the vineyard owner in Italy who boasts to his daughter—in Italian—about having completed his graduate work at Indiana University, with the help of a modem and IBM. We line up for copies of Windows '95 and, in a more primitive imitation of *Neuromancer*'s Case, jack into Netscape. What Ellul prognosticated has come to pass: the cyberpunk, following his glamorous entry onto the scene in movies like *Tron* and fiction like Gibson's, has been normalized—neutralized—by the sheer profusion of software and hardware that has flooded the market.

Of course, the "we" that I associate above with cyborgs and cyberpunks is actually what Arthur Kroker and Michael Weinstein call the "virtual elite," those with the resources to get "wired." At the same time, this "we" is a universalized conception of the desired product of education in advanced societies: California, which as Baudrillard reminds us, is the original site of Disneyland and thus a leader in the worldwide proliferation of simulacra, has now legislated the statewide computer networking of its schools, a de facto branding of noncyborg/cyberpunks as uneducated and illiterate. In *Neuromancer*, technoilliteracy is a severe disability, the mark of poverty and hopelessness.

When Case looks down on the poor Middle Eastern city of Beyoglu, with its "walls of patchwork wooden tenements . . . grim housing projects, [and] walls of plyboard and corrugated iron," he notices that "a few letter-writers had taken refuge in doorways, their old voiceprinters wrapped in sheets of clear plastic, evidence that the written word still enjoyed a certain prestige here. It was a sluggish country" (87–88). Writing, even with what seems to be a mechanical dictation translator, is associated with the disenfranchised and is a sluggish practice indeed, in contrast to the conception of cyberspace that is taught to schoolchildren: "Cyberspace. A consensual hallucination experienced daily by billions of legitimate operators, in every nation, by children being taught mathematical concepts. . . . A graphic representation of data abstracted from the banks of every computer in the human system. Unthinkable complexity. Lines of light ranged in the nonspace of the mind, clusters and constellations of data. Like city lights, receding . . ." (51).

Of course, Gibson's emphasis on cyberspace as a hallucination maintains some distinction between the virtual world and the real world and implies that any symbol system adopted as a universal literacy is a shared delusion. The positing of cyberspace as the realm in which basic childhood education is conducted stresses the penalty for being excluded from it; that penalty is illustrated by the poor writers of Beyoglu and by the Case we meet at the beginning of the novel, a denizen of Chiba City, where expatriates sit and drink and make deals centered on the petty thefts of data software and "proscribed biologicals."

Case is a twenty-four-year-old Prometheus type: Prometheus steals from the gods and is punished by having his body eaten away. His is the theft of power reserved to the superhuman, and in some versions of the myth Prometheus steals *magic* or *writing* and gives it to humanity, thus making himself, and the human race at large, rivals to the gods. In Case's world, it is the possession of information, "the names of programs . . . that owners seek to conceal," that constitutes social and economic power. As the novel opens, Case has stolen information from his employers, who have the power of life and death over him. For his crime, Case's body is altered, so that he can no longer "pilot" a computer console into cyberspace. His initial despair, then, is his desire for the cyberpunk literacy he once knew; Case longs to "reach the console that wasn't there," to become the Promethean demigod who—by virtue of his ability to enter the consensual hallucination of cyberspace—escapes the "meat" world of wasting bodies. The loss of cyberpunk literacy has left Case an outcast from cyberspace, where wealth, power, and pleasure are brokered.

The question that continues to attend debates over the value of cyberpunk, and larger debates over the promise of technology, is whether—apart from the specific problem of whether cyberspace is too exclusively a masculinist realm— new technological literacies can disrupt what Donna Haraway calls the "informatics of domination" (161), those oppressive regimes that produce both weapons systems and computer software in order to maintain political and ideological control. In other words, can cyberpunk literacy function as a force for positive change? Given that cyberpunk literacy is featured in *Neuromancer* and elsewhere as rife with magico-religious associations, while it also represents the implicitly sacrilegious attitude of the sociocultural rebel, this question requires some attention to the relation between cyberpunk literacy and *piety*, which, as Kenneth Burke presents it, is an impulse that locates magico-religious behaviors in the secular realm and is present in even the most ostensibly irreverent or "utilitarian" behaviors. For Burke, piety is a conditioned associational orientation, connected with the wish to return to a prior, Edenic state of being. This wish—based on childhood experiences—governs our adult sense of "what properly goes with what"; thus piety is "a response which extends through all the texture of our lives but has been concealed from us because we think we are so thoroughly without religion and think that the 'pious process' is confined to the sphere of churchliness" (74–5). Burke notes that "we cannot speak the mother-tongue without employing the devices of a Roman orator" in order to stress that some considerable measure of piety is inherent in every action, because all have foundations in the psychological, historical, and cultural "sources of our being." A pious attitude is particularly apparent in those for whom "a job" becomes not only a utilitarian necessity but also "a calling" (82).

In a state of suicidal despair, *Neuromancer*'s Case gets a job offer that is also an appeal to his piety. His body will be fixed, his cyberpunk literacy returned, if he joins a high-level information-theft mission. With this setup, Gibson's version of cyberpunk literacy locates the potentially radical individual within the constraints of a matrix that define his talent and energy as forms of servitude. Case is unaware that he has been picked—called—for this mission by Wintermute, an artificial intelligence that appears throughout the novel in parodies of the biblical God, as a virtual reality that a Rastafarian religious cult worships as "the Mute" and in various guises that Wintermute itself compares to the Bible's "burning bush." A parody of spiritual calling occurs well into the mission, when Case is standing in a hotel lobby near a row of pay phones:

> The phone nearest him rang. Automatically, he picked it up.
> "Yeah?"
> Faint harmonics, tiny inaudible voices rattling across some orbital link, and then a sound like wind.
> "Hello, Case."
> A fifty-lirasi coin fell from his hand, bounced, and rolled out of sight across Hilton carpeting.
> "Wintermute, Case. It's time we talk."
> It was a chip voice.
> "Don't you want to talk, Case?"
> He hung up.
> On the way back to the lobby, his cigarettes forgotten, he had to walk the length of the ranked phones. Each rang in turn, but only once, as he passed.
> (98)

In connection with the deified Wintermute, then, Case himself is a parodic version of the chosen, those in the biblical tradition who experience the revelation of the deity. And his piety is guaranteed by the urgency of his desire, his yearning to return to what Burke would call the pietistic "sources of his being," to the console keyboard, that altar that pays homage through its very operation to the corporate-cosmological matrix and its deities.

As the mission proceeds, finding the secret code comes increasingly to represent, for Case, discovering the source and center of the symbolic order that is governing his behavior. Infiltrating the matrix brings the hope of some vague sort of liberation, because somewhere in there is the magic word that just might deliver Case from the oppressive monotony of his existence. He screams at 3Jane, the corporate leader who knows the magic word, "I got no idea at all what'll happen if Wintermute wins, but it'll *change* something" (260). The possibility that cyberpunk literacy is a vehicle for change is one that Gibson finally rejects, but not without featuring the ultimate cyberpunk achievement—the discovery of the magic word and the reordering of the matrix—as an act that requires the transcendence of human language altogether.

With his desperate argument for *change*, Case finally gets 3Jane—who wants some relief from her own boring entombment in the grotesque recesses of corporate headquarters—to give up the Word. However, the Word is no word but a song: "three notes, high and pure. A true name" (262). This series of tones activates an ornate jeweled bust, a computer terminal that speaks the changes that will transci-fiorm the matrix: "piping melodically, endlessly, speaking of numbered Swiss accounts, of payment to be made to Zion via a Bahamian orbital bank, of passports and passages . . ." (262). With this scene, Gibson adapts the traditional magic notion of sound and music as cosmological forces and features the alphabet of nature generated by song as merely a recitation of money transci-fiers and travel arrangements. Like the song of Yeats's nightingale in "Sailing to Byzantium," the terminal also sings "of what is past, or passing, or to come." And the song of Yeats's nightingale, like the song of the bejeweled terminal, is merely a vehicle for relieving boredom, used in the poem "to keep a drowsy Emperor awake." As in Yeats's eternal magic city, nothing changes in *Neuromancer*'s world; after his mission is accomplished, Case hears from Wintermute again:

> "I'm not Wintermute now."
> "So what are you." . . .
> "I'm the matrix, Case."
> Case laughed. "Where's that get you?"
> "Nowhere. Everywhere. I'm the sum total of the works, the whole show.". . .
> "So what's the score? How are things different? You running the world now? You God?"
> "Things aren't different. Things are things."   (270)

Cyberpunk literacy is not a force for change in a world where corporate reorganization is the only change possible. It is, rather, a diversion, an entertainment, a stimulation, because while the matrix may need the individual in order to effect change, the change itself finally keeps the matrix in control and the individual pious. Finally, then, cyberpunk literacy merely serves the purposes of stimulation and entertainment and represents the ability of a talented individual to amuse himself in a world that is—with reference to any substantive change in material conditions—always the same. After Wintermute wins, Beyoglu is still backward, Chiba City is still "the color of television, tuned to a dead channel" (3).

The cyberpunk can, perhaps, gain some personal integrity by rejecting the piety of his literacy: Case ultimately tells Wintermute, "I don't need you" (270). But Case is at last just another Orwellian "prole," whose resignation is expressed by the strikingly flat, bemused account of his return to ordinary life:

> He found work.
> He found a girl who called herself Michael.   (270)

Cyberpunk literacy, like its magico-religious precursors, would seem to offer transcendence and power, but finally the working-class cyberpunk remains just that, adept at infiltrating a "consensual hallucination" he cannot really affect. In Derrida's terms, Gibson's Case has exposed the "historico-metaphysical character" of cyberpunk writing-riding in the matrix; through his desperate piety, he has confronted the source of his own being and finds his own metaphysical desire "ousted" by the sheer power and stability of the matrix he worships. He has met a deity that we might call, after Derrida, the "theory of cybernetics itself," which in *Neuromancer* renders writing-riding a grim parody of the old desire to dominate the symbolic order.

It seems appropriate finally to ask how our understanding of the confrontation between Case and Wintermute might inform the teaching of rhetoric and writing, especially as we work in an electronic age in which the obsolescence of traditional oral and print literacies is impending, if not apparent, and the evangelism associated with cyberliteracy grows from a sociocultural movement into a commonplace. Gibson's cyberspace is a version of Roland Barthes's "docuverse," that "galaxy of signifiers" that comprises the materials of our reading and writing, and, in this connection, cyberspace becomes itself a *call to writing*, a vast space for the construction of meaning. The question Gibson prompts is one of motives: Do we ride the matrix—do we write—from an impulse to conquest? Transcendence? Piety? Change qua change? Certainly, these impulses remain even as the technologies of literacy change, and seeing their pursuit in *Neuromancer* should remind us that we cannot launch our students into the new matrix without raising the old question, the question that ensures some reflective hesitation before the matrix makes us its own: why write?

Works Cited

Aristotle. *On Rhetoric*. Trans. George Kennedy. New York: Oxford University Press, 1991.

Barthes, Roland. *S/Z*. Trans. Richard Miller. New York: Hill and Wang, 1974.

Baudrillard, Jean. "Disneyworld Company." Trans. Francois Debrix. *CTheory* 19, nos. 1–2. Online posting 27 Mar. 1996.

Blair, Hugh. *Lectures on Rhetoric and Belles-Lettres*. 2 vols. 1783. Repr., Carbondale: Southern Illinois University Press, 1965.

Bolter, Jay. *Writing Space: The Computer, Hypertext, and the History of Writing*. Hillsdale, NJ: Erlbaum, 1991.

Booth, Wayne. *Modern Dogma and the Rhetoric of Assent*. Chicago: University of Chicago Press, 1974.

Burke, Kenneth. *Permanence and Change: An Anatomy of Purpose*. 3d ed. Berkeley: University of California Press, 1984.

Bukatman, Scott. "Amidst These Fields of Data: Allegory, Rhetoric, and the Paraspace." *Science Fiction Studies* 33, no. 3 (1992):199–219.

———. *Terminal Identity: The Virtual Subject in Postmodern Science Fiction*. Durham: Duke University Press, 1993.

Bunyan, John. *Grace Abounding to the Chief of Sinners*. 1666. Repr., Grand Rapids: Baker, 1986.

Coudert, Allison. "Some Theories of a Natural Language from the Renaissance to the Seventeenth Century." In *Magia Naturalis und die Enstehung der Modernen Naturwissenschaften*. Wiesbaden: Steiner, 1978. 56–114.

Covino, William A. "Grammars of Transgression: Golems, Cyborgs, and Mutants." *Rhetoric Review* 14, no. 2 (1996):355–73.

———. *Magic, Rhetoric, and Literacy: An Eccentric History of the Composing Imagination*. Albany: SUNY Press, 1994.

Csicsery-Ronay, Istvan. "Cyberpunk and Neuromanticism." *Mississippi Review* 47/48 (1988):266–78.

Derrida, Jacques. *Of Grammatology*. Trans. Gayatri Chakravorty Spivak. Baltimore: Johns Hopkins University Press, 1976.

Ellul, Jacques. *The Technological System*. Trans. Joachim Eugroschel. New York: Continuum, 1980.

Gibson, William. *Neuromancer*. New York: Ace, 1984.

Gray, Chris Hables, ed. *The Cyborg Handbook*. New York: Routledge, 1995.

Haraway, Donna J. "A Cyborg Manifesto." In *Simians, Cyborgs, and Women: The Reinvention of Nature.* New York: Routledge, 1991. 149–81.

Hollinger, Veronica. "Cybernetic Deconstructions: Cyberpunk and Postmodernism." *Mosaic* 23, no. 2 (1990):29–44.

Kroker, Arthur, and Michael A. Weinstein. *Data Trash: The Theory of the Virtual Class.* New York: St. Martin's, 1994.

Landow, George. *Hypertext: The Convergence of Contemporary Critical Theory and Technology.* Baltimore: Johns Hopkins University Press, 1992.

Leary, Timothy. "The Cyberpunk: The Individual as Reality Pilot." In *Storming the Reality Studio: A Casebook of Cyberpunk and Postmodern Science Fiction.* Ed. Larry McCaffery. Durham: Duke University Press, 1991. 245–58.

McCaffery, Larry, ed. *Across the Wounded Galaxies: Interviews with Contemporary American Science Fiction Writers.* Urbana: University of Illinois Press, 1990.

The Net. Dir. Irwin Winkler. Columbia, 1995.

Nixon, Nicola. "Cyberpunk: Preparing the Ground for Revolution or Keeping the Boys Satisci-fiied?" *Science Fiction Studies* 19 (1992):219–35.

Plato. *Gorgias.* Trans. W. C. Helmbold. New York: Liberal Arts Press, 1952.

——. *Phaedrus.* Trans. Harold North Fowler. Cambridge: Harvard University Press, 1914.

——. *Sophist.* Trans. Harold North Fowler. Cambridge: Harvard University Press, 1921.

Ross, Andrew. *Strange Weather: Culture, Science, and Technology in the Age of Limits.* London: Verso, 1991.

Schroeder, Randy. "Determinacy, Indeterminacy, and the Romantic in William Gibson." *Science Fiction Studies* 21 (1994):155–63.

Sprat, Thomas. *History of the Royal Society.* 1667. Ed. Jackson Cope and Harold Jones. St. Louis: Washington University Press, 1958.

Suvin, Darko. "On Gibson and Cyberpunk." *Foundation* 46 (autumn 1989): 40–51.

White, E. B. *The Elements of Style.* New York: Macmillan, 1959.

Wiener, Norbert. *God and Golem, Inc.: A Comment on Certain Points Where Cybernetics Impinges on Religion.* Cambridge: MIT Press, 1964.

Wargames. Dir. John Badham. United Artists, 1983.

Tron. Dir. Steven Lisberger. Disney, 1983.

Yeats, William Butler. "Sailing to Byzantium." In *Norton Anthology of English Literature.* Ed. M. H. Abrams. New York: Norton, 1986. 1951.

4   Writing in the Hivemind

Don Byrd and Derek Owens

Hive, *sb.*: 1. An artificial receptacle for the habitation of a swarm of bees; a beehive. 2. *fig.* A storehouse of sweet things. 3. *transf.* a. A place swarming with busy occupants. b. A place whence swarms of people issue; the nursery of a teeming race . . . d. *spec.* A breeding-place for oysters. . . . 5. A capsule or case containing many cells. . . .

    Hive, *v.* . . . 4. *intr.* To enter the hive, take to the hive, as bees. b. To live together as bees in a hive; also *transf.* to lodge together.   —*Oxford English Dictionary*

Taking the Labor out of Collaboration

The emphasis on collaborative writing is so prevalent in composition studies that many of us can't imagine teaching in environments that don't have students interacting in groups, swapping drafts, and generally composing in teams at every stage of the writing process. While many of us can remember stoic grade-school encounters where stern teachers forced us to write in silent isolation, increasingly our students have no memories of such situations. Some of them walk into our courses having never been in a writing classroom where students did *not* break into small groups, exchange papers, and pass back and forth editorial comments. And now that computers play an increasingly central part in writing instruction, collaborative writing happens more efficiently and with greater variety than before. Email correspondence, new writing software (Daedalus, Aspects, Storyspace, CommonSpace, Norton Textra Connect), MUDs and MOOs, HyperNews, enhanced electronic conferencing techniques, the ease of incorporating sound and video within the written text—these technologies situate collaborative writing at the center of computer-supported composition pedagogy. Clearly, composition theory has moved away from the romantic image of the sequestered, solitary writer toward a sense of writing as a tribal practice—to an extent.

    But while all this editorial exchange and virtual conversing on networks has significantly altered the way teachers and thus students think of themselves as writers, much of this activity remains predicated on rather conventional assumptions about the nature and purpose of composing. No matter how much we might stress process over product, for example, or admit uncertainty as a necessary element of the writing process, we still honor fairly entrenched ideas about what our students' finished texts ought to look and sound like. Most of us would probably like it if their writing were to move toward some central idea, defining terms and advancing claims supported by a degree of evidence, and generally demonstrating some sophistication about readerly expectations. We want students to construct texts that will succeed according to prior standards. We have become adept at inventing ways to use collaboration and technology to refine what we already do, but we still have far to go when it comes to inventing new objectives for the practice of writing.

When multiple minds cohabitate within the same writing space, it follows that unpredictability should manifest. When multiple psyches, agendas, and histories cross-pollinate within a shared zone of activity, who can predict the outcome? The composing process is unpredictable enough for a single writer working in a relatively controlled environment; bring together several minds within the same compositional space, and the result is chaos. Not chaos in any pejorative sense (we now know that chaos is not the absence of logic), but rather chaos as the proliferation of multiple logics ever in flux and open to mutation. Yet the fact that so many of the texts students create as a result of collaborative work ultimately resemble—rhetorically, formally, thematically—the kinds of writing made before our recent forays into collaborative writing underscores just how carefully teachers continue to shape these collaborative encounters. That students working collaboratively do not end up with wonderfully strange and heretofore unseen textual performances indicates just how much we unwittingly contain the social energies we claim to promote in our classes. To a large extent, our understanding of collaboration remains at the level of co-labor: more than one person working together toward a shared task. Innovation is encouraged but only en route to an assumed product; the resultant look and feel of the final product remain more or less anticipated, and thus fixed.

Some will contest this, claiming that collaboration does indeed change the final product, often radically so; that multiple writers working together will invariably alter the direction of their activity in profound ways. And no one can deny that collaborative writing creates a largely unpredictable map of rhetorical possibilities. But no matter how many unexpected twists and turns occur along the way as a result of other writers sharing their desires and experiences, chances are good that the final outcome will resemble something we have seen before, something we can safely characterize as an essay, a research paper, a short story, or some other classifiable entity. These forms exist prior to the collaborative activity, and teachers (often unconsciously) assume them to be given; as a result, student writing tends to fall into one of a very few appropriate rhetorical boxes. We bring a limited number of formal vocabularies to the new technologies, and instead of exploring how these technologies might create hybrid forms, often we use them to preserve old paradigms of rhetorical construction.

What happens when people collaborate in writing groups—or hives—that lead to the construction of texts that could never have been anticipated prior to the group's assemblage? How might current technologies be used to create not only different kinds of texts but radically different modes of writing and reading experiences? What happens when collaborative encounters occur in such a way that no product remains after the activity of communal improvisation; all that exists is writing as a heterarchic social consciousness, mutually conceived and simultaneously realized? How might we reconceptualize collaboration not as co-labor but as the transformation of labor into heretofore unanticipated modes of communal ludic meditation?

We were fortunate enough to be part of a writing experiment that brought these questions to our attention.

The Hivemind

As an experimental writing group, the hivemind met every week or two for nine months. A handful of friends and colleagues, poets and fiction writers mostly, we spent evenings in a computer lab experimenting with Daedalus, an interactive computer application that was new to us at the time. Marketed for teachers and students of writing, Daedalus is a tool that, among other things, permits users to share comments and feedback with one another on a network: using the Interchange function, each writer types in a comment of any length and then sends it through the program to all the users, where it appears in an ongoing queue of comments submitted by other users of the program. This technology has been reproduced and improved in many ways since; anyone familiar with chat rooms or MOOs knows the experience, which is rather like watching the chronological scrolling of simultaneous conversations at a cocktail party or a salon made manifest on one's computer.

What makes our experiment noteworthy is that from the beginning we sought to use the software for ends other that its intended purpose. We were not interested in chatting with one another or discussing some topic. We were not much concerned with meeting to create publishable texts. Rather, we wanted to work with a communal language that would grow spontaneously from each encounter, to work with that material as it evolved, rather than letting the software force us to interpret our language as a tool applied to the resolution of some problem. It was the measure of the act we were interested in, as well as how all that communal input altered the way we thought and acted in language.

We were curious to see what would happen if a number of us used this program not to facilitate discussion but to engage in a jam session. Seven turned out to be our ideal number. The commentary became too difficult to follow with more; less than that, and the group became too self-conscious. It was a jam session in which we intentionally avoided perpetuating any particular genre and concentrated on working within whatever rhythms and cues surfaced as a result of collective improvisation—something not too unlike what William Carlos Williams might have had in mind when he spoke of the "variable foot," except that our ears were trained to a variable crowd. We wanted to know if we could collaborate in the tradition of the Ornette Coleman double quartet in their classic *Free Jazz* recording, where eight musicians jammed simultaneously for one uninterrupted free improvisation, with no scores and for no predetermined length of time. Of that recording Coleman has said, "The most important thing . . . was for us to play together, all at the same time, without getting in each other's way, and also to have enough room for each player to *ad lib* alone—and to follow this idea for the duration of the album" (Williams). How could collaborative writing software help us understand composition as simultaneous, collective invention, where there is no product, just the shared experience of spontaneously synchronized elaboration and variation, the mutual awareness of process-in-the-making? How might such an experiment lead us to reconsider the writing process not as a series of procedures ultimately headed toward a more finished draft but as a collective state of mind, evolving but without goals, multiple but self-contained?

For these experimental sessions, we would arrive at the networked classroom and begin writing at our terminals. Sometimes someone would be chosen to kick things off; at other times we would all just begin to write. We set the software so that our entries would appear on everyone's screens anonymously: including our names would have made our experiment amount to just another online chat room, and, besides, we were trying to let go of our egos so as to concentrate on how all our voices could combine with each other in a polyvocal chorus. This chorus is what we came to call the hivemind.

We allowed ourselves to write anything: sentences, stanzas, queries, paragraphs, fragments. Whether writing consciously in response to someone else or creating something entirely out of the blue, we would keep writing for several hours. It took several seconds for an entry to materialize on all the other computers. Sometimes only one comment would appear; at other times multiple entries would pop up on the screen at the same time. When we wrote fast, submissions would appear on the screen so quickly that it was hard to keep track. On other occasions, long pauses between entries introduced a different sense of pace. One of the interesting temporal conditions of the medium was that the present seemed to stretch, because so many intersections from various sources were being assembled along an evolving, unbroken string. The moment that was conceived as containing simultaneities thus had to be stretched beyond the usual conversational or dialectical duration. The present was dense with multiple vectors of argument, confirmation, and elaboration.

The entire event moved between the poles of inertness and alertness, distance and intimacy. The participants were not like participants in a conversation. Their scope of attention broadened to flows of energy: the entries were responses not so much to other comments as to what might be called the atmospheric forces at play in the passage of time, larger rhythms, flows, oozings, and sludgy viscosities, on the one hand; tap dances, fast edits, and quick blurts on the other.

Our interest in pushing the possibilities for synergized writing are by no means new. Precursors for this sort of thing can be found in traditional Japanese *renga*, algorithmic programs of the Oulipo school, and other contemporary fusions: the Beats (Burroughs's cutups and writing machines), the New York School (Ted Berrigan and Ron Padgett's *Bean Spasms*), and the Language poets (*Legend*, by Bruce Andrews; Charles Bernstein; Ray DiPalma; Steve McCaffery; and Ron Silliman). But so far written collaboration has entailed the hinging of two or more authors working in relative isolation, goaded by the exchange of manuscripts or disks. Even hypertext, which would seem to lend itself so splendidly to simultaneous construction among multiple writers, often remains largely another avenue for solitary authorship (and still largely less interesting than older hypertexts such as Pound's *Cantos*, Williams's *Paterson*, or Olson's *Maximus*). The problem with single authors, whether working in isolation or in accordance with traditional collaborative modes, is that a painfully (although to be sure an often exquisitely rendered) self-reflective voice or stance remains engaged in an act of self-definition or self-question. Either way it is inevitably an act of self-promotion (*author* coming from the Latin *auctor*, "promoter").

Instead of self-promotion—which was impossible in the hivemind in that no self was ever in control and neither was there any overarching self to promote—we tried to put our selves on hold in order to get to know this curious collective of which we were all part. If anything, the synergistic nature of our enterprise made it seem that the groupuscle was authoring *us* into shape. Something we called "the groupuscle effect" occurred when writers began to lose some fix on their authorial selves and begin to commingle with the rest of the tribe. This was assisted by the anonymity of the enterprise as well as the willingness of the participants to work, immediately and directly, off of each other rather than their own private agendas. That writers could not, in retrospect, often remember which passages were theirs indicates that some wonderfully corrupting invisible hand had momentarily readjusted once-fixated psyches. For some members of the groupuscle the goal was nothing less than to leave one's ego behind—or at least, to get the self, for a short while, to disremember its name:

> now I can begin
> have always desired to exit the form
> that chased me since conception
> now it hits me that form was never an it to escape:
> no distance between the molecules of my fingerpads
> and those of that lilypad
> ug ug ug[1]

From First Person to Third Mind

After we had spent several months getting used to the technology, the novelty wore off, and we were able to concentrate more on the language that would grow out of these sessions. What struck us was not how strange the writing was but how new it always felt. We have already told how, occasionally, when reading over the transcripts of our sessions, some of us could not recall having written certain passages. On some nights it felt as if there were not so much seven separate writers contributing to a multilayered polylogue as one synergistic arena from which a narrative—or, rather, a feeling—evolved, in fits and starts, to which all contributed but none possessed. The whole was larger than the sum of the parts; all writers were present, all contributed, and yet none could take control of the assemblage. The effect has parallels with what Brion Gysin and William S. Burroughs called the "third mind," when the two writers collaborated so intensely that some force greater than either one seemed to take over the composing process. Gysin felt that this mysterious agent of orchestration and invention was not the product of collaboration per se but the result of two writers literally mutating into a collective consciousness. Consequently, a literary pairing could not be considered a

> literary collaboration but rather the complete fusion in a praxis of two subjectivities, two subjectivities that metamorphose into a third; it is from this

collusion that a new author emerges, an absent third person, invisible and beyond grasp, decoding the silence.

The book is therefore the negation of the omnipresent and all-powerful author—the geometrist who clings to his inspiration as coming from divine inspiration, a mission, or the dictate of language.

It is the negation of the frontier that separates fiction from its theory.

It is, finally, the negation of the book as such—or at least the representation of that negation.   (18)

Just as Gysin and Burroughs's cutups could not in their eyes be considered texts written for books, our jams were properly speaking neither works nor texts but occurrences, a gathering of collaborators within a mediated social event. The proposal was to reveal spontaneously the content of the particular occasion of the writing itself. There were no preconceived themes or literary methodologies other than to read and cooperate in the production of the event within the limits imposed by a particular piece of software. In effect, whatever was possible was allowed. Hacker ethics prevailed as all were permitted to submit entries in any fashion. Anything that was possible was permitted, even if it meant tinkering with the system or submitting writing done in another person's style. And even here the styles of one's collaborators were in turn often derived from others; the more we worked with each other, the more the idea of an individual, "true" voice became increasingly unfathomable. Whereas even the most progressive of writing assignments are typically bound by laws, or expectations housing implicit laws, we worked within a strictly anarchistic realm. When we did create rules we almost never followed them. As children know so well, the joy lies more in inventing new logics than in adhering to them.

We emphasized the creation not of image or idea, except pragmatically as the stuff of the writing, but of community. The structuring materials became the *contents* of the community, not its formal limits. As it turns out, the insides of much of our software are empty, like most of the cyberspatial caves in the world. Most of the data in the world is mailing lists, inventories, and records of dental appointments. Word processing and collaborative writing programs are largely spaces with different tools and operatives for making things with those spaces. The great problem for the hacker is the poverty of the information to be found. Ours was an attempt to overcome this problem, to put something on the networks worth discovering.

The ancient theme of technology is the transformation of consciousness. We need to take mind back from the darkness. There is only consciousness and

the trillionically complex structurality that it finds in itself in finding itself. Now we know there is no pejorative chaos. All complexity is formal, multiple, and it is ours.

> Seek the primary mind; speak the primary mind.
> There was never mind before now,
> never knowledge before here.

> Empty the content of mind
> to empty computer screen,
> empty the screen full with first mind.

What Is the Value of an Unreadable Text?

With the hivemind, any resultant printed texts were not the definitive versions of the events from which they transpired but only one possible performance of the score created on the VDTs. Other performances could have consisted, for example, of public readings by multiple readers—readings that could be performed at least in part simultaneously, perhaps—or documents transferred in either linear or hypertextual formats to computer disks where any could edit the material at will.

The reading of such texts is thus deeply uncertain from the outset. All the traditional reading postures are of dubious value. Even the illusion that we are the subject of a communication of another "person" is disrupted, and the conception of a writerly "voice" is inappropriate. Our hivemind compositions were severely *written* events, but the writing did not exist for the creation of some final product: that would have been impossible as no one participant was ever in control of the entire design. Sense of property was called constantly into question, and, when the session ended, even the faces of one's collaborators appeared slightly defamiliarized. One could no more claim authorship for any recorded version of a groupuscle encounter than one could videotape a conversation at a party and claim to own that conversation. One could certainly publish something taken from a disk on which the remnants of a hivemind encounter occurred, just as one could own the rights to such a videotape, but in neither case could anyone be considered the author of the event under consideration. Although these were strictly written events, here writing took place as a procedural engagement, a collective, exploratory meditation. Writing in this case is not the representation but the enactment of community. The writing happens as the community seeks to know itself; it is not maintained for reasons of posterity.

The remains of our hivemind activities were something like textual clouds produced by many hands, just as clouds in the sky are produced by multiple air currents, topographical features, and so forth. The cloud is far more definite than the forces that produced it, and we now know from dynamic systems theory that such striking visual formalities as clouds arise from states of disorder that can only be accounted as chaos. Just such a reordering of this sort is encountered in the hivemind phenomenon.

How then to read such works, the hardcopies that remained after the sessions? Traditional structuralist devices are of no use in this case. The principles of the text's material production preclude the possibility of discovering a cohering and ordering structure. It has all the complexity of highly evolved language practices emerging into an identifiable, public shape, or cloud. On the other hand, poststructuralist methodologies are also of questionable value: we do not have even the illusion of a transcendental signifier to expose. Such texts do not call for deconstruction. They are without the illusion of depth. They project no image of subjective unity. Like beauty, they are only skin-deep. *There was no unconscious at work here.* If there were signs that suggested Oedipal depths, they had no place literally but in consciousness and had to be dealt with in consciousness.

Ultimately the question is raised, does this writing have any value? Of course, the answer is no, not if by *value* we mean its ability to be exchanged for retribution. And this is precisely what made these encounters so worthwhile, and so unlike almost any writing that occurs in the classroom for a grade, among colleagues for publication, or even by people chatting on online: what we sought was the construction of group consciousness through art, art in this case manifested as a delight in shared language. Unlike texts produced in the creative writing workshop, filled with writers typically hungering for group approval, or by the student, whose writing always ultimately gets exchanged for some kind of grade, or by the academic, whose value is determined by publication, here writing exists only as the contact among people who realize a shared consciousness within the sustained event of that writing. That this work did not exist for publication but as a catalyst for some kind of temporary, unmediated communal synthesis made it utterly worthless. Which is why we kept returning for nine months to explore its possibilities.

Collaboration for Communion, not Compensation

The benefits of conventional approaches to collaborative pedagogies are obvious. Our interest is not to debate the merits of using collaborative writing in the classroom nor to challenge writers who use collaborative methods for purposes unlike those addressed here. We do however want to supplement such writing pedagogies with additional means of making meaning through composition. So far little has been done in exploring collaboration as primarily a means of moving toward communities devoid of any concern for compensation, whether in the form of receiving grades, achieving publication, or getting or holding a job. What can happen when we think of collaboration as nothing more or less than a way to move beyond our self-absorbed psyches into a working space where contact with other humans becomes an art form? The claim has often been made that in many primitive tribal communities concepts such as art, poetry, religion didn't exist because the natives seemed to live in a perpetual state of higher awareness. How might we reinvent our current technologies to help us regain a sense of what it might be to experience human contact through collaborative enterprises, solely for the sake of knowing consciousness differently?

Our hivemind found itself seeking modes of immediate communal exchange and shared intellectual (fore)play, many of us having grown impatient with the fetishization of the published text found so often in the academy and among writers. The communal *jouissance* that at times grew out of these encounters was strong, evident in a comment in one of our early sessions:

> If the words could be as physical as we are. That's always what I want from poetry. A way to make love with everyone, without the confusion of just simple promiscuity. When it works (as I have seen it work a couple of times in my life), it can be without all of the confusions of gender and plumbing. . . . Not to replace the other kind of sex, to be sure, but the only kind of a community that seems worth having. . . . Mind and body sex in the groupuscle. I mean you can talk a lot and share big important ideas. . . . But I think of Whitman, saying "Whoever touches this book touches a man," and so forth.

Ultimately, we are interested in how to use new technologies so that we might further enhance our relationships with others and not move further from human contact by disappearing into virtual reality. Any technology that seeks to replace face-to-face contact is one we have no patience with. After spending several hours at our machines, our hivemind was always eager to sign off, drained by the hypnotic blue terminals and the fluorescent lights, irritated by the monotonous buzzing of the electrical equipment. It was not the computers that brought us together week after week—there is nothing lovely about a room full of brand-new IBMs—nor the software itself, which, like all software, is essentially a tool designed to get one from here to there. What kept us coming back was that, for a period of time anyway, we had found a way to make technology serve as a catalyst for the realization of our little tribe. The potentialities of the technology pulled us together each week, got us thinking in ways that were impossible without it, and then, after we had grown tired of the equipment, made us come face to face again with our friends, ready for some beer and conversation.

Our goal is to teach ourselves how to reach inside the new technologies and, aiming for the electrons, suddenly grab hold of someone's hand. Hakim Bey reminds us that

> computers, video, radio, printing presses, synthesizers, fax machines, tape recorders, photocopiers—these things make good toys, but terrible addictions. Finally we realize we cannot "reach out & touch someone" who is not present in the flesh. These media may be useful to our art—but they must not possess us, nor must they stand between, mediate, or separate us from our animal/animate selves. We want to control our media, not be controlled by them. And we should like to remember a certain psychic material art which stresses the realization that the body itself is the least mediated of all media.
>
> (10)

If we look at the various definitions of the word *hive* we find the term refers to more than just architecture for societies of bees. A hive is "the nursery of a teeming race," a "breeding-place for oysters"; "to hive" is to "lodge together." As writers and teachers and humans who dwell with other humans in our various "capsules containing many cells," we want to use the technologies at our disposal to rediscover what it means not just to work collaboratively with others but to *think* with them, as a group: to make contact with a group that matters to us, for no other reason than because we love them, because we need them to keep us from falling into narcissism and cynicism. There is something to be said about company:

> now we sew our selves together
> advance conglomerate
> one immense and writhing
> ball of names and skin
> catching all debris in our path
> gummy tumbleweeds drunk on intimacy

Notes

1. Unless otherwise indicated all quotations are taken from hivemind encounters. For obvious reasons, no attempt has been made to attribute these quotations to

any authors. A list of hivemind regulars, though, is worth mentioning: David Bookbinder, Don Byrd, Eric Douglas, Nancy Dunlop, Christopher Funkhouser, Tom Kincaid, John Mason, Derek Owens, Ed Sanders, Sharon Stenson, John Torquato, and Katie Yates.

Works Cited

Bey, Hakim. *Immediatism*. Edinburgh, Scotland: AK, 1994.
Williams, Martin. Liner notes to *Free Jazz*. CD, Atlantic, 1961.
Gysin, Brion, and William S. Burroughs. *The Third Mind*. New York: Seaver, 1982.

Literacy and the Body Electric   **TWO**

5   We Are Not Just (Electronic) Words: Learning the Literacies of Culture, Body, and Politics

Beth E. Kolko

The version of cyberspace allowed by current technology requires that we become more aware of how the physical world is embedded within our language. Such technologies are largely text-based; email, MOOs, MUDs, newsgroups, and other widely available forums for computer-mediated communication (CMC) are predicated on textual exchanges. While graphical interfaces for the World Wide Web are slightly changing the evolution of communication technologies and the shape of virtual space, the vast majority of online interaction still occurs with and through words. Yet despite this reliance on reading and writing, the emerging global network has rarely been characterized as a space of literacy. Nevertheless, because interaction in virtual spaces is conducted through language, learning to write the world of cyberspace necessitates learning how to read the intersection of language with culture, bodies, and politics. In addition, the notion that the body disappears in virtual interaction has dominated a great deal of scholarship. Researchers have also settled on other arguments, namely, that text-based virtual realities such as MUDs and MOOs (see chapter 7 in this volume for discussion of MUDs and MOOs) generate a multiple and fluid subject and that the physical self is implicated in online interactions. These two threads of scholarship open a variety of questions, many of which ask what role rhetoric can play in recuperating the notion of accountability within cyberspace. The center of such inquiry begins with that which is no longer centered: the subject.

When Mark Poster announced the second media age by showing the inadequacies of subject-pair binaries from the first media age, he encapsulated his argument by stating, "subject constitution in the second media age occurs through the mechanism of interactivity" (88). Perhaps appropriately, then, questions of subjectivity in online cultures have formed the core of research regarding text-based virtual realities—interactive reading and writing spaces that they are. A variety of academics in disparate humanities and social science disciplines have approached cyberspace curiously and with a version of Seyla Benhabib's "supposing the subject" question in mind. MOOs and MUDs as teaching tools, however, were not required to initiate writing specialists' interest in subject construction. In the teaching of writing, subject construction has long been a central focus. Compositionists from a variety of perspectives have examined how composing allows the writer to work through and among versions of the self, whether it is the voice of Lester Faigley, critiquing a modernist conception of the self, claiming that "the self in student autobiographies . . . is not one that emerges like a butterfly as a chrysalis . . . but one that is discursively produced and discursively bounded" (129) or that of Susan Miller, critiquing a similar concept and asserting that in "the traditional freshman composition course, the textual carnival of correctness, propriety, and 'good breeding,' has served just as well to further the end of neutralizing the public participation of its students" (91). From this perspective, writing is a matter of creating the self. In a text-based virtual reality, not just the self (the internal) but the world (the external) is written by participants. This is perhaps the simplest explanation of why MUDs and MOOs have captured the imagination and professional interest of writing teachers. MOOs provide us with a way to play out the stakes of students' literacy in tangible and visible ways. What is written in a MOO is all that exists. The stakes are necessarily high.

While MOOs seem to raise the stakes of students' literacy acts, there is also a growing body of scholarship that threatens such claims: namely, the argument, heard from so many quarters, that because the online self is dispersed, ultiple the question of accountability is left dangling. In ke to show some of the ways the decentered subject of the l then discuss some strategies for recuperating both political accountability from these arguments. The implications for numerous. If rhetoric and composition specialists were s because of the all-importance of reading and writing in , the argument that physical selves have no claim to and no e words thrown into a virtual environment threatens the an instrument of literacy instruction. In the light of such s to claim we are educating students to be responsible rhetors ring hollow; it is imperative that we develop a clear conception of how literacy instruction is served by emerging communication technologies such as MOOs.

Fragmented Subjects

Poster is a central voice in the growing chorus of commentators documenting the fragmented, multiple, and fluid subject chronicled by postmodern theory and cemented with the growth of electronic communication technologies. Poster characterizes what he terms the second media age by giving us a twentieth-century where

> electronic media are supporting an equally profound transformation of cultural identity. Telephone, radio, film, television, the computer and now their integration as "multimedia" reconfigure words, sounds, and images so as to cultivate new configurations of individuality. If modern society may be said to foster an individual who is rational, autonomous, centered, and stable . . . then perhaps a postmodern society is emerging which nurtures forms of identity different from, even opposite to, those of modernity. And electronic technologies significantly enhance those postmodern possibilities.   (24)

When Poster later discusses MOOs and MUDs specifically, his argument frames the issue of subjectivity within virtual environments, but it also, in its tone, hearkens to what I have come to call conversion narratives of online experiences. For some, like Poster, these narratives are third-person, displaced. For others, like Sherry Turkle, Allucquère Rosanne Stone, Shannon McRae, and Rob Shields, these narratives are first-person chronicles of scholarly observation. It seems likely that the predominance of conversion narratives is a stage in research about cyberspace. Quite simply, we lack frames of reference for research in virtual communities; consequently, first-person qualitative studies abound. Certainly this chapter would have had a different shape were there statistics on which I could draw. For the time being, though, the conversion narratives, the stories of observation and participation, are the text from which we must begin reading.

   Poster's displaced narrative asserts that "observers of and participants in Internet 'virtual communities' repeat in near unanimity that long or intense experience with computer-mediated electronic communication is associated with a certain fluidity of identity" (35). As a commentator, rather than one of the observers, he draws on others' work to recapitulate one of the central themes of virtual scholarship. His is simply one of a growing number of voices that uses a variety of participatory and cyberethnographic work to substantiate arguments.

One of the more unapologetically personal critics of cyberspace, Allucquère Rosanne Stone, returns to Donna Haraway's cyborg in order to begin conceptualizing the body and self's relation to cyberspace. Stone's work is disarmingly playful and yet incisive; her discussion of the multiple self as the counterassertion to "location technology" builds on Poster's conception of dispersion through interactivity. She asserts that the "cyborg, the multiple personality, the technosocial subject, Gibson's cyberspace cowboy all suggest a radical rewriting, in the technosocial space . . . of the bounded individual as the standard social unit and validated social actant" (43). Stone is (like Raul Sanchez in chapter 7 of this collection) disturbed by the "old Cartesian trick" of separating the body from the mind, and she is careful to introduce real political stakes into her theorizing. Her compelling use of border identities and her recognition of valences of technological desire provide key vocabularies for further discussion. And while she is careful to explore both the productive and destructive potential of CMC, she conceives of cyberspace as a space that is, ultimately, more masked than that which a writing teacher might conceive.

Sherry Turkle, similarly, is concerned with the enactment of identity online. Turkle's has become one of the best-known names in the burgeoning world of cybertheorizing; her book, *Life on the Screen: Identity in the Age of the Internet*, is an articulate and well-researched treatment of the fragmentation of identity in online interaction. Her claim that in "computer-mediated worlds, the self is multiple, fluid, and constituted in interaction with machine connections" (15) is a sort of rallying cry for celebrants of the postmodern distributed presence that is the cyborg. In concert with Poster and Stone, Turkle announces the theme of the moment for scholars examining online interaction. Consider, for example, Heather Bromberg, who echoes the same claim as she writes that for a certain portion of the online population, MUDs "allow the exploration of alternate identities and personae, offer the promise of connectivity and community and allow users to experience the feeling of mastery over their environments. . . . This medium clearly allows for this exploration of alternate or preferred identities" (146, 148). Like Turkle, Bromberg's voice is that of a conversion narrative. "My own observations," she writes, "along with the responses of informants, suggest that some people do, in fact, experience altered states of consciousness while connected to virtual worlds. The promises of eroticism, mastery, connectivity and identity exploration are significant as they all have the potential to contribute to producing these altered states, with the computer as the interface" (149). Bromberg's article weaves a bit more of the pattern begun by Turkle, Stone, and Poster. All together, though, these critics propose a disturbing theme: that the self in cyberspace is not just multiple but *re-writable*, somehow separate from the situated self behind the typist. While a certain fluidity of identity in text-based virtual realities is incontestable, the question remains as to how and whether the physical self can be completely masked by acts of linguistic passing.[1] I don't claim to have an answer to that question, though I do think it is one that merits a great deal more attention. What I can provide, however, is a way to think through the impasse caused by the dislocation, to whatever extent, of the embodied self from the virtual self.

(Re)Enter the Body

At the same time that Stone, Turkle, Poster, and others are tracking and, to some extent, celebrating, the dissolution of the coherent subject in cyberspace, another set of cultural commentators has come to recognize the visceral component of online interaction. Poster's interactivity of the second media age is not, it turns out, a hermetically sealed experience. The body that is displaced by technology is not effaced. It seems we have at least reached this consensus: that while physical characteristics that mark our bodies are not immediately visible in computer-mediated communication, the traces of this physical self are not inconsequential.[2] What seems to be the argument these days is that, instead, the body goes along for the virtual ride.

In the variety of conversion narratives published as part of cyberspace theory today, we can see a range of experiences, most of which center around the theme of "this stuff really matters." I use the word *matter* advisedly. This "stuff," this online interaction, affects the meat left behind. It impinges not just on the consciousness of the self but on the body as well.

Katie Argyle and Rob Shields provide a framework for thi? cussion as they refute the contention that "alienation and de often associated with computer-mediated communication, body and mind." They continue:

> Nonetheless, "presence" doesn't just vanish. Technology me Within computer communication technology, there are ways be present to each other, with our bodies, interacting in a ho
> Bodies cannot be escaped, for we express this part of oursel ence together. Although some attempt to conceal the status of betrayed unless we resort to presenting another kind of body i cations. There is no loss of body in and through virtual reality te........... (50)

Argyle has embedded her conversion narrative within this coauthored article; as she moves from the contemplative to the confessional, she focuses on the social aspects of her interaction. "Sex, sadness, elation: the important trivialities which make everyday life are opportunities for contact, for people to make themselves felt-presences to others, translating themselves from absent and abstract computer addresses into engaged interlocutors" (59). Here, once again, we have Poster's interactivity, the central characteristic of the second media age. What we also have, though, is the recognition that bodies are present, but this recognition is located in the physical rather than the linguistic. Argyle goes on to describe the self that she presented online, "Kitty," as a persona. She found that "many people trusted this 'other' that I gave them of myself, and they revealed parts of themselves to me in turn. What we exchanged was *real*. I felt it in my body that they were honest about the facts of their lives, their confessions, their dreams, as I was" (59). Argyle's body is affected by her online interaction; she does not draw distinctions between the personae and the meat.

Similarly, programmer Ellen Ullman tells the story of how she "fell in love by email." Although the Other in this story is someone she had known in a variety of mediated technologized formats, she had never physically met him. "It was as intense as any other falling in love," she says, going on to claim "no, more so. For this love happened in my substitute body, the one online, a body that stays up later, is more playful, more inclined to games of innuendo—all the stuff of romantic love" (12). While Ullman differentiates her online body, she does not *separate* it from herself. The linguistic interaction of her online body effects ramifications with which her physical body must deal: desire, longing, the shock and anxiety of voice contact, the escalating panic before a first date, the efficiency-threatening need to read and write email with increasing regularity. Although while discussing *actions* Ullman can bracket off the online consciousness from the self that inhabits the physical world, there is no separation when it comes to assessing *reactions*.

Ullman's experience occurred via email, an arena of CMC that is asynchronous and, as such, less immersive than the environments of MUDs and MOOs. In MOOs, for example, participants can type messages to one another, but they can also type emotions and narrate movements of their discursive bodies. Use of the particular communicative style of emoting is one of the subjects taken up by Shannon McRae. McRae, a longtime participant in virtual worlds, approaches the affects of CMC in an article that lyrically details the enactment of gender as a poetic and sexual act. She writes:

> Emoting [in a MOO] allows for a richness and variety of communicative nuances not easily conveyable in other electronically mediated environments. Players become conscious of having "bodies" and, just as they do in "real life,"

express themselves with physical gestures as often as they speak. Sometimes the sense of presence is so vivid that you feel as if you really are touching, smelling, tasting, seeing whatever is around you, in a complex interchange of experience between a physical and an imaginary body.   (247)

Later in her article, as McRae cycles out of any remnant of the conversion narrative and instead relates the experience of an informant named Elaine, a man who adopts the persona of a woman online, she notes that "what she [Elaine] experiences as her female side seems to be part of herself that her socialization as a male somehow excluded." Or, in Elaine's words, "God only knows what weird stuff I'm saying about femaleness and [maleness] and myself and who knows what, but I feel it . . . strongly" (250). Once again, participants in this virtual space attach physical reactions to the interaction. Elaine is merely one of the number of subjects of McRae's study of eroticism and the enactment of gender. Her focus on the "dislocated eroticism" of virtual sex allows her to explore this notion of feeling in specific and magnified ways and, finally, to conclude that "most people who spend any amount of time on MUDs discover, often to their own surprise, the emotions involved when people become sexual with each other can be very, very real" (254). Descartes is shunted aside by such formulations; the cyborg becomes the focus of ontological inquiry. The enactment of virtual gender, or whatever variable of virtual identity, becomes an integration of the technologized self and the embodied machine.

Yet another version of the physicalized virtual self is told by Argyle in a single-authored piece that relates a particular story of her online life. She talks of her experience with the heavily trafficked mailing list Cybermind and what occurred in the wake of the list coowner's death. She performs a reading of various list members' reactions, acutely aware of the voyeuristic nature of her actions. But her analysis culminates in the juxtaposition of a Gibsonesque characterization of the body as meat—something inadequate, left behind by the emergence of cyberrelations—with the very real grief she and others feel at the physical passing of the online presence. The visceral reaction to this unseen body's disappearance is testimony to the remaining and retained power of the situated knowledge of the flesh.

Love. Sex. And Death. All effected within the realm of cyberspace via communication in virtual environments. All implicate and involve the physical self, the meat, obviating claims of bodily transcendence, complicating claims to a cyborg existence.

This discovery, located either within the frame of personal experience or ethnographic data, is discussed in Cartesian and Foucaultian terms, but only in-

frequently and haphazardly has the connection been discussed in poststructural linguistic terms. Candace Lang argues that the body and the text are "one and
the same" in a MOO, asserting that "computer-mediated-communication of
this type revives, rather than deadening, our awareness of ourselves as physical
bodies" (248). She speaks of the MOO as "a world in which words are things
and things are words, where words are made flesh and vice-versa, where if you
try to see or touch something that has not been described by an author/pro-
grammer, it simply does not exist" (248). Or, as I have argued elsewhere, "cyberspace is not . . . just willing a world into action, but into being. When we
write in cyberspace, we create" (106). This act of creation occurs wholly and
completely through the deployment of language, and this is the connection that
merits deeper exploration.

Political Selves

There is, within these two narratives about online interaction, something of a
contradiction. If the self is multiplied, fragmented, dispersed, then how does
online interaction come to be characterized repeatedly as being able to evoke
visceral reactions? How do we locate a fragmented self long enough for its interactions to refer back to the physical body? The contradiction here may not
seem particularly noteworthy; after all, we are only beginning to understand the
nuances of communication in virtual worlds. This gap may be one that is best
approached in work such as that of the linguist Lynn Cherny or theorists such
as Candace Lang, Marie Ryan, and Cynthia Haynes, researchers who have
found ways to discuss the very complex and impossibly amorphous connections between words, social codes, and virtual space. Alternatively, there is a
particular combination of rhetorical and legal theory that can provide a framework for addressing questions of how these two narratives relate.

Evelyn Fox Keller and Jennifer Mnookin have both asked how, if the cyber-
self is multiple, we can hope to develop a theory of accountability for the virtual self. Crucially, their questions have tremendous import for theories of online
literacy. Mnookin, during a symposium on gender, cyberspace, and the law,
claimed that "only single, accountable selves can be accountable to the law."
Given that the self inhabiting cyberspace is fragmented, decentered, she asked,
how do we hold that self to a conception of justice? What is it, precisely, that can
be done to and with the virtual self? The issue is not just, how do we think about
the virtual self? but, actually, what can we *do* with it? How can we act on the dispersed self of virtual culture? How can we incorporate a conception of accountability into online communication protocols?

It is important to begin this conversation by bracketing the ways in which the variety of researchers have discussed the effects online interaction have on the body of the typist. While the consensus among researchers is certainly that the body is affected by online interaction, the nature of that effect has not been explored. For instance, when Bromberg concludes her article with the following passage, she merely hints at the implications for rhetoric in her study; she notices but does not interrogate the connection between the way language is used in a MOO and the way users' selves are affected. In some ways this is the magic to which Marcos Novak refers, but, more crucially for the argument in this chapter, this connection is the crux of why writing theorists can play an important role in conceptualizing how media like MOOs and MUDs can be used productively.

> Almost all respondents said that they gained some kind of personal insight and awareness as a result of their interactive participation in virtual worlds that changed the way they responded to their physical, material worlds. . . . The consensus among both theorists and users of virtual reality who assert that it is capable of producing altered states is that this is caused as a result of intense and immediate and interactive feedback that responds to the user's individual commands. This is also what differentiates it from other, more passive, entertainment and communications technologies. The importance of language and the prevalence of mythic themes and symbolism in the design of virtual worlds should be more thoroughly examined to further understand the virtual reality experience from a cultural/psychosocial perspective.
>
> (150)

Bromberg is not alone in her passing acknowledgment of language's importance in this medium. Argyle and Shields refer to the way writing can "transmit the body" (66); Lori Kendall talks of social codes that are manifest in the enactment (via language) of gender. What is missing from these and other discussions is an awareness and analysis of the *rhetorical* nature of the interaction;[3] we have an incomplete understanding of the fact that, through all these kinds of contact—love, sex, and death online—the substance of the living is words. When Susan Miller critiques writing pedagogy that considers the student to be "a presexual, preeconomic, prepolitical person" (91), she is asserting compositionists' understanding that when we write, our words embody our selves in significant ways. This is the truth to which cyberspace researchers are reacting. But without the link made between the writing and the effect, we lose a valuable point of efficacy.

During the symposium on gender, law, and cyberspace that I mentioned earlier, Fox Keller, intrigued by the assertion that words can hurt, questioned a panel of lawyers who had talked about cyberspace as a zone of "plasticity," as a place where "communications technologies exist to eliminate borders," as a "frontier" zone that does more to redefine community than identity: "Does cyberspace give words *more* power to wound?"[4] She rephrased, restated, circled around her question: "What is the nature of words' power to wound?" And when we make this claim, that words can hurt, is it "a real body upon which the words are being written"? She toyed with this question over and over, each reshuffling of words delivering a new cadence of meaning. "What is the power of words that affect the body? Is it a virtual body being wounded? Or a real body?" Or, as one of the lawyers claimed, is what is wounded the name (or the reputation) rather than any conception of a physical body? Or is it, as Julian Dibbell, author of the famed "A Rape in Cyberspace" article, claimed in the same forum, that cyberspace simply reminds us that the "body is not just a physical object, but a social machine." Could this recognition be the lesson cyberspace teaches us about the body in "meat space"? he asked. The body is not just a physical object but also a social machine: the self is not a biological or even an ontological creation; it is a social creation. That is, after all, one of the central lessons of postmodern theory.

When urban historian M. Christine Boyer frames the cyberbody as an instantiation of the "bodily disenchantment that haunts our postmodern era" (80), she echoes Dibbell's formulation. And when she goes on to argue that in cyberspace "the self is unstable, dephysicalized, and thus beginning to disappear, making projection from it ambiguous and unclear" (80), she articulates the concerns raised by both Fox Keller and Mnookin. And Mark Lajoie's concerns are similar, if not identical, when he writes, "the danger, as I see it, is the atomization of the public sphere through the misguided use, or rather overuse, of technologies which eliminate face-to-face interaction. The danger of mediated communications, to the extent that they replace rather than augment face-to-face interactions, is the elimination of public space, and the consequent reduction of citizens to the status of atomized entities, ill-equipped for collective politics or public life" (154). Lajoie's focus on geographical placement is a thoroughly embodied critique. Like Mnookin, Fox Keller, and Boyer, he recognizes the importance for real bodies to be implicated in the communication that is mediated by technology. Lajoie's assertion that "denying bodies is easy for the master, but impossible for the slave" (167) is crucial, and it correlates with Stone and Haraway's arguments. But I would assert that it is not necessary to see cyberspace as bodiless; nor is it necessary to see the displaced body as a repudiation of the physical self. It is possible to be dispersed and situated. That, it seems, is at the root of Haraway's cyborg.

Dan Thu Nguyen and Jon Alexander, in their article "The Coming of Cyber-spacetime and the End of the Polity" echo many of Lajoie's concerns. Nguyen and Alexander critique the political effects of virtual space, claiming that the public sphere that is being created on the Internet is a "conversational, demassified, non-representational democracy" (111) that holds little potential for political efficacy. They acknowledge some of the positive potential of the medium, including the ways in which shifting subjectivities allow for a break from hegemonic structures, but, ultimately, they see the geographical unrootedness and decentralization of the virtual communities as destroying the concept of the polity and thus essentially depoliticizing. They write:

> Now the wildly proliferating fields of cyberspacetime are . . . not only ex-tremely social, they are also profoundly apolitical. In cyberspacetime, the so-cial realm is engulfing and overwhelming the political realm. The "social" is decomposing the body politic. Decay of politics is proceeding quickly as the matrix is growing. . . . Millions of people have made drifting in and out of dig-ital realities a significant part of their everyday lives. This is a global retreat from our now empty public lives, from roles we once acted out in a real-life political realm. It is a retreat from nations, from nationalism and from poli-tics itself. This is a retreat from civilization. It places millions in a tribalized fantasy culture, a theatre of the bizarre and the absurd. Fantasy culture be-comes universal by making all the world a proliferation of cyberstages, an in-authentic virtual simulation of Shakespeare's *theatrum mundi*. . . . Online, Logos reduces to increasingly nihilistic play.   (109, 116, 117)

Such critiques are strong, and they give pause. As teachers who are concerned with responsible public discourse, we must heed warnings of this tenor. The stakes for writing teachers are high. If CMC disperses and depoliticizes, if the online self cannot be traced back to a physical self, then students lose the abili-ty to recognize the importance of their words, the idea that their language has power and effect. Nguyen and Alexander's cautionary tale emerges from their belief in the importance of public discourse and the necessity for such dis-course in democratic institutions, a concern that is central to many teachers of writing and rhetoric. There is a good deal in their argument that is worthy of at-tention. We must, indeed, make sure that online interaction does not replace face-to-face connections. We must also find ways, as Mnookin and Fox Keller urge, to think through how to reconcile the fragmented subject in a MOO with questions of accountability. As rhetoricians, these questions are, necessarily, at the center of our focus. And, in fact, it is as writing teachers that we are best poised to counter the assertions made by Nguyen and Alexander, and Lajoie, when they argue that virtual communities imperil public institutions, that because of the fractured nature of identity in online discourse, there can be no accountability. In this sense, the questions of accountability asked by Mnookin and Fox Keller can be seen as a direct counterthesis to arguments that cyberspace effaces public institutions; their queries urge a rethinking of fractured subjectivity online precisely in the interests of assigning responsibility to virtual actions. By ignoring the arguments of how online interaction is embodied, critics of virtual communities are preoccupied with only half the narrative. Writing theorists' reclamation of discursive resistance is precisely the point at which we can reconcile multiple selves with accountability for words and actions.[5]

Linda Brodkey speaks of this need for discursive resistance, calling for concrete projects of such interventions. In her characterization of such resistance, Brodkey introduces perhaps the thread of composition theory most meaningful to a project that seeks to design a framework of accountability for online interactions. Her formulation illustrates how discursively creating a self can be an embodied act and how such a self, although geographically displaced, can counter the fears of critics such as Lajoie and Nguyen and Alexander who see the growth of virtual communities as leading to the destruction of face-to-face communities. She urges:

> those individuals who are ambivalent or threatened by their subject positions in a given discourse to interrupt the very notion of the unified self—the traditional Cartesian notion that the self is a transcendent and absolute entity rather than a creation of language and ideology—in their spoken and written texts. . . . Studies of these and other interruptive practices, rhetorics of resistance in which individuals shift subject positions from one discourse to another or within a discourse in their speaking and writing, would constitute empirical inquiry into the postmodern speculation that language and discourse are material to the construction of reality, not simply by-products reflecting or reproducing a set of nondiscursive, material social structures and political formations.`   (90–91)

This, it seems to me, is both the answer to Mnookin's question of how to extract accountability from online interaction and a rejoinder to Lajoie's and Nguyen and Alexander's pessimistic projections that cyberspacetime bleeds a progressivist impulse from public life. When Kendall discusses gender passing in MOOs, she grounds her discussion in matters of social codes, expectations, roles. And when Laurel Sutton speaks of the power of having one's voice heard in a newsgroup or email forum, she concentrates on the breakdown of social barriers, on the amazement of having one's voice heard in a forum not generally considered welcoming. When L. Jean Camp chronicles the value of the Systers listserve, her focus is on virtual geography, on creating "space" within which women can speak and be heard. What none of these researchers adds to the formulation is an awareness of the speech act that comprises these environments. I would argue, in fact, that each of these media could be considered sites of Brodkey's discursive resistance.

The symposium mentioned earlier concerned gender, law, and cyberspace. The inclusion of law was no accident. Introducing law into a discussion of a text-based medium is a strategy specifically designed to tie practical solutions to theoretical issues. For example, in her larger body of work, Brodkey focuses on legal discourse in order to show how language, via policy, leaves tangible marks on our lives. That is, legal scholarship overlaps substantially with rhetorical theory; the melding of language theory and practice in both realms has decidedly real-world implications. Perhaps, in fact, retracing the steps of J. L. Austin can help us here, drawing on his notion of the performative utterance, a concept Lang evokes when she says the MOO seems as if "this text were composed, not of *mots*, but of *paroles*" (248). Indeed, Austin specifically refers to legal discourse as a way of understanding his claims about language. He writes:

> It is worthy of note, as I am told, [that] in the American law of evidence, a report of what someone else said is admitted as evidence if what he said is an utterance of our performative kind: because this is regarded as a report not so much of something he *said*, as which it would be hear-say and not admissible as evidence, but rather as something he *did*, an action of his. . . . The more we consider a statement not as a sentence (or proposition) but as an act of speech (out of which the others are logical constructions) the more we are studying the whole thing as an act.   (13, 20)

Legal scholars are currently grappling, in much more concrete ways, with questions of accountability in cyberspace. Their concerns are, necessarily, tied to rhetorical theory as the space they examine is that space of reading and writing, that space comprised, almost entirely, of literacy acts. M. Ethan Katsh, in *Law in a Digital World*, writes of how "new information technologies" will affect law. He takes the time to illustrate how previous changes in technology—namely, the printing press—have altered "cornerstones of modern law" (8). That is, he claims that, because law is centrally occupied with communication, changes in communication technologies will dramatically affect how we conceptualize legal practice. I would like to propose that the changes Katsh anticipates, yet names only minimally, are linked to poststructural and rhetorical claims and that interruptive practices such as the discursive resistance cataloged by Brodkey, can become a way to frame online interaction. Such a claim might affect a number of spheres; for the purposes of this chapter, however, I would like to concentrate on the repercussions for literacy theory and practice. In other words, the dual realizations, by Austin and Katsh, that the legal system reflects changing conceptions of language, can be used as a way to articulate the stakes of literacy in a technologized world.

Katsh argues that looking at law in electronic spaces, rather than in the static artifacts of books, will change the way we conceptualize what law is. He writes, "the medium employed by the law colors how distant we are from it and whether it is accessible or remote, friendly or hostile, tolerant or demanding. It affects when we can navigate through the law by ourselves and when professional assistance is needed. It shapes whether we are satisfied with traditional modes of conflict resolution and with existing artifacts of legal culture or whether we will begin to feel that new practices are needed" (93–94). Law in the digital age, then, becomes more dialogic. As he goes on to distinguish between the umbrella of print and the umbrella of different media—electronic media— he writes of the difficulty of such changes.

> Traveling into cyberspace involves moving away from a view of information and law as being fairly static and fixed to a model where information is hard to hold on to, where it can be accessed quickly and easily but possessed over time with great difficulty. We will, of course, continue to use information by reading, thinking, and responding to it in some way. Many skills that came into wide and general use in the print era will continue to be valuable as information becomes increasingly accessible in electronic form. Yet, interaction with information in electronic form will present us with new options and make new demands on us. What we read, how we think about information, and how we respond to it will gradually change. More particularly, as we take from the knowledge trees of cyberspace, we will be challenged to develop new skills and habits of thought, patterns of acting and patterns of thinking, that will be reflected in institutional processes and practices.   (94–95)

Those new habits and patterns of thought will create a dialogic space that will change the nature of literacy. I draw from legal writings in order to address these changes precisely because of the way law ties rhetoric to a physicalized world. Like Mnookin and Fox Keller, I believe it is utterly imperative that we interject accountability into that formulation of cyberspace as a place of multiple selves. Writing theorists have pointed out for some time that it is precisely through writing—whether on parchment or a VDT—that we work out and through the various components of who we are, that as we write, we create personae. The electronic age, in many ways, simply makes more obvious the transformations of the self to which writers have always been subject. But we cannot leave off at the point of a fluid identity. Students' (written) interactions online must *matter*, just as their writing in the classroom (and outside of it) must matter—to them and to others. We must not allow an embracing of the dialogic voices of electronic writing to cost us that crucial sense of impact and consequences in our writing; to do so is to do ourselves, our field, and our students a disservice.

As a postscript to this article, I want to point out a curious confluence I found in the scholarship concerning CMC. Turkle's book has already been widely cited and circulated. Her conclusions and speculations regarding the attendant real-world aspects of online interaction have opened up new and energized recurrent conversations regarding cyberspace. The argument in her book can be encapsulated by the following sentence: "While electronic discourse explodes the belief in a stable unified self, it offers a means of exploring how identity is multiply constructed and how agency resides in the power of connecting with others and building alliances." That sentence, however, is from page 199 of Faigley's book, published four years earlier. I do not take the scholarly prescience of Faigley's statement to indicate anything amiss. Rather, I read the preempting of Turkle's claims as an indication of the role compositionists can play in making meaning of changing patterns of literacy. That is, the MUDs and MOOs that all these theorists discuss, the curiosities of interaction, the power of the medium, the social and moral transformations identified are all occurring in text-based environments. Rhetoric and composition scholars have an understanding of language and its use in public fora that is not always seen in its nuances by other disciplines. I move from Miller and Brodkey, from compositionists, to Katsh, however, in order to make the realization stark that our theorizing, and our teaching in these spaces, has dramatic and tangible consequences outside classroom space. The dialogic nature of CMC, and the dialogic space of the MOO, is fertile ground for reconceptualizing how language can be used as a political tool. To turn the other way, to lose the opportunity of shaping these spaces for productive educational practices, would be a loss of composition's intellectual birthright.

Notes

1. Lisa Nakamura assesses the complex way race is "adopted" in virtual space in an attempt to investigate what she calls "identity tourism" that is enabled by online

interactions. Her argument effectively demonstrates that language is not enough to create or mask elements of identity; Amy Bruckman makes a similar analysis with respect to gender. Both authors analyze the way discursive actions (rather than identities) have tangible effects on the physical world and physical selves.

2. Recent scholarship in rhetoric and composition has explored quite comprehensively how computer-mediated communication transforms classroom dynamics. Such research has focused on the way CMC allows students who would otherwise feel silenced because of the ways they are variously "marked" to participate more fully in classroom discourse. The mediation of the technology, it is argued, masks difference and provides a venue for traditionally underrepresented voices.

3. For detailed discussions of the dynamics of linguistic interaction in cyberspace, see the work of linguists such as Lynn Cherny and Susan Herring.

4. These comments are taken from the final session of that symposium, during which Fox Keller, panelists, and audience members participated in an informal discussion. Their comments are quoted here from notes taken by the author at the time.

5. In its analysis of a writing class that used a MOO, Tari Fanderclai's essay "Like Magic, Only Real," in *Wired-Women: Gender and New Realities in Cyberspace,* comes closest to demonstrating both the dynamic and the potential of a pedagogy informed by such a perspective.

Works Cited

Argyle, Katie. "Life After Death." In *Cultures of Internet: Virtual Spaces, Real Histories, Living Bodies.* Ed. Rob Shields. London: Sage, 1996. 133–42.

Argyle, Katie, and Rob Shields. "Is There a Body in the Net?" In *Cultures of Internet: Virtual Spaces, Real Histories, Living Bodies.* Ed. Rob Shields. London: Sage, 1996. 58–69.

Austin, J. L. *How to Do Things with Words.* Ed. J. O. Urmson and Marina Sbisa. 2d ed. Cambridge: Harvard University Press, 1994.

Benhabib, Seyla. *Situating the Self: Gender, Community and Postmodernism in Contemporary Ethics.* New York: Routledge, 1992.

Boyer, M. Christine. *Cybercities: Visual Perception in the Age of Electronic Communication.* New York: Princeton Architectural Press, 1996.

Brodkey, Linda. "On the Subjects of Class and Gender in 'The Literacy Letters.' " In *Writing Permitted in Designated Areas Only.* Pedagogy and Cultural Practice 4. Minneapolis: University of Minnesota Press, 1996.

Bromberg, Heather. "Are MUDs Communities? Identity, Belonging and Consciousness in Virtual Worlds." In *Cultures of Internet: Virtual Spaces, Real Histories, Living Bodies.* Ed. Rob Shields. London: Sage, 1996. 143–52.

Bruckman, Amy. "Gender Swapping on the Internet." In *Proceedings of INET '93.* Reston, VA: The Internet Society. Presented at meeting of the Internet Society

(INET '93), San Francisco, California, Aug. 1993. ftp://ftp.media.mit.edu/pub/asb/papers/gender-swapping.txt.

Camp, L. Jean. "We Are Geeks, and We Are Not Guys." In *Wired-Women: Gender and New Realities in Cyberspace*. Ed. Lynn Cherny and Elizabeth Reba Wiese. Seattle: Seal, 1996. 114–25.

Cherny, Lynn. "Objectifying the Body in the Discourse of an Object-Oriented MUD." *Works and Days* 13, nos. 1–2 (1995): 151–72.

Dibbell, Julian. Unpublished remarks at the "Virtue and Virtuality: Gender, Law and Cyberspace" symposium, MIT, Cambridge, MA, Apr. 20–21, 1996.

Faigley, Lester. *Fragments of Rationality: Postmodernity and the Subject of Composition*. Pittsburgh: University of Pittsburgh Press, 1992.

Fanderclai, Tari Lin. "Like Magic, Only Real." In *Wired-Women: Gender and New Realities in Cyberspace*. Ed. Lynn Cherny and Elizabeth Reba Wiese. Seattle: Seal, 1996. 224–41.

Fox Keller, Evelyn. Unpublished remarks at the "Virtue and Virtuality: Gender, Law and Cyberspace" symposium, MIT, Cambridge, MA, 20–21 Apr., 1996.

Haraway, Donna. *Simians, Cyborgs, and Women: The Reinvention of Nature*. London: Free Association Press, 1991.

Haynes, Cynthia. "pathos@play.prosthetic.emotion." *Work and Days* 13, nos. 1–2 (1995): 261–76.

Herring, Susan. "Bringing Familiar Baggage to the New Frontier: Gender Differences in Computer-Mediated Communication." In *CyberReader*. Ed. Victor Vitanze. Needham Heights, MA: Allyn and Bacon, 1996. 144–52.

Katsh, M. Ethan. *Law in a Digital World*. New York: Oxford University Press, 1995.

Kendall, Lori. "MUDder? I Hardly Know 'Er! Adventures of a Feminist MUDder." *Wired-Women: Gender and New Realities in Cyberspace*. Ed. Lynn Cherny and Elizabeth Reba Wiese. Seattle: Seal, 1996. 207–23.

Kolko, Beth E. "Building a World with Words: The Narrative Reality of Virtual Communities." *Works and Days* 13, nos. 1–2 (1995): 105–26.

Lajoie, Mark. "Psychoanalysis and Cyberspace." *Cultures of Internet: Virtual Spaces, Real Histories, Living Bodies*. Ed. Rob Shields. London: Sage, 1996. 153–69.

Lang, Candace. "Body Language: The Resurrection of the Corpus in Text-Based VR." *Works and Days* 13, nos. 1–2 (1995): 245–60.

McRae, Shannon. "Coming Apart at the Seams: Sex, Text and the Virtual Body." *Wired-Women: Gender and New Realities in Cyberspace*. Ed. Lynn Cherny and Elizabeth Reba Wiese. Seattle: Seal, 1996. 242–64.

Miller, Susan. *Textual Carnivals: The Politics of Composition*. Carbondale: Southern Illinois University Press, 1991.

Mnookin, Jennifer. "Bodies, Rest and Motion: Law and Identity in Virtual Spaces." Cyberlaw session at the "Virtue and Virtuality: Gender, Law and Cyberspace" symposium, MIT, Cambridge, MA, 20 Apr., 1996.

Nakamura, Lisa. "Race in/for Cyberspace: Identity Tourism and Racial Passing on the Internet: The Resurrection of the Corpus in Text-Based VR." *Works and Days* 13, nos. 1–2 (1995): 245–60.

Nguyen, Dan Thu, and Jon Alexander. "The Coming of Cyberspacetime and the End of the Polity." In *Cultures of Internet: Virtual Spaces, Real Histories, Living Bodies.* Ed. Rob Shields. London: Sage, 1996. 99–124.

Novak, Marcos. "Liquid Architecture in Cyberspace." In *Cyberspace: First Steps.* Ed. Michael Benedikt. Cambridge: MIT Press, 1991. 225–54.

Poster, Mark. "Postmodern Virtualities." *Cyberspace/Cyberbodies/Cyberpunk: Cultures of Technological Embodiment.* Ed. Mike Feathersone and Roger Burrows. London: Sage, 1996. 79–96.

——. *The Second Media Age.* Oxford: Polity-Blackwell, 1995.

Ryan, Marie-Laure. "Immersion vs. Interactivity: Virtual Reality and Literary Theory." *Postmodern Culture* 5, no. 1 (1994). http://muse/jhu.edu/journals/postmodern_culture/v005/5.1ryan.html.

Shields, Rob. "Introduction: Virtual Spaces, Real Histories, and Living Bodies." In *Cultures of Internet: Virtual Spaces, Real Histories, Living Bodies.* Ed. Rob Shields. London: Sage, 1996. 1–10.

Stone, Allucquère Rosanne. *The War of Desire and Technology at the Close of the Mechanical Age.* Cambridge: MIT Press, 1995.

Sutton, Laurel. "Cocktails and Thumbtacks in the Old West: What Would Emily Say?" *Wired-Women: Gender and New Realities in Cyberspace.* Ed. Lynn Cherny and Elizabeth Reba Wiese. Seattle: Seal, 1996. 169–87.

Turkle, Sherry. *Life on the Screen: Identity in the Age of the Internet.* New York: Simon and Schuster, 1995.

Ullman, Ellen. "Come in, CQ: The Body on the Wire." *Wired-Women: Gender and New Realities in Cyberspace.* Ed. Lynn Cherny and Elizabeth Reba Wiese. Seattle: Seal, 1996. 3–23.

6 prosthetic_rhetorics@writing.loss.technology

Cynthia Haynes

When the word *prosthesis* is casually tossed into a conversation, you begin to notice discomfort in the air, sometimes leading to dead silence. The artificial limb is an obscene and repulsive object in our culture. It signals a lack, a loss, and a profound (and anguished) recognition that we cannot regenerate. I suppose this accounts for the collective gasp in the audience at a 1994 MLA session when, after briefly scolding Baudrillard for disavowing (and forgetting) the lived body, Vivian Sobchack calmly announced that she had recently had her left leg amputated. In the published version of her talk, "Beating the Meat/Surviving the Text; or, How to Get Out of This Century Alive," Sobchack even goes so far as to say, "I wished the man a car crash or two, and a little pain to bring him (back) to his senses" (207). After her surgery, as she lay in her hospital bed amid physical and psychological pain, it occurred to her that she was struggling to make her loss of flesh "mean" something. In other words, as she put it, her prosthetic leg represented "a hermeneutic problem to be solved" (210).

I begin with this story because it situates us uncomfortably between loss, language, and technology in computer-supported literacy instruction. Why do I invoke discomfort to introduce my topic? The answer lies somewhere between the fact that we are too comfortable with our role in serving the academy (as prosthetic agents) and that we are not yet comfortable with the role of technology (as prosthetic extensions of us) in education. Still, we serve and are served by prosthetic rhetorics. Thus, the prosthesis is a metaphor that captures our postmodern dilemma. With this word, we may gaze on the scars of an old debate with regenerative eyes, and re/member the body of composition theory and its prosthetic arm, the field of computers and writing. Or we may desire to incorporate the prosthetic by rhetorical means and inject it with new tropological currency in a network of overloaded circuitry. That is the beauty of the term, its resistance to serving us in any one particular way. It is *transgenic*. It is a generic user ID of a re/generate address. As Donna Haraway explains, "Email is one of the passage points . . . through which identities ebb and flow in the Net of technoscience" (4). All the terms in my address (title) represent narrative figures that, as Haraway suggests, are tied to each other by the passage of bodily substance, they "share bodily fluids," they have a "common circulatory system" (22).

My aim is to propose a similar *transgenic* body, that is, a body that is genetically engineered so that organic discourse and prosthetic rhetorics share a circulatory system and an address, a body in which writing, loss, and technology exchange bodily fluids in the disciplinary field of composition. We cannot hope to outline a hermeneutic, something as personal as Sobchack's hermeneutic problem. Those meanings arise strictly from her body. Only a rhetoric can arise from this (our) body. Only a rhetoric can share a circulatory system that courses through the body of a prosthetic field whose members function like prostheses replacing absent (lost) literacies.

Enter password: *amnesia*

Amnesia is a word that evokes concern, anxiety, trauma, and fear of memory loss. It also shares a hermeneutic kinship with *amputation*, with the feeling of losing a limb, which Sobchack says "is not not-feeling, but the feeling of not-feeling" (207). This may account for the double gesture I wanted to read into the title of Deborah Holdstein's 1995 *College English* review of several books on composition and technology, "Technology, Utility, and Amnesia." While amnesia signals a loss, in her employ it registered much more than that. Holdstein means it to signal an active forgetting, a careless lapse in scholarly homework resulting in dangerous scholarship. In her opening remarks, Holdstein contends that the texts she reviews are (to some extent) guilty of "neglect and forgetfulness," and she wonders whether "we further delay radical impact by a form of memory loss—passing as theory restated old contentions in newly-packaged contexts" (588). She is tired of the "plaintive cries for credibility or discipline-bashing" in the "scuffle between the technology-friendly and the technology-hostile" (589). In short, Holdstein wants to "move on" (589).

But there is moving on, and then there is moving *on*. When it comes to computer-supported literacy instruction, we cannot afford to move on if it means pushing aside. Much critical work remains to be done, and there are good reasons for continuing the debate. When Holdstein writes that "we no longer need to convince allegedly recalcitrant department heads that computers are 'useful'" (590), she errs in assuming that all faculty who use computers in teaching understand how to use them and why. In this respect, Holdstein overlooks the necessity of continuing to theorize and to agitate for this emerging field within composition. Instead of moving on, we need to enter the space of amnesia, to consider the scuffle itself and negotiate a deconstructive movement beyond the friendly/hostile binary. We need to re/member the loss, to understand the phantom literacy that haunts students as they learn the prosthetic rhetorics of critical literacy. In short, we need to understand the loss of some literacies, even though we re/member (*as* prosthetic subjects) newer forms of literacy that we are only beginning to visualize by means of computer-supported writing instruction.

Unfortunately, what Holdstein values (and wants to preserve at all costs) are *existing* literacies, namely, those that pay homage to the history of a field, those that situate "work, discourses, and activism within the political realities and useful 'literacies' of various scholarly, institutional, and hierarchical contexts; that [embrace] the well-articulated *ethics*, theories, and forms of practice that we profess for composition studies in general" (598). But is this not a kind of cryoliteracy? Would Holdstein have us freeze literacies in order to advance the work of computers and composition? What is the original problem that computer-assisted instruction must defrost before it can "move on"?

In 1982 James Berlin called our attention to the problem when he claimed that many writing teachers "look upon their vocations as the imparting of a largely mechanical skill, important only because it serves students in getting them through school and in advancing them in their professions" (766). To counter this attitude, Berlin argues that writing instruction carries a far greater responsibility in that "we are tacitly teaching a version of reality and the student's place and mode of operation in it" (766). In 1992 Lester Faigley offered a slight variation on Berlin's argument. According to Faigley, literacy instruction has been historically linked to nationalistic values from the early national period through most of the nineteenth century, but process pedagogy drew our attention away from the broader goals (113). In his view, teachers today are not as quick to admit that, like their predecessors, "writing teachers were as much or more interested in *whom* they want their students to be as in *what* they want their students to write" (113). What Berlin and Faigley imply is that many teachers of writing assume that by teaching writing as a skill, they avoid the pitfalls of ideology.

Thus teaching composition has become like fitting each student with a pros-thesis that provides a solid arm of literacy where there was none before. This kind of service-oriented rationale for teaching writing is a too-familiar dilemma for composition programs and the faculty who teach within them. Foremost there is the hope that good writing will aid students in their other college coursework, but, in addition, administrators pressure English departments na-tionwide to maintain the philosophy that improved writing will improve stu-dent retention, which means a stable tuition base. The public perception of writing instruction also reinforces the service-oriented dogma about composi-tion, namely, that writing well will get you a good job.

In the nineties, to make matters more complex, the growing proliferation of computer-assisted instruction further reifies the prosthetic function of compo-sition curriculum in the academy. At best, the field of rhetoric and composition has fought a shaky battle against institutional politics and public perceptions of the value of writing instruction. It should not surprise us, then, when comput-ers become just another prosthesis to assist an already prosthetic field of in-struction. The irony is that computer literacy is often seen as more empower-ing than the writing instruction in which it is but one element among many in the broad spectrum of goals and strategies for teaching writing. Still another irony lies in the fact that computers are sometimes viewed as threats to auton-omy. Thus, as Holdstein suggests, we have perpetual tangles between technophiles and technophobes. These are complex problems that frequently spawn incompatible opinions that fan the flames of cultural and institutional attitudes and threaten the idea that the teaching of writing is *intrinsically* valu-able. I have to agree with Holdstein in one sense: it is time to do something. But moving on is not going to implode these problems sufficiently. We must enter the space of amnesia, of phantom pain, and ask some cold titanium questions. Is it enough to resist seeing composition and the computer as tools of empow-erment or to resist seeing technology as a threat to autonomy? Or is it time to risk the final amputation of a decaying pedagogy?

Resistance to technology is not new. Resistance to debates about resistance is not new either, as evidenced in Holdstein's review. In her suggestion that we "move on," I find a disturbing repression of the deeper structure in these resis-tant rhetorics. When Holdstein asks: "What rough beasts are we that will slouch toward cyberspace?" (592), I hear not just a technophobic mantra but, even worse, a disingenuous attempt to laud technology out of one side of the mouth while speaking against those willing to theorize new technoliteracies. I find my-self wanting to ask Holdstein, What is at stake in moving on in the name of "preserving existing literacies" (598) by a "self-critical practice" (590) that seems uncomfortable revisiting issues that are not yet resolved? If it is time to cut off the notion of composition instruction as "service-oriented," as I have implied, then it is also time to see the *transgenic* prosthesis as more than a hermeneutic problem. It is time to see it rhetorically, not just to exercise critical reflexivity but to see *transgenesis* as a diffraction (to use Haraway's term) in which the light and the lens register not a reflection but the history of passage, of interaction, and of difference. It is time to ask what it means to slip the prosthetic arm of technology onto the deconstructed self and to ask what lies at the threshold of this joining.

I employ three organic metaphors to discuss prosthetic rhetorics in recent debates on composition and computer pedagogy. First, I take on the dominant model: the perception of computers as tools of empowerment in the teaching of writing. I call this the *vivogenic* model because it tends away from pathology, because it seeks to vivify, nurture, create, regenerate, and empower. Second, I outline a more sinister model that I call the *pathogenic* perception of computers (and technology in general) as threats to the body, as threats to a well-defined self.[1] Finally, I propose a *transgenic* nonmodel in which composition instruction becomes a process of educating the machine,[2] where students create their own agents, sending them across cultural and technological borders. Unfortunately, too many in our field prefer *cryogenics* (*cryocritique*?), the freezing of a printcentric mentality with a modern tool that only results in a kind of *cryoliteracy*. There is a thaw, however, in this wintry scenario. I believe we are witnessing the biogenetic engineering of a new literacy, a prosthetic literacy in which writing, loss, and technology course through the veins of a strange new body.

Enter password: *vivogenic*

It is not surprising that one of the primary sites of struggle in rhetoric and composition concerns the value of technology and how to adapt our pedagogies in response to cultural and political mandates to technologize education and increasing pressures to provide distance education. As I have indicated, writing courses have long been perceived as the handmaiden to other disciplines. Now that composition pedagogy has allied itself (more or less) with technology, composition programs have even more at stake in the perception that they perform a service to other disciplines in the academy. Institutional budgets and politics seal this bond because the very survival of writing programs is often linked closely with their ability to produce student writers who enter the workplace well prepared—which today often means being computer literate.

The complex nature of the service-oriented perception of writing instruction is not limited to institutions of higher education. In fact, this perception is perhaps cherished the most by the political forces that dominate cultural beliefs about liberatory pedagogy. Hardly any writing instructor would disagree with Ann Ruggles Gere that "citizens in a democracy need to be literate" (90). Making the case that writing instruction is intricately tied to democracy, Gere quotes from the 1990 mission statement of the government-established Center for the Study of Writing: "The ability to write effectively is a major aspect of the literacy skills people need to acquire information, to learn other skills, and to function independently in the everyday world" (90).

Interestingly, technology has come to stand metonymically as a sign of such independence. Gere explains that "research tell us that computers improve students' attitudes toward writing and computers make some aspects of writing easier. We know that word processors diminish the labor of recopying/retyping successive drafts and enable the uncertain speller to produce a reasonably polished piece of writing. The least able writers have the greatest need for the kind of assistance computers can provide, but institutions often fail to make it available, thereby exacerbating the differences between the haves and have-nots" (94). Sharon Crowley associates this with a naive belief that an "inoculation with literacy will somehow solve this country's social problems" (195). She goes so far as to compare this kind of liberal hope for literacy to "the false magic reflected in the 'Just Say No' campaign. Proponents of this willfully ignorant and arrogant policy seem to think that 'just saying no' can protect an eight-year-old ghetto child from the horrors of drug trafficking" (197). John Clifford warns, also, that the goals of a democracy and the goals of teaching composition may be incompatible. He reminds us of Kenneth Burke's chilling analogy, "The shepherd, qua shepherd, acts for the good of the sheep, to protect them from discomfiture and harm. But he may be 'identified' with a project that is raising the sheep for market" (Burke 27; qtd. in Clifford 38).

What Gere argued in 1990 is important in terms of access to technology and class struggle but still typical of the field today when it comes to perceptions of the benefits of technology in education. Attitudes like Gere's do not reflect an understanding of the deeper strata of electronic textuality or how virtual spaces can disrupt power relations, technify pathos, and morph identity. Nor do they reflect the concerns that Clifford and Crowley raise. In a sense, then, rather than *vivogenic*, the focus on technology as a tool for the unempowered masses is actually a quite benign and misguided argument for using technology in the writing classroom. More recent examples of *vivogenic* attitudes toward computers and composition are focused on the benefits of

LANs (local-area networks), the ability of computers to be networked for file-sharing capabilities, and Daedulus Integrated Writing Environment (DIWE), where students talk in real-time in an integrated writing environment. Going even further, computer-assisted instruction now often means access to broader networks like the Internet, where students may access email discussion lists, bulletin boards, the World Wide Web, and multiuser domains such as MOOs. As the trend to network classrooms to the Internet spreads, it is crucial to supply critical scholarship in this area in order to provide balanced views about the use of technology in writing instruction. This also holds true for those for whom computer-assisted writing instruction is not a blessing but a costly, unnecessary, threatening, and frivolous blip on the screen of composition pedagogy.

Enter password: *pathogenic*

The utilitarian perspective of technology that grounds a *vivogenic* model of composition pedagogy is familiar. That is, much of our current composition scholarship is fairly overt about the value of computers in the writing classroom. On the opposite end of the spectrum, those who view the union of technology and composition as a threat are less apt to commit those opinions to print. While it is rare to read such arguments in our journals, ironically, it is not unusual to hear *pathogenic* arguments on email lists such as MBU (Megabyte-U), a list dedicated to computers and writing issues. Here is a sampling of a few common objections to network technology in writing classrooms from an MBU exchange that took place in the fall of 1994:[3]

- If the whole class is online and one continuous and changing virtual text, are we effectively teaching students anything?
- If there is nothing *but* process—i.e., students and instructors never stop to dialogue, to step back and examine their words in the form of a product like a paper—is the process itself justified?
- If the computer is being used only as a way to deliver a response to a student paper more efficiently, is this significantly different?
- We can't evaluate as instructors the process without an interruption of product.
- After all, a grade is still a grade is still a product.
- I just don't see the point. It's chaos, we're losing control.

From these comments, it is not difficult to see that for some teachers, using computers in composition pedagogy feels like wearing a prosthesis that is supposed to compensate for a lack of control but ends up frustrating them when they can't control it. If we add another layer of complexity here—the fact that many computer-networked writing classes are taught by graduate teaching assistants with varying degrees of training—the *pathogenic* plot thickens. In the effort to use the latest in technology, we end up marching into our pedagogical techno pep rallies with little or no understanding of the pitfalls. Then when the technology fails to "liberate" students as expected, we make it the scapegoat for our own teaching failures, for being underprepared and not invested in the technology to begin with. The *pathogenic* model is characterized, then, by suspicious motivations for using technology coupled with quick attempts to blame the computers with little or no analysis of what went wrong.

Let me engage in a little casuistic stretching here and draw on a rather far-fetched analogy, one that reveals the dark side of these rhetorics. Peter Sloterdijk's study of post–World War I Weimar Germany, *Critique of Cynical Reason*, provides an interesting analogue against which to weigh this syndrome. Sloterdijk's analysis does two things: it throws our compensatory (*vivogenic*) motivations into question and reveals the threat of the *pathogenic* reaction. As in composition teaching, the prosthetic mentality of post–World War I German culture is charged with a positive attitude and a patriotic motivation. Sloterdijk explains:

> Two things were recommended to the mutilated survivors by the standard psychotechnical textbooks: a will to live as hard as steel and the training of the body to handle artificial limbs. . . . With deadly earnest, grimly humorous, patriotic doctors turned to the cripples: The Fatherland requires your services in the future, too: one-armed, one-legged men and wearers of artificial limbs can fight again on the production front. . . . A man is a man. In the textbooks on the maimed and the writings of the medical-technical industry, a highly apposite image of the human being emerges: Homo prostheticus, who is supposed to say a wildly joyful Yes to everything that says No to the "individuality" of "individuals."   (445–46)

Compare this next passage from a 1915 primer to the 1990 mission statement of the Center for the Study of Writing discussed earlier: "The present booklet . . . wants to show [the amputee] . . . that one-armedness is not the worst thing by a long shot. . . . To gain independence in every respect is the first commandment, the highest aim of the one-armed man" (447). In this next passage, Sloterdijk reveals what underlies the *vivogenic* hope in technology: a *pathogenic* fear of the deepest loss possible: of the self. But worse than that, Sloterdijk's analysis uncovers something perhaps more unthinkable: that the prosthesis is closer to us than we imagined. According to Sloterdijk: "The human body in the society of labor and war had already long been an artificial limb even before one had to replace damaged parts with functioning parts. . . . With elegant, easy-care, light metal legs . . . thinking hobbles along behind reality, and thus personality as well as soul are kept in operation as usual. The bourgeois philosophy of technology thoroughly breathes in the spirit of the one-armed primer. Personality amputated? No problem—we have another one for you in stock" (447–49).

It seems that much of the neo-Luddite fear of technology as a prosthesis in composition instruction is grounded in an even deeper psychological fear: that technology will eliminate the self. When online, some experience a psychological phantom pain and associate this with a threat to the self. The question is whether we experience this as a loss or as a redefinition of self. In his essay "Final Amputation: Pathogenic Ontology in Cyberspace," Mark Pesce (of Ono-Sendai Corporation) explains this phenomenon as he encountered it while designing and implementing the first home Virtual Reality systems marketed by Sega. Pesce discovered in his test studies of VR users that "any technological amputation always has a consequent effect in the structure of the self, as the reconfiguration of the senses produced by self-amputation introduces a new gestalt, or world view. . . . It is the overloaded self crying out for final amputation within cyberspace."

So what do we do if the machine is simultaneously perceived as both a *tool* of invention and an inherent *threat* to it? Sloterdijk reminds us of what happens when a philosophy overlooks "the destructive aspect of 'invention.' . . . The more [the fighting subject] threatens to break under the massive suffering of the technical, dominated world, the more optimistically it simulates the heroic pose. At the heart of this theory stands a subject who can no longer suffer because it has become wholly prosthesis" (449). The problem with the heroic pose is that much violence has been done in the name of heroic struggles against a technical, dominated world. The opposite is also true. As Paul Virilio suggests, "To be a subject or to be subjected? That is the question" (11). To be served is also to be subdued (9). When technology plugs us into the dome of the world, Virilio argues, prostheses "turn the overequipped, healthy (or 'valid') individual into the virtual equivalent of the well-equipped invalid" (4–5).

The machinic transformation seems to threaten, then, on all sides. The question to consider is how rhetoric and composition, as a field, can productively understand our relation to *techné* in order to critique the service-oriented attitudes that drive the claim of technology as a *vivogenic* tool of empowerment and to quit the cycle of scapegoating that causes us to fear technology as a *pathogenic* amputation of the self.

Enter password: *transgenic*

In our students' world, hybridization is the norm. The academic world of rigid disciplines has yet to understand this fully, even in the most interdisciplinary programs. We want the *transgenic*, but we are afraid; too much is at stake in forestalling the decay of disciplinarity itself. Bruno Latour put it best: "In the eyes of our critics the ozone hole above our heads, the moral law in our hearts, the autonomous text, may each be of interest, but only separately. That a delicate shuttle should have woven together the heavens, industry, texts, souls and moral law—this remains uncanny, unthinkable, unseemly" (5).

The *transgenic* (non)model represents a distributed field of figures of hybridization and genetic engineering and thrives in the matrix of rhetorical and textual writing technologies. It is a field made up of technicians, sociotechnologists, cyborg anthropologists, hypermedia software designers, cyberfeminists, hypertext authors, VR theorists, linguists, historians, sophists, and MOO wizards. It barely resembles composition as we presently understand it, yet all of these people teach writing. In Haraway's terms, *transgenic* figures are double agents, that is, "inside the stories where they circulate, they trouble kind and force a rethinking of kin. Gender, i.e., the generic, is askew in the transgenic. . . . They do not rest in the semantic coffins of finished categories, but rise in the ambiguous hours to trouble the virginal, coherent, and natural sleepers" (43). In short, they are unnatural: compounds of the organic, technical, mythic, textual, and political.

The *transgenic* includes new *genres* (such as hypertext), new *tropes* (such as speed), new *morphings* of identity (such as software agents or emissaries). Marilyn Strathern describes in one irritated remark the nature of hypertext: "You cannot spill coffee on this text, or glance back at an earlier chapter, or suspend judgment, or just let it wash over you: you have to interact with the thing" (42). The problem of interaction is twofold: we are used to the passive consumption of texts, and we are suddenly faced with "infoglut." We in the field have somewhat (albeit cautiously) embraced hypertext, the speed of MOO conversations, and the infinite maze of available texts on the World Wide Web. But are we prepared for artificial intelligence now entering the market in the form of software agents and emissaries?

In her study of virtual systems, Allucquère Stone identifies three ways that the "space and character of human social interaction" have been radically altered in technological space: (1) the development of prosthetic speech (i.e., the acoustic transducer); (2) the development of prosthetic writing as text on monitor screens; and (3) the development of prosthetic proxemics in the form of interactive video ("Virtual Systems" 609). Now studying the effects of what she calls UB-Comp—"ubiquitous computing"—Stone predicts that "two things happen as we start down the road to 'ubi-tech.' We do a certain amount of letting go and forgetting, and so does the 'tech' " ("Techno-Prosthetics"). In other words, a symbiotic relationship with ubi-tech emerges. In one sense, then, we have circled back to amnesia—but a ubiquitous amnesia.

The question remains whether our amnesia, our loss, can be reconceived in the writing classroom to stay in step with the development of prosthetic agents and intelligent rooms. In a 1995 interview in *WIRED* magazine, Pattie Maes discussed her work in artificial intelligence at MIT. Maes explained that AI research is changing, backing away from its early attempts to produce agents that are very intelligent or omniscient. She, for example, works on designing software agents that learn about their user's habits, interests, and behaviors with respect to certain tasks. They can detect patterns and then offer to automate them on behalf of the user. Maes notes, however, that "we think it's important to keep the users in control, or at least always give them the impression they are in control" (Berkun 117). Thus users can instruct agents using soft or hard rules, "soft being accepted as a default that can be overwritten by what the agent learns, hard meaning it cannot be overwritten by the agent" (117). The Internet makes it impossible for people to deal with the complexity of the online world, so we "need agents that are our alter egos; they will know what we are interested in, and monitor databases and parts of networks" (117). Delegation is the answer. Agents may also collaborate, that is, they can share knowledge about their respective users, which helps in groups of people who share habits or interests.

If we may now delegate to our own agents, perhaps in the near future we may even delegate tasks to the very rooms we work in. Another MIT artificial intelligence project involves the development of "intelligent rooms" capable of "interpreting and augmenting activity occurring within it" (MIT Artificial Intelligence Projects). The applications include "computer-assisted brainstorming, automatic meeting minutes, automatic camera direction for remote meeting teleparticipation, multimedia presentation support, and the physical embodiment of virtual agents."

If agents make it into the writing classroom and the classroom turns into an intelligent agent as well, the question is, how can we use them to teach writing? Can students use them to write? Or will they learn the habits of other "authors" and plagiarize? Will students send agents out to troll the databases to do research for them? In one sense, agents are already present. For those who use text-based virtual reality programming, such as MOOs (where students log on in real time and discuss topics, receive tutoring on writing projects, and build virtual communities), delegated virtual personae, morphs, avatars, and agents are realities. In a recent talk, Lynn Cherny took the notion of "character as pros-thesis as a given" and moved on to analyze the MOO discourse at Jays House MOO (154). She explained that some people program their players to automate null emotes (154–58) or they write programs that move them out of crowded rooms once they get too loud (160). Other sorts of automation include "idle twitches" (161), where players code their characters to do or say things when triggered by mentions of their name while they are idle—or in some cases when they are not connected at all. Cherny concludes that the body has become what Katherine Hayles calls "flickering signifiers" of identity (151).

It is one thing to move on as Cherny did—moving from a given premise of prosthetic character—and yet another to move on as Holdstein would have us do. Moving on under her terms would be moving back into the hands of print-centric histories, where giving a nod to scholarship is more important than keeping in step with new technologies, new pedagogies, and new theories. We are not in a position to hold back what Pesce witnessed as the phantom pain of self-amputation when "those in the grip (or thrall) of a technology *willingly* un-dergo a painful psychological amputation" (emphasis mine). What have we got to lose? If we think we will lose the self, think about Vivian Sobchack, whose struggle to make her loss of flesh "mean" something is far more significant than our struggle to preserve literacies (and selves) in the name of *cryogenic* re/membering. It takes courage to forget disciplinarity, history, and "the" self in the name of *transgenic* dis/membering.

Let us begin to invoke the literacies of our future critically, limited only by our imagination and a dialogic fantasy. Let us imagine a listserv moderated by prosthetic rhetoricians, writing email messages to phantom subscribers of the list. They all believe in the listserv. It serves the list members by its prosthetic memory, dutifully storing in its archives the amnesiacal data flung into the ether by one quick press of a button. Control X. Send message? Y or N? I don't remember what to do here. Why are there no other options? I need my agent/emissary to make this decision. I don't remember why the listserv serves me. I have amnesia? Perhaps I am an emissary. Hmmm. I am a prosthesis? I have replaced a lost append/age with writing. Yes. Writing message to disk.

[1 new message! from prosthetic_rhetorics@ . . .]

Notes

1. Both of these metaphors—*vivogenic* and *pathogenic*—I borrow from Mark Pesce's work at Ono-Sendai Corporation, where he conducts research on the physi-

ological and psychological effects of full-immersion virtual reality games on children, specifically the recent products marketed by Sega.

2. I take this phrase from Jan Rune Holmevik's groundbreaking thesis, *Educating the Machine: A History of Computing and the SIMULA Programming Language* (Center for Society and Technology, University of Trondheim, 1994).

3. I have purposely left these paraphrased comments unattributed because of the inflammatory nature of this particular exchange.

Works Cited

Berkun, Scott. "Agent of Change: Interview with Pattie Maes." *WIRED* 3, no. 4 (Apr. 1995):116–17.

Berlin, James A. "Contemporary Composition: The Major Pedagogical Theories." *College English* 44 (Dec. 1982):765–77.

Burke, Kenneth. *A Rhetoric of Motives*. Berkeley: University of California Press, 1969.

Cherny, Lynn. " 'Objectifying' the Body in the Discourse of an Object-Oriented MUD." *Works and Days* 13, nos. 1–2 (Mar. 1996):151–72.

Clifford, John. "The Subject in Discourse" in *Contending with Words: Composition and Rhetoric in a Postmodern Age*. Ed. Patricia Harkin and John Schilb. New York: MLA, 1991. 38–51.

Crowley, Sharon. "Reimagining the Writing Scene: Curmudgeonly Remarks About Contending with Words." In *Contending with Words: Composition and Rhetoric in a Postmodern Age*. Ed. Patricia Harkin and John Schilb. New York: MLA, 1991. 189–97.

Faigley, Lester. *Fragments of Rationality: Postmodernity and the Subject of Composition*. Pittsburgh: University of Pittsburgh Press, 1992.

Gere, Ann Ruggles. "The Politics of Teaching Writing." *Focuses* 3, no. 2 (fall 1990):89–98.

Haraway, Donna J. *Modest_Witness@ Second_Millennium.FemaleMan_Meets_OncoMouse: Feminism and Technoscience*. New York: Routledge, 1997.

Holdstein, Deborah. "Technology, Utility, and Amnesia." *College English* 57 (Sep. 1995):587–98.

Latour, Bruno. *We Have Never Been Modern*. Trans. Catherine Porter. Cambridge: Harvard University Press, 1993.

MIT Artificial Intelligence Projects. "The Intelligent Room: Intelligent Enhanced Reality." http://www.ai.mit.edu/projects/hci/hci.html (1 Feb. 1998).

Pesce, Mark D. "Final Amputation: Pathogenic Ontology in Cyberspace." *Speed* 1, no. 1. http://tunisia.sdc.ucsb.edu/speed/1.1/pesce.html (1 Feb. 1998).

Sloterdijk, Peter. *Critique of Cynical Reason*. Minneapolis: University of Minnesota Press, 1987.

Sobchack, Vivian. "Beating the Meat/Surviving the Text; or, How to Get Out of This Century Alive." *Body & Society* 1, nos. 3–4 (Nov. 1995):205–14.

Stone, Allucquère Roseanne. "Techno-Prosthetics and Exterior Presence: A Conversation with Allucquère Rosanne Stone." *Speed* 1, no. 2. http://tunisia.sdc.ucsb.edu/speed/1.2/stone.html (1 Feb. 1998).

———. "Virtual Systems." In *Zone 6: Incorporations.* Ed. Jonathan Crary and Sanford Kwinter. Cambridge: MIT Press, 1992. 608–21.

Strathern, Marilyn. *Reproducing the Future: Anthropology, Kinship and the New Reproductive Technologies.* New York: Routledge, 1992.

Virilio, Paul. "The Third Interval: A Critical Transition." In *Rethinking Technologies.* Ed. Verena Andermatt Conley. Minneapolis: University of Minnesota Press, 1993. 3–12.

7 Our Bodies? Our Selves? Questions About Teaching in the MUD

Raul Sanchez

In *Data Trash: The Theory of the Virtual Class*, Arthur Kroker and Michael Weinstein discuss the current and potential hazards of our culture's rush toward virtuality. Among these is a reaffirmation of the notion that mind and body are distinct entities, the latter acting as a brake on or even a prison for the former. As they see it, this idea derives its persuasive power from the pervasive sense of isolation felt by many in the atomistic world of late twentieth century capitalism: "The appeal of electronic networking operates in inverse proportion to the disconnectedness of people from each other, of the recombinant sign from the human species, and of the body digitized from the abandoned site of the organic body" (39). In such a scenario, freedom is equated with an escape from the body, the capacity to move into and out of realms that are not obliged to honor the exigencies of corporeality. The mind travels over fields of data, collecting information or accumulating experience without leaving the house. Kroker and Weinstein see this as symptomatic of what they call the Recline of the West: technological society's dependence on increasingly sophisticated forms of mediation between self and experience. As our notion of experience takes us further from our bodies, we become in a sense invalid, and "culture is reduced to a standing reserve of prosthetic devices" (41).

Yet, as postmodern theories insist, mediation is the sine qua non of our existence, the starting point rather than the goal of discussions about perception, knowledge, agency, subjectivity. We no longer try to remove the so-called obstacles that keep us from apprehending reality. Rather, we seek to understand the ways in which the apprehension of reality is intimately linked to our perceptions of it, knowing (perhaps *believing*) that all our ontological ruminations take place within the boundaries of a generative and not merely descriptive set of discourses. And so to speak pejoratively of mediation is not to engage in useful critique. However, *forms* of mediation can be examined. Their ideological dimensions can be questioned. For example, we can determine what Julian Dibbell calls "socially meaningful differences" between the bodies we conceive of in cyberspace (virtuality) and our more mundane physical ones, applying "our late modern ontologies, epistemologies, sexual ethics, and common sense," inadequate though they may seem, to the problems at hand (238). Here at the intersection of mind, body, and technology, such procedures seem especially important because they can help us arrive at appropriate individual and collective visions of ourselves in a world experiencing rapid and constant change, a world where the struggle among cultural and political and economic forces of liberation and domination is by no means resolved.

In this chapter I will suggest that we may be reinscribing the centuries-old split between mind and body via our computer-oriented writing pedagogy. Specifically, I will look at how MUDs and similar synchronous communication programs can help contribute to a sense of self (or selves) that relies less and less on one's bodily configurations and limitations. I will also suggest that while there are clear advantages to such a strategy of self-identity, eventually we run the risk of deepening the alienation that may have driven us and our students there in the first place. Finally, I'll consider some of the ethical issues that arise when one chooses to teach students (in) these kinds of environments.

The Body as Meat

Kroker and Weinstein are not alone in formulating a critique of virtuality while denying neither its potential value nor, to some extent, its inevitability. In an examination of the cyborg metaphor, Kevin Robins and Les Levidow point out the idealism and utopianism that underlie our visions of a virtual future, a future that overcomes physical limitations. In the image of the cyborg, they argue, "we combine an omnipotent phantasy of self-control with fear and aggression directed against the emotional and bodily limitations of mere mortals. Through regression to a phantasy of infantile omnipotence, we deny our dependency upon nature, upon our own nature, upon the 'bloody mess' of organic nature" (106). In an effort to demonstrate the consequences of such an outlook, Robins and Levidow then go on to trace the metaphor's military applications, specifically in the Gulf War. Here the activity of war is technologically transformed into a video game where there is "closer visual proximity between weapon and target, but at the same time greater psychological distance" (107).

On a larger scale, Jean Baudrillard notices similar effects of the dizzying acceleration of data exchange in media-saturated environments, including the mind. While it might be tempting to say that this phenomenon has the capacity to alter our sense of reality, Baudrillard argues instead that it obliterates the notion of reality altogether, since our conceptual apparatus is now embedded in media logic. Even our visions of the past are constructed and routed via the channels of high-tech communication. The wish for a return to a simpler, unmediated past is recast as one more option in the range of possible sensations, a nostalgia effect to be employed in our continuous quest for the ecstatic.

In Baudrillard's scenario, the body becomes a liability, the reminder of a discarded ontology: "The human body, our body, seems superfluous in its proper expanse, in the complexity and multiplicity of its organs, of its tissue functions, because today everything is concentrated in the brain and the genetic code, which alone sum up the operational definition of being" (*Ecstasy* 18). We appear to have rationalized ourselves out of our bodies, so that the body itself achieves significance only as a function of mind. Synchronous communication programs—pure mind, pure text (for now)—seem to offer an environment from which the last vestiges of corporeality have almost been purged, reduced to the visual process of reading, the tactile sensation of typing, and the aural experience of hearing keys click.

While questioning the disembodiment on which this kind of communication seems to depend, I am trying not to fall back into the very mind/body dualism that thus far has characterized many of our visions of cyberspace. My aim is not to shun the technological after having declared it the latest development in the history of Western thought and oppression; mine is not a holistic, primitivist, or mystical discourse. It is, however, an attempt to examine the potential reification of traditional Western values through computer technologies. Despite this, my critique might be seen as fresh form of Luddism, defined here as a straw man, a construction arising from a particular attitude toward technology, one that relies on an unreflective idea of "progress." As Iain Boal notes, "it is a lie that direct action against the instruments of production has always been hopeless or that it somehow entails being 'antitechnology,' as if that were a possible position *in general*" (11). The last phrase of this quotation is important. It highlights the impossibility of the oppositional relationship on which the idea of Luddism is constructed. It also points us in the direction of Donna Haraway, whose vision of the cyborg is complex and potentially liberating although it is not yet a vision that informs our perceptions of MUDspace.

Like Boal and others, Haraway sees the potential danger of new technologies that reproduce masculinist, atomistic ideologies. For instance, she notes that "the culture of video games is heavily oriented to individual competition and extraterrestrial warfare," resulting in "high-tech, gendered imaginations" that become militarized, as are the realms beyond psychological boundaries (168). Yet for Haraway the answer to this threat is not a retreat from science to humanism, mysticism, or the kind of pretechnological mythos out of which goddess narratives are woven. Instead, she argues for an end to the dualisms from which oppressive and gendered manifestations of technology emerge, citing the potential of technological culture itself to subvert such formations. In the high-tech environment, "it is not clear who make and who is made in the relation between human and machine. It is not clear what is mind and what body in machines that resolve into coding practices. In so far as we know ourselves both in formal discourse . . . and in daily practice . . . we find ourselves to be cyborgs, hybrids, mosaics, chimeras" (177). And this, for Haraway, is all to the good. As we move away from an ontological and epistemological imperative toward a more fluid conception of self and agency, we come to more sophisticated understandings of body and mind, understandings that have heretofore only been coded according to the specific cultural and intellectual requirements of an exclusionary ideological formation.

Likewise, Judith Butler attempts to arrive at an understanding of the body that includes it in the process of signification, where its status as an ongoing construction project of historically situated hegemonic forces is first articulated and then questioned. However, it is customary, she argues, to posit the body and materiality as ontologically prior categories that fall beyond the purview of discourse, of representation, thereby rendering them absolute and thus closed to interpretation or investigation. Through her readings of Plato and Irigaray, Butler argues that this is a preeminently discursive move, an attempt to ontologize the "gendered matrix" through which materiality is constructed, to establish the feminine "as that which is necessary for the reproduction of the human, but which itself is not human, and which is in no way to be construed as the formative principle of the human form that is, as it were, produced through it" (42). The feminine, which is to say the womb, which is to say the body, is written as the nonconstitutive vessel from which the masculine, which is to say the mind, emerges. Matter assumes the proportions of a "metaphysical concept that serves a phallogocentrism" (47). It is reasonable to suggest that this understanding of the composition and relationship of mind and body underlies our current visions of online pedagogy, primarily because it forms part of the foundation on which the technology of cyberspace itself is constructed. Kroker and Weinstein articulate this situation clearly and succinctly in their dystopic vision of the body as meat: an untheorized, untheorizable, strictly functional vessel fit for all kinds of figurative consumption; the latest frontier on which the colonialist drama of manifest destiny can be enacted and celebrated.

Yet this thing called the body remains attached to us. It has yet to be obliterated, precisely because it marks the boundary of and therefore defines that which we call the mind. The body is the necessary other of the colonizing mind. Because of this we are willing, through our actions and our ontologies, to abandon it (as if we could); we want to deliver ourselves and our students into a potentially disembodied future. Moreover, we too often are not asking what interests other than the ones we value as educators are being served by this immersion into virtuality, by our capitulation to the idea that our "minds" can travel great distances while our "bodies" stay at rest, docile. Allucquère Rosanne Stone reminds us that "forgetting about the body is an old Cartesian trick, one that has unpleasant consequences for those bodies whose speech is silenced by the act of our forgetting; that is to say, those upon whose labor the act of forgetting the body is founded—usually women and minorities" ("Will" 113). Has this crusty old notion of a mind/body dualism acquired high-tech trappings in which to advertise its promise of unlimited and unmediated apprehension of the real? Do we stand to learn something "real" about our "selves"? By now we might have realized that the road to this horizon is paved with the bodies of the powerless and the disenfranchised. However, it is easy for those of us traveling on it to not recognize or worry about our complicity in the processes of domination that make the trip possible. And we do this at our own peril, of course. As Stone notes, "no refigured virtual body, no matter how beautiful, will slow the death of a cyberpunk with AIDS. Even in the age of the technosocial subject, life is lived through bodies" ("Will" 113).

Perhaps our embrace of virtual pedagogies has to do with our desire to overcome what Susan Miller calls the feminization of composition. In her article by that name she discusses the "prevailing negative cultural identity" that the feminine and composition share in their respective spheres (39). Miller rightly notes that, as currently constituted in the field of English studies, composition "is the counterpart, the handmaiden, and low-order basement attached to vernacular literary study" (42). Because of its historical ties to remediation and its identification as a primarily pedagogical rather than theoretical activity, composition is often quietly and institutionally categorized under the sexist title of "women's work." Furthermore, she argues, in its attempts to embody a "pow-

erful, masculine academic position," especially over and against its rivals in literary studies, composition has in the past adopted a scientific and empirical approach to research that, ironically, mimics the strategy of New Criticism earlier
in the century as it struggled to legitimate itself in the face of the scientific disciplines (50).

It is not difficult to see composition's embrace of computer technology as
a similar move in the quest for departmental and institutional legitimation.
For example, at my institution some of the most advanced computer technology on campus is housed in the English department's multimedia classroom,
and most of the courses taught in it are composition courses. Writing teachers are eager to have classes scheduled in it, not only because of the pedagogical opportunities the technology makes possible, but because it is considered
a good vita line in this time of shrinking employment opportunities and pro-
liferating educational technologies. In addition, being familiar with (if not
mastering) computer-assisted writing instruction is a mark of distinction
within the rank and file of the department, thus contributing to the formation
of professional hierarchies. Finally, it might be argued that computers make
composition "safe" for men, as they bestow a respectable veneer of high technology on the work itself. As Miller points out, the bulk of the lower-level composition teaching in this country is still performed by underpaid and under-
valued women (41).

As teachers of computer-mediated composition, we stand to find ourselves
confronted with technologies that may or may not support the philosophical
and educational principles by which we care to live and teach. But we are susceptible to the allure of computer technologies, and, as Gail Hawisher and Cynthia Selfe have pointed out, much of our scholarship on the subject adopts a
noncritical and even utopian tone. They argue that "unless it is used carefully
and critically," computer technology "can and will support any number of negative pedagogical approaches that also grow out of our cultural values and our
theories of writing" (56). Our failure to understand that computers are "cultural artifacts embodying society's values" makes us susceptible to forms of control and domination that we might otherwise resist, both for our own sakes and
those of our students (55).

In the MUD

Still, it may not be the case that communicating via a MUD constitutes a whole-
sale rejection of the body in favor of the textual pleasures of the mind. Staunch
defenders of the medium insist that the body is very much a part of the com-

munication process, despite the fact that it is not materially copresent with other bodies. And this is true, to an extent. Angry, affectionate, and comedic exchanges elicit bodily responses from a person sitting at a computer, typing and reading text. It is not uncommon to hear people laugh out loud in the middle of a university computer lab: the corporeal effect of a particular situation or statement they have just read on their screens. Likewise, it is possible to feel tangible anger from offensive words whether they be on a computer screen or in the mouth of a materially present person.

Yet there does seem to be some difference, and how we gauge that difference may have to do with whether we see the computer, in McLuhanesque terms, as a "hot" or a "cool" medium. For McLuhan, a hot medium is "low in participation" because it provides the receiver with most of the information, leaving very little for her or him to fill in (23). A cool medium, then, "demands involvement in process," requiring the participant to provide information not accounted for in the communicative gaps (31). It seems to me that a vision of the computer as a hot medium is possible if we question the nature of the interactivity taking place between the person at the keyboard and the computer before her or him, if we make claims about the kind and quality of engagement that goes on. Ironically, however, this would be to ignore the possible cliché but still useful notion that the medium itself *is* the message.[1] This idea allowed McLuhan to argue that television required the sort of multisensory engagement that had only been dreamed by Western artists. As he saw it, television offered "a daily session of synesthesia" despite the fact that much television programming was and is considered base, vulgar, and corrupting (315). I prefer McLuhan's inclination, at least in part, because it allows me to discuss the content of synchronous discourse programs and the interaction that takes place through them in terms of another "content": the fact of the textual computer environment itself.

With this in mind, we might consider the actual goings-on in a MUD.[2] At first glance, the emotional and intellectual highs and lows one experiences there seem significant and real. However, even at a remove of a few minutes the gravity and even the content of these situations often seem to disappear, and what was unforgivably insulting moments before suddenly seems insignificant and barely memorable in the face of other real-world or virtual exigencies. This ability to move unproblematically between states of emotional or intellectual stimulation would seem to be less common in the realm of face-to-face interaction, and to some it might signal the MUD's inherent inability to accommodate and foster the full range of human communicative complexity. And yet this is not true of all users. Some experience profound "real-life" effects from their activities in the MUD and are moved either to stay away completely or to alter their behaviors profoundly, reacting just as they might to any other significant off-line event. Despite this similarity, however, we might still ask if it is possible to make meaningful distinctions between what happens online and off. If so, how might these distinctions relate to the ways we and our students envision the relationship between our bodies and our minds?

Stone identifies what she sees as differences in "the density of communication, or the bandwidth," of face-to-face and computer-mediated conversation (*War* 93). Bandwidth, defined by Stone as "the amount of information exchanged in unit time," is wide in face-to-face communication because participants have access to the greatest possible range of modes and can mix and use them simultaneously (*War* 93). It is narrow in text-based computer-mediated communication and in telephone conversation because communication is restricted to lines of writing on a screen in the first instance and disembodied, distorted, and compressed voices in the second. Because of this narrow bandwidth, Stone argues, participants are forced to raise their level of interpretive engagement, creating and absorbing maximal meaning from minimal symbology. If we link this idea of increased interaction to the idea that what we call "the body" is at least in part a constructed phenomenon, then the distinctions between computer-mediated and physical forms of embodiment seem less rigid. To the extent that our notion of the "self" is fundamentally distinct from our notion of the "body," then it is hard to argue that one extra step of mediation, this time via MUD technology, can make that much difference in what is already a flawed perspective.

Furthermore, one can argue that the relevance of this mind/body issue takes a conceptual backseat when we think of certain practical applications of MUD technology. I'm thinking here of distance learning projects that allow people in remote areas access not only to the institutional structures of the university but also (and perhaps more importantly) to each other. Clearly, people can be brought together in meaningful ways, whether their bodies are directly involved or not. Even here, however, we have to ask ourselves careful and serious questions about how and why such connections might be made. We do not have to be mathematicians or accountants to understand that if a teacher's classroom is not bound by traditional notions of space or geography, then the possibility for increasing the size of what constitutes a class rises dramatically, in turn increasing the amount of revenue an institution stands to earn. Given the belt-tightening fiscal climate in legislatures around the country, coupled with the revival of a back-to-basics approach to education that frowns on the kinds of dialogical pedagogical innovations that progressive and radical educators have been struggling to promote for the last twenty years, it is not hard to imagine

MUD technology being used in the service of an aggressively dualistic vision of education that treats distant and disembodied minds as receptacles of prepackaged but cost-efficient information bits. And despite what some optimistic advocates might claim about the liberatory inevitabilities of high technologies, I think it is fairly obvious that the technology itself makes this kind of unfortunate political and cultural transformation possible: distance learning as a panoptical nightmare of highly accurate detection, increased accountability, continual assessment, and the perpetual threat of surveillance (as Taylor discusses in chapter 8). And so even when discussing issues of the mind we find ourselves, not surprisingly, squarely in the realm of the body.

In arguing against the conventional notion that media derive their societal impact solely according to how they are implemented by people, McLuhan notes that the "effects of technology do not occur at the level of opinions or concepts, but alter sense ratios or patterns of perception steadily and without any resistance" (18). That is to say, a technology is a sort of *episteme*. However, the epistemological consequences of computer-mediated communication will possibly never be fully understood, as that would imply an ability to perceive and evaluate our current situations from some exterior vantage point. But I think we can take periodic, if incomplete, glances at how our bodies are being reconfigured in and by new technologies, especially under the guise of education. And I think that, as long as we are part of the educational institution, we have some hope of determining the course of future arrangements.

We might begin by asking ourselves how we implement MUD technology in our classrooms. Many teachers hold class discussions online, even when their students are all materially present in one room. One often-cited reason for this practice is that by having their conversations textualized, students are made more aware of their own discursive processes. Synchronous conversation combines the textuality of writing with the spontaneity of speech, and placing students at the nexus of these two modes presumably heightens their awareness of the workings of discourse. Another reason for bringing physically copresent students into a MUD-type environment is that such exposure might allow otherwise silent or silenced students, particularly women and people of color, to express themselves in a way that is perhaps less threatening than the face-to-face environment of the traditional classroom. I think that both of these scenarios are valid, and in the interest of promoting both I have taken my students into the MUD, so to speak. My aim, therefore, is not to invalidate them. Rather, I want to ask what we stand to give up in relation to what we gain.

I must begin by stating what seems to be the obvious: that the very idea of putting people in one room and then asking them to communicate via computer is somewhat bizarre, if not (for lack of a better term) unnatural. We don't use telephones to speak to people if we can see and hear them directly, so why do the same with computers? If part of the function of an education is to introduce and inculcate people into normal and accepted forms of human interaction, if the medium of the educational institution is (at least in part) its message, then what are we and our technologies transmitting to our students when we tell them it is acceptable and perhaps even preferable to communicate by means of the computer prosthetic even when it is not necessary? It seems to me that this approach encourages a kind of atomistic sense of self that disengages from the materiality of daily existence. Students get cut off from other students, more so than they already are, because they know each other in large part via electronic print. Furthermore, we can ask what concept of self this kind of pedagogy encourages as it increasingly requires the student to find and develop a voice that is intimately linked to the technological device. Finally, it could be argued that simply changing the environment of a class discussion constitutes an evasion rather than a confrontation of the social and cultural forces that silence some students while empowering others to speak. We might be exchanging one set of sociodiscursive circumstances for another, or we may not. In either case, the circumstances themselves are not being addressed, only displaced or moved around.

Another argument for the use of MUDs and, more specifically, MOOs suggests that such technology allows students to explore multiple subjectivities, to explore and develop a character or characters that might differ in slight or significant ways from that of their "real" lives. This perspective constitutes an attempt to theorize MUDspace in specifically postmodern terms that critique and undermine the unified and ontological notion of self that is in part a legacy of Enlightenment rationality. By immersing students in the hyperdiscursive MUD environment, we allow them to confront the constructed dimensions of subjecthood as they watch themselves and others become (re)creations of the discursive exchanges in which they participate. This is a subtle point, more so than the previous pedagogical justifications, I think, and more convincing. Yet I wonder to what extent we can accurately maintain the correspondence between our postmodern notions of the subject and the discursive dimensions of MUD subjecthood.

While the subject in most postmodern configurations is fluid, shifting, and largely a function of discourse, this is not to say that people merely pick and choose their identities as they would garments or masks. In fact, the idea that subjecthood and identity are inextricably discursive rather than ontological places limits on the subject's ability to exert, to express anything like a "will."

Facile notions of postmodern subjecthood have people changing costumes and confusing that kind of change with what we might call socioepistemic shifts and movements. It is true that in a MUD one can change one's name, description, even behavior. However, this is of a fundamentally different order from the complex movements of the postmodern subject, movements that occur not necessarily of her or his own volition. While this kind of transformation may happen just as well in a MUD as anywhere else, what usually passes for multiple subjectivity in a MUD is in fact the illusion of a unified Enlightenment subject trying on different roles but nonetheless maintaining the idea of a core being that exists apart from discursive exigencies.

Conclusion: The Carceral?

I'm standing in the middle of our multimedia classroom, surrounded by students and computers lined up against the walls. The students are typing, "talking" to each other on a MUD. I see screens glowing beyond my students' backs. The hum of the computers provides a frigid sonic backdrop for the percussive sound of fingers hitting keys. Now and then someone laughs out loud or one student will turn to another and say something like, "Really?"

My students are communicating via computer technology, taking steps toward the future. I'm doing my job, preparing them for the discursive worlds of the next century. I am making it all possible, providing the framework for their understandings of computerized textuality, exposing them to a communication environment that had heretofore not been dreamt in composition's philosophy. I recall Lester Faigley's characterization of composition's modernist project: "Hard work aimed at producing an enduring object" (191). Not here. This is writing that is barely writing: transient, temporal, contingent, ephemeral. It will never be hard copy. Most of it will not exist when we log off. I remember Elizabeth Reid's nicely accurate observation: "MUD interaction is not intended for an audience uninvolved in it. MUD interaction is not enacted to be read but to be experienced" (171).

But I am bothered by this student "discussion." At my own terminal, strategically situated so that I can monitor activity, I once again survey the classroom: human backs and glowing fragments. As if for the first time, suddenly I realize that we are actually in the same room. So why don't we just talk to each other, face-to-face? I think of Michael Heim's assertion that "the face is the primal interface, more basic than any machine mediation. The physical eyes are the windows that establish the neighborhood of trust" (102). I am not sure I buy into this idea completely, but it has its appeal.

Then I wonder about the cultural and ideological implications of this computer-assisted pedagogy. I wonder what kinds of literacy I am disseminating and promoting when I throw students into this MUD. Why am I doing it? Maybe I'm simply training them to be more efficient stay-at-home online consumers of pizza and dry goods. Kroker and Weinstein have a grim vision of a world hardwired for mass consumption: "Not a wired culture, but a virtual culture that is wired shut: compulsively fixated on digital technology as a source of salvation from the reality of a lonely culture and radical social disconnection from everyday life, and determined to exclude from the public debate any perspective that is not a cheerleader for the coming-to-be of the fully realized technological society" (4–5). The students in the room are learning to be alone together, and I am showing them the way. I wonder if there are any alternatives that don't simply turn a blind eye to the technological realities in front of me and my students, that offer possibilities for resistance. I would hate to think that the Unabomber's warped vision is all that remains outside the system, beyond signification, although even that Othered, violent subject will soon be swallowed and co-opted under the socially tolerable and understandable category of pathology, illness, disease.

Notes

1. It also suggests that McLuhan's distinction between *hot* and *cold* eventually collapses, as the difference between low interactivity and high becomes difficult to gauge in any meaningful way. On the one hand, McLuhan seems to suggest that the quality of a medium's engagement with its recipient is unrelated to its status qua medium; hence the idea that the medium is the message, regardless of how its recipients engage it. On the other hand, he suggests that the ways and degrees in which recipients engage a medium determines its status as either "hot" or "cool." Rather than risk getting mired in such unnecessarily evaluative questions, I find it easier to assume a potential "coolness" in any medium, especially the computer. Yet the distinction is initially useful to my point, if for different reasons than McLuhan perhaps intended.

Interesting commentary on McLuhan's theory can be found in Kenneth Burke as well as Baudrillard ("The Implosion of Meaning in the Media"). Essentially, Burke dismisses McLuhan for not deriving a formula or method as complete as his own notion of dramatism, while Baudrillard explains why McLuhan's ideas don't go quite far enough toward describing the relationship between medium and reality.

2. From here on I will use the term *MUD* generically to indicate all kinds of text-oriented, synchronous-communication programs, including MOOs and local-area

programs such as Daedalus Interchange. I will make explicit reference to these types of programs when necessary.

Works Cited

Baudrillard, Jean. *The Ecstasy of Communication*. Trans. Bernard Schutze and Caroline Schutze. New York: Semiotext(e), 1988.

———. "The Implosion of Meaning in the Media." In *Simulacra and Simulation*. Trans. Sheila Faria Glaser. Ann Arbor: University of Michigan Press, 1994. 79–86.

Boal, Iain A. "A Flow of Monsters: Luddism and Virtual Technologies." In James Brook and Iain A. Boal, *Resisting the Virtual Life: The Culture and Politics of Information*. San Francisco: City Lights, 1995. 3–15.

Brook, James, and Iain A. Boal. *Resisting the Virtual Life: The Culture and Politics of Information*. San Francisco: City Lights, 1995.

Burke, Kenneth. "Medium as 'Message.'" In *Language as Symbolic Action: Essays on Life, Literature, and Method*. Berkeley: University of California Press, 1966. 410–18.

Butler, Judith. *Bodies that Matter: On the Discursive Limits of "Sex."* New York: Routledge, 1993.

Dibbell, Julian. "A Rape in Cyberspace; or, How an Evil Clown, a Haitian Trickster Spirit, Two Wizards, and a Cast of Dozens Turned a Database into a Society." In *Flame Wars: The Discourse of Cyberculture*. Ed. Mark Dery. Durham: Duke University Press, 1994. 237–61.

Faigley, Lester. *Fragments of Rationality: Postmodernity and the Subject of Composition*. Pittsburgh: University of Pittsburgh Press, 1992.

Haraway, Donna J. *Simians, Cyborgs, and Women: The Reinvention of Nature*. New York: Routledge, 1991.

Hawisher, Gail E., and Cynthia L. Selfe. "The Rhetoric of Technology and the Electronic Writing Class." *College Composition and Communication* 42 (1991):55–65.

Heim, Michael. *The Metaphysics of Virtual Reality*. New York: Oxford University Press, 1993.

Kroker, Arthur, and Michael A. Weinstein. *Data Trash: The Theory of the Virtual Class*. New York: St. Martin's, 1994.

McLuhan, Marshall. *Understanding Media: The Extensions of Man*. New York: McGraw-Hill, 1964.

Miller, Susan. "The Feminization of Composition." In *The Politics of Writing Instruction: Postsecondary*. Ed. Richard Bullock and John Trimbur. Portsmouth, NH: Boynton/Cook, 1991. 39–53.

Reid, Elizabeth. "Virtual Worlds: Culture and Imagination." In *CyberSociety: Computer-Mediated Communication and Community*. Ed. Steven G. Jones. Thousand Oaks, CA: Sage, 1995. 164–83.

Robins, Kevin, and Les Levidow. "Soldier, Cyborg, Citizen." In James Brook and Iain A. Boal, *Resisting the Virtual Life: The Culture and Politics of Information*. San Francisco: City Lights, 1995. 105–13.

Stone, Allucquère Rosanne. *The War of Desire and Technology at the Close of the Mechanical Age*. Cambridge: MIT Press, 1995.

——. "Will the Real Body Please Stand Up?: Boundary Stories about Virtual Cultures." In *Cyberspace: First Steps*. Ed. Michael Benedikt. Cambridge: MIT Press, 1992. 81–118.

THREE

8 The Persistence of Authority: Coercing the Student Body

Todd Taylor

It seems that literacy theorists may be eternally sentenced to contend with issues of classroom authority, and over the last twenty years we have certainly witnessed a variety of responses to this struggle. In the mid-1970s, Peter Elbow's *Writing Without Teachers* suggested that classroom authority should be almost completely leveled if we want to facilitate effective learning about writing. Patricia Bizzell's *Academic Discourse and Critical Consciousness* chronicles varying attempts throughout the 1980s and early 1990s to reconcile advantages and disadvantages inherent in classroom authority, as well as in the authority transferred and maintained through academic discourse. More recently, literacy theorists such as J. Elspeth Stuckey have gone so far as to claim that the exercise of traditional academic authority can exert a type of violence on certain students. Yet other critiques, such as Min-Zhan Lu's "Conflict and Struggle: The Enemies or Preconditions of Basic Writing?" counter Stuckey's position by arguing that the students she hopes to protect from "violence" are actually being sheltered from exposure to the very discourses of authority that they must confront if, in fact, they are to gain power.

Thus issues of classroom authority continue to be especially problematic for instructors. Judging from the messages in much of the scholarship in the field today, we might expect that instructors who have a solid grounding in contemporary composition theory and practice would support pedagogies that delegate authority in increasingly more democratic ways, but if we look closely we might be surprised by some of the practices of these educators.

As one of these educators myself, I must confess that I am surprised by some of my own uses of authority. Consequently, the reader will find in this chapter a confession, a self-conscious examination of issues of authority that I face as an instructor in a developing computer-assisted writing program. After describing some of these problems through a brief personal narrative, I then turn to Michel Foucault's analysis of authority in *Discipline and Punish* in an attempt to answer a central question: "How is it that writing instructors sometimes find themselves subverting their own goals?" In order to answer this question, I take a close look at new methods of coercion and control that have recently been devised to maintain traditional types of authority in computer-assisted classrooms. This chapter concludes by questioning the degree to which it makes sense to continue discussing classroom authority in terms of teacher-centered versus student-centered models.

Building Panopticons in Your Own Backyard

In the summer of 1994 I was asked to design our department's first-ever computer-supported writing classroom. This new facility was to serve as a full-time classroom, rather than as the more familiar computer lab, meaning that it would be dedicated almost exclusively to class meetings. Consequently, I searched for a floor plan that would support contemporary views of teaching and learning: namely, student-centered pedagogies that emphasize active participation and democratic distribution of classroom authority. During the previous academic year, I had been teaching in another department's computer classroom, a facility arranged according to an amphitheater- or proscenium-type floor plan wherein the instructor occupies a pit in the front of the room and the students sit in rows ascending away from the pit, with their workstations directly in their faces. The amphitheater design involved a good deal of stretching, jogging, and stair climbing; it also made teaching difficult. From the front of the room I would try to help students operate rudimentary writing software while asking the same question over and over again: "Who out there is not looking at the same screen I am?" Inevitably, no one would reply. I would look up and see only the glowing foreheads of students whose faces were buried in their monitors. I found myself giving instruction down in the so-called teacher station and then climbing up to the back of the room and peering over shoulders to see who was not on the same screen, for I was not even close to winning the competition with the computer for their attention.

The amphitheater design was not only chaotic and physically demanding, it also made me anxious about my pedagogy. After reading a number of articles and talking with a number of colleagues about problems with instructional technology, I had become acutely aware of the idea that computer-assisted pedagogies run the risk of reducing writing courses to classes in software skills. This critique led me to question devoting class time to software instruction even of the most basic kind; it was as if whenever we were learning about the programs a timer was running in my head, clocking the minutes invested in what felt like the wrong type of activity. And because the amphitheater design extended the amount of time required to get everyone on the same screen, I became even less confident about the soundness of my computer-assisted pedagogy.

In a deliberate response to the annoying amphitheater classroom, I designed the floor plan of our new writing facility so that students worked at stations along the perimeter of the classroom with their backs to the center of the room. One advantage of the perimeter design was that it allowed me to tell instantly and easily whenever someone was on the wrong page. However, I secretly knew that there was a problem with my design, a problem that I could not seem to avoid. In the course of generating the new design, I had carefully studied Linda Myers's *Approaches to Computer Writing Classrooms*. Myers's book offers an intriguing collection of twelve narratives, each describing a different computer-assisted writing program and focusing in particular on classroom architecture. A number of these narratives tended to argue for the superiority of either a perimeter or a cluster design as compared to other options. The cluster floor plan, which divides the classroom into workstations arranged in pods of four, five, or six students, is intended to encourage the type of small-group collaborative activities that are integral to contemporary writing instruction. Promoters of the cluster plan claim that the design is inherently student-centered because it lacks an obvious facility-wide center of attention for the teacher to occupy. These proponents argue that the perimeter arrangement is inferior because it enhances teacher authority through surveillance and control (Hawisher and Pemberton 39–41). These arguments notwithstanding, based largely on my frustrating experience in the amphitheater classroom as well as a sense that our college's upper administrators would oppose a cluster design as too costly and too unconventional, I went ahead with the perimeter design despite my awareness that it is manipulative in ways similar to Jeremy Bentham's panopticon as analyzed by Foucault in *Discipline and Punish*.

But how could someone who intended to design a classroom that would explicitly support student-centered pedagogies consciously select a panoptic floor plan? It seems that despite the high-minded goals of decentering classroom authority and empowering students, reconfigurations of the postmodern classroom often replace traditional methods of coercion with others that are not significantly different. It is instructive to examine certain aspects of computer-mediated writing pedagogy and to highlight the ways in which traditional forms of authority are often unconsciously reinscribed and punitive measures reinvoked. For example, while in *Fragments of Rationality* Lester Faigley labels, with a hint of irony, the computer-networked classroom an "achieved utopia," some teachers and administrators have recently begun to scramble to create restrictions to the Internet, known as "firewalls," that are designed to confine students to areas of safe and tractable electronic discourse.

The point here is not especially original: when we try to improve pedagogy significantly, we often take two steps back for every step forward; when we try to change the structure of authority in our classrooms, we may believe we are countering mechanisms of control when, in fact, we are simply reinventing or reinscribing them in different ways, regardless of our good intentions. And it is important to point out that this phenomenon can be identified in many, if not all, classrooms, computerized or not. Computer-assisted writing classrooms, however, provide a particularly revealing example of this phenomenon because they currently represent a place where the "rubber" of rhetorical theory "hits the road" of pedagogical reality: at these sites we gain the opportunity to test-drive shiny, new theories on snazzy, new (information) highways, with the hope that we will be able to improve on traditional approaches to learning.

On the one hand, one might point out that attending to details as trivial as classroom architecture is not very revealing; after all, one could argue convincingly that the instructor determines the nature of authority in a classroom more than physical space does. On the other hand, because computer-assisted instruction currently represents an area of pronounced pedagogical growth and change, the warrant for striving to understand the intimate details of the issues it raises is that such investigations can be both diagnostic and predictive. The rationale for carefully monitoring the growth of computer-assisted pedagogy is analogous to the grounds for microscopically studying new cell growth: we need to identify what may be very subtle patterns in the most recently and rapidly developing areas in order to understand the forces at play as well as to predict and perhaps to alter future growth.

The question then becomes, How does this happen? How does an instructor, despite contrary intentions, find himself or herself creating and maintaining panopticons? Foucault himself may provide some clues. Because many readers will no doubt be quite familiar with Foucault's examination of power and authority in *Discipline and Punish*, I provide only a brief sketch of the principles and observations discussed there, particularly in his chapter on panopticism. According to Foucault, the effective creation and maintenance of authority operates according to a pattern. While it would be difficult to delimit this pattern in absolute terms, a panopticon can be defined more or less as an architectural as well as a psychological arrangement of people in such a way that authority and disciplinary power can, from an apparently central position, watch over the population for the purposes of maintaining control. The first element in the panoptic pattern is thus *surveillance*. The second element is *willful conformity*; that is, in order for authority to be exercised most effectively over a political body, its constituents must feel that authority naturally belongs in a position from which it can perform surveillance. The body conforms to the belief that surveillance is beneficial to the degree that such measures of control become almost invisible, though very much present. Foucault argues that conformity is encouraged by a belief in *maximum efficiency*, that is, that authority is secured according to the notion that by placing bodies in certain arrangements, maximum efficiency of individual as well as collective bodies can be achieved. And lastly, the primary mechanism of panoptic control is not so much punishment, such as imprisonment or torture, as much as it is a calculus of *microphysics* (139). According to Foucault, a microphysics of panoptic control can be defined as a complex, widespread system of forces and impulses that function on the small scale of day-to-day human interaction, maintaining control by injecting measures of surveillance and willful conformity into the transactions between bodies on the smallest scale. Thus apparent locations of central authority, such as traditional academic discourse or the guard tower at the hub of Bentham's panopticon, function more as *symbols* of mechanisms of authority that are actually more ubiquitous than central: "Power has its principle not so much [as] a person as in a certain concerted distribution of bodies, surfaces, lights, gazes; in an arrangement whose internal mechanisms produce the relation in which individuals are caught up. The ceremonies, the rituals, the marks by which the sovereign's surplus power were manifested are useless. . . . Consequently, it does not matter who exercises power. Any individual, taken almost at random, can operate the machine" (202).

As presented so far, these key elements—surveillance, willful conformity, maximum efficiency, and microphysics—require examples in terms of writing pedagogy, and we can return to the computer-assisted classroom to examine them. One of the most recent and pressing developments regarding instructional technology and classroom authority concerns institutional policies about the use of the Internet. As an infamous *Time* cover story titled "Cyberporn" suggests, the wildness of the Internet is frightening some people, most notably parents and legislators. Some lawmakers have rushed to try "to ban the smut from cyberspace with new legislation—sometimes with little regard to either its effectiveness or its constitutionality" (Elmer-Dewitt, "Cyberporn," 38). Obviously, the first amendment and the courts are going to hamper the ability to introduce legislation that will suddenly assert control over the Internet; in fact, early rulings on the controversial Internet Decency Act suggest that such legislation will be overturned. It is more likely that, in the short term, other measures, such as firewalls, will be more effective to snuff out the so-called smut.

Firewalls are simply filters that can be placed on any connection to the Internet; they were originally invented and are currently used primarily as security devices to protect institutional and corporate systems from outside saboteurs. Firewalls have the ability to monitor all transactions coming in from and going out to the Internet, and, as Foucault might have predicted, they achieve this surveillance without being readily detected. In other words, if a student were dialing up pornography (or, worse yet, a socialist newsletter) through a school account, an institutional firewall could produce a report of this student's activity. But it is unlikely that firewalls configured to create such McCarthyesque reports are in place or would be very efficient themselves at carrying out such heavy-handed disciplinary control; all that is really required is the mere *rumor* that these types of firewalls exist, thereby invoking willful conformity and a calculus of microphysics to manage student bodies effectively. According to such a scenario, it will become the responsibility of the writing teacher who integrates the Internet into his or her courses to inform students about the possible existence of such firewalls.

If this sounds like paranoia, consider the well-publicized case of a University of Michigan undergraduate who was expelled, arrested by the FBI, and incarcerated for twenty-nine days, though eventually acquitted, for sending a fantasy story over the Internet that depicted the rape of a female classmate ("Cyberblotter" C4). In light of the violent and sexist dimensions of this case, computer-assisted writing programs, including my own, would be well advised to adopt clear policy statements warning students about their responsibilities and the nature of networked discussions as public discourse, especially given that the lone writer at his or her workstation often operates under the illusion of privacy.

As many instructors who work in computer-assisted writing classrooms can attest, "flaming," typically defined as vicious electronic commentary (although rarely as severe as in the Michigan incident), is fairly common. But, because of the multimedia potential of the Web, we might encounter flaming of a different kind. Recently, I witnessed a male student bringing up pornographic images from the World Wide Web specifically to antagonize female students sitting at adjacent workstations. While the incident was over almost as quickly as it occurred, it gave me pause, particularly since I am responsible to a degree for such things. What do I do if such problems continue or escalate? Should I look to install firewalls to repel such "flames"? At one point, my writing program was forbidden from allowing students to build pages on the World Wide Web because our systems administrators were afraid that students might create sites that could make headlines as negative as the ones from Michigan. Their fear was based on the implied threat that the legislature might pull the plug on our Internet funding.

And the impulse to control information through legislation is only gaining momentum. Alongside the Internet Decency Act, Congress also approved legislation that would require television manufacturers to include a controversial "v-chip" that would allow parents to block violent programs from appearing in their homes (whether or not the v-chip becomes a reality remains to be determined). Similar measures are being considered for the Internet. The *Time* article reports on the popularity of a brand of firewall software for home computers called, predictably, "Net Nanny." The article also reported that legislators are currently considering a rating system for the Internet similar to that used for movies. The Internet rating system could work in combination with software such as the Net Nanny to block information just as the v-chip will. However, promoters of v-chips, electronic nannies, and rating systems are not likely to influence writing pedagogy *directly* as much as they will *indirectly* control classrooms through particular constructions of technology. For instance, the *Time* cyberporn story was based on "exclusive" access to a Carnegie Mellon study that supported the fear that pornography on the Internet is out of control. Two weeks later, Philip Elmer-Dewitt, *Time*'s senior editor for technology and author of the original article, published a mild retraction of the cyberporn cover story based on the revelation that the Carnegie Mellon study was the product of questionable data compiled by an undergraduate ("Fire Storm" 57). However, readers of *Time* are less likely to remember the retraction on page 57 than they are to retain the sensationally doctored cover image of a prepubescent child glaring bug-eyed at an implied computer screen full of flesh. In short, a persistent construction of the Internet as a bastion of pornography is likely to exert more authority over the use of computers than firewall mechanisms or legislation.

The point here is not whether pornography on the Internet represents an immediate problem in the writing classroom. Rather, it is to identify in this situation ways that writing instructors find themselves serving as new conduits of

surveillance and control despite the liberatory visions we have of emerging pedagogy. It seems as though the drive to exercise authority is, in fact, irresistible.
Notice in the following passage how Gail Hawisher and Charles Moran are unable to suppress the temptation to institutionalize some control over electronic
discourse, despite the fact that they are quite aware that they may be colonizing
a formerly genuine territory of dialogic exchange: "Our overarching assumption is that email, as a medium for exchange in written language, is a proper
subject of study in the field of composition theory. One could argue that we
should leave email to the students, as an underground medium where they will
use writing to achieve their own ends, far from our governing gaze. Yet historically we have brought into our first-year writing courses any and all genres that
seem pandisciplinary" (629). It seems that the closer one looks, the more one
can identify new methods of coercion and control used to manipulate student
bodies in writing classrooms. In other words, the confessions may never end.

And mine have only just begun. For example, I confess that I have invested
significant effort in devising ways to keep students on task during electronical-
ly networked discussions; in fact, I have developed for this purpose a mechanism that might be called an *electronic panopticon* (see Provenzo for a different
discussion of electronic panopticons). Whenever one of my classes is, for the
first time, about to enter into a networked interchange, I preface the session
with a rather demonstrative policy statement concerning online decorum ("ne-
tiquette") and public discourse. The soon-to-be-online interlocutors are also
told that I have the ability to store and retrieve transcripts of these exchanges
and that these transcripts will be used to enforce policy as well as to encourage
everyone to participate fully in the class ("anything you say can and will be used
against you"). Thus I have created a panopticon not just in the physical classroom but also in the developing landscape of pedagogical cyberspace. This
arrangement actually maintains control quite well because students themselves
will rush almost without exception to corral class members who begin to veer
away from prescribed courses. On almost a daily basis, a student will correct
others by writing something akin to "Professor Taylor wants us to do *x*; so, student *y*, stop goofing around!" And this electronic panopticon is efficient precisely because the students micromanage each other without my having to
crack many whips. Students have also on occasion asked me privately to inter-
cede more actively in order to quiet irritating online comments made by other
classmates. As one of the more experienced instructors in my department's
computer classroom, I am constantly asked by new teachers for strategies to
keep networked discussions on task. After encountering these questions as
many times as I have, I find myself wanting to develop a handout for new in-

structors that would present the blueprints for my electronic panopticon. Thus these pressures illustrate how a complicated web of microphysical mutual manipulation among students, some of whom I will never meet, influences instructors in the program who in turn compel me to design and disseminate new methods of coercion.

As this electronic panopticon demonstrates, the calculus of microphysics is a powerful force, one to which even instructors are not immune. And what is more, the persistence of the microphysical web wears on all of us to the point that we eventually consider the recently invented electronic panopticon a natural part of our local segment of cyberspace. Further, this web seems to have no end. I myself did not program the software to compile the transcripts that serve as the critical feature of the electronic panopticon. The software, some of which was created by teachers of writing, arrives packaged with the electronic panopticon already embedded as an essential element, an ideological feature that users are unable to suppress or counter in significant ways. As Cynthia Selfe and Richard Selfe, Jr., point out, software supports and creates ideological landscapes that can "enact—among other things—the gestures and deeds of colonialism, continuously and with a great deal of success" (484).

But my confession has become too bleak. Our computer and writing program is, of course, not looking foremost to promote colonialism, coercion, and control. When other instructors ask me for advice on corralling students, I counter by pointing out that dialogic and, yes, chaotic interchanges are what we are after in the first place. I ask them to read Marilyn Cooper and Cynthia Selfe's "Computer Conferences and Learning: Authority, Resistance, and Internally Persuasive Discourse" in order to remind everyone, myself included, that the entire purpose for (re)inventing computer-assisted pedagogy is to strive toward positive change. And so my chapter in the form of a confession is not intended to wage an attack on contemporary pedagogy as much as to deconstruct what is taking place in the tiny realm of my courses and, by extrapolation, what may be taking place in other locations.

Therefore, within the boundaries of this chapter, the ultimate question has finally become, What do we gain by trying to understand the ways in which we sometimes subvert our own goals? That is, what is the purpose of such deconstructive turns? Selfe and Selfe, citing Henry Giroux, claim that the goal of the deconstructive enterprise—defined in their article as a "critical reading" and "continual mapping and remapping of educational, political, and ideological spaces" that educators themselves are complicit in creating—is to counter "oppression based on class, race, and gender" (500). However, I would argue that the deconstructive turn is actually more limited in its potential: as long as we continue to operate in a culture wherein authority is still very much a function of class, race, and gender, the most we can reasonably expect to gain is a better understanding of the utter persistence of ideological control as microphysical rather than central. Selfe and Selfe are not completely unaware of the limits of this potential. Having conducted an analysis of computer interfaces similar to my analysis of a local computer-assisted pedagogy, they write, "Our continuing efforts toward revealing the interested nature of computer interfaces will, in part, contribute to concealment because 'as carriers of tradition, we cannot be objective observes of it' " (501). But Selfe and Selfe execute a utopian end around when they conclude that "this realization cannot provide an excuse for inaction" (501), as if the incomprehensibly widespread microphysical ideological powers that they have just examined might, after all, surrender to admittedly quixotic campaigns of resistance. They continue to operate under the very assumption that their critical reading has just challenged: the misguided notion that authority, power, and control can be located primarily in a system of central hegemonies, that it makes sense to continue to discuss classroom authority in the terminology of teacher-centered and student-centered pedagogies. Their analysis of ideology, like my examination of new methods of pedagogical control, demonstrates that authority seeps and insinuates much more than it wrenches and dictates. Thus we will continue to fail to invent truly student-centered classrooms because authority does not have a center. As Foucault suggests, authority does not primarily inhabit central storage houses, although certain symbolic structures and architectures come to be mistaken for the power they only reflect; rather, it occupies the interstices between bodies and shapes the spaces used to align them. In fact, in this light, proposing the possibility of a teacher-centered pedagogy appears to be merely an expression of self-absorption rather than an acute observation. Almost without exception, students do not enroll in, pay for, and attend classes primarily because of teachers. They do so, at best, to grow intellectually or, at worst, to gain economically. And we should admit that both the intellectual and economic drives are fueled by authorities far more omnipresent than educators or even educational institutions.

Contracting to Build Panopticons

My confessional analysis of a computer-assisted pedagogy is intended to lead to interrogations of other composition pedagogies. Consider, for example, a cornerstone of process theory: peer editing and collaborative group work. While the architecture of the computer facility I confessed to earlier might have seemed panoptically manipulative, I failed to mention that the chairs in the room swivel and roll in order to provide a variety of possible arrangements. I, of course, had collaborative pedagogy in mind when I insisted on this type of chair for the new facility. Even in a noncomputerized classroom, however, using institutional authority to *contort* student bodies into a variety of face-to-face groupings, even for the purpose of empowerment through dialogic collaboration, amounts to a fairly tangible act of coercion, one that may actually be more violent than allowing them to arrange themselves in the secured rows and fixed seats of a proscenium classroom. That too is certainly a manipulative arrangement, but it is also one with which they are already accustomed and that they may have already re-created in individual ways.

Coercion discovered within either process approaches or computer-assisted pedagogies is typically excused as long as it is generally agreed that these measures are in the best interests of students. In fact, despite all my confessions, I must admit that, at present, I still support my panoptic designs precisely because I believe they improve on alternative arrangements of student bodies; I believe that as coercive as my designs may be, they serve the best interests of students, "best interests" being determined by what I perceive to be an operational consensus in our profession. But my unabashed reendorsement of coercive mechanisms should not be all that surprising, for the entire enterprise of institutional education is a function of contractual and implicit agreements to coerce and to be coerced. As I have argued, authority is exercised through a microphysics that permeates and operates on all levels, not just from the top down. Foucault claims that "the disciplinary gaze" requires "relays" arranged in "an uninterrupted network" distributed across "multiple levels" and "over the entire surface to be supervised" (174). Authority is therefore like a pyramid: while it appears that the entire purpose of the structure is to establish the pinnacle, the structure itself cannot exist apart from its constituents. The supporting structure, the "docile bodies" of our students, are as much a part of the classroom panopticon as are instructors, program administrators, process theorists, legislators, parents, and the manufacturers of firewall software. And all these constituents, all these individual parts, work together to create and maintain authority. Therefore we can be fairly certain that almost everyone will eventually come to endorse ideas such as firewalls or collaborative pedagogy. We are likely to conform to these ideas (or may have done so already) as a result of panoptic surveillance, and after this conformity has been achieved, we are likely to believe that the new arrangement is of maximum efficiency.

Thus the answer to the question "How is it that we find ourselves undermining our own goals and re-creating panopticons?" is that we are inevitably bound up in mechanisms of authority, punishment, coercion, and control. But the real surprise is that even if we are somewhat aware of these mechanisms and attempt to alter them through ideals such as student-centered pedagogies, we are unable to travel very far toward the realization of such ideals, regardless of how radical we might think our pedagogies are or how radical we hope to make them. For example, many faculty are surprised to discover the degree to which they do not actually own their own classes. Although entities such as the tenure system support the concept of academic freedom, this freedom applies mostly to scholarship and not so much to teaching. Course catalogs, syllabi, and other documents such as signed grade sheets are de facto contracts that the teacher enters into with students, and these contracts encompass much more than the instructor and his or her intellectual freedom. Institutions have specific course policies and descriptions to which the teacher subjects himself or herself once he or she agrees to teach a particular class. Thus *we may be surprised by not only the degree to which we find ourselves building and maintaining panopticons but also the degree to which we have actually contracted to do so*, even though teachers often consider such contracts as signifiers of nothing more than the mundane and the clerical. But as Foucault reminds us, the more commonplace and natural such disciplinary mechanisms feel, the more powerful they become. Through an understanding of authority as persistent and ubiquitous, perhaps we can begin to identify more readily specific mechanisms of coercion. Some of these mechanisms, such as firewalls and electronic panopticons, will be easy to identify at first because they represent a sudden change in the landscape. However, the real trick is to identify other types of firewalls, ones that may exist in more familiar places, such as noncomputerized classrooms, in which limitations and boundaries may not be as new or as easy to identify as an electronic firewall.

Works Cited

Bizzell, Patricia. *Academic Discourse and Critical Consciousness*. Pittsburgh: University of Pittsburgh Press, 1992.

Cooper, Marilyn, and Cynthia Selfe. "Computer Conferences and Learning: Authority, Resistance, and Internally Persuasive Discourse." *College English* 52 (1990): 847–69.

"Cyberblotter." *Pittsburgh Post-Gazette*, 25 July 1995, Sooner ed., C4.

Elbow, Peter. *Writing Without Teachers*. New York: Oxford, 1973.

Elmer-Dewitt, Philip. "Cyberporn." *Time*, 3 July 1995, 38–45.

———. "Fire Storm on the Computer Nets." *Time*, 24 July 1995, 57.

Faigley, Lester. *Fragments of Rationality: Postmodernity and the Subject of Composition*. Pittsburgh: University of Pittsburgh Press, 1992.

Foucault, Michel. *Discipline and Punish: The Birth of the Prison*. Trans. Alan Sheridan. New York: Vintage, 1979.

Hawisher, Gail E., and Charles Moran. "Electronic Mail and the Writing Instructor." *College English* 55 (1993):627–42.

Hawisher, Gail E., and Michael A. Pemberton. "Integrating Theory and Ergonomics: Designing the Electronic Writing Classroom." In *Approaches to Computer Writing Classrooms: Learning from Practical Experience*. Ed. Linda Myers. Albany: State University of New York Press, 1993. 35–52.

Lu, Min-Zhan. "Conflict and Struggle: The Enemies or Preconditions of Basic Writing?" *College English* 54 (1992):887–913.

Myers, Linda, ed. *Approaches to Computer Writing Classrooms: Learning from Practical Experience*. Albany: State University of New York Press, 1993.

Provenzo, Eugene F., Jr. "The Electronic Panopticon: Censorship, Control, and Indoctrination in a Post-Typographic Culture." In *Literacy Online: The Promise (and Peril) of Reading and Writing with Computers*. Ed. Myron C. Tuman. Pittsburgh: University of Pittsburgh Press, 1992. 167–88.

Selfe, Cynthia L., and Richard J. Selfe, Jr. "The Politics of the Interface: Power and Its Exercise in Electronic Contact Zones." *College Composition and Communication* 45 (1994):480–504.

Stuckey, J. Elspeth. *The Violence of Literacy*. Portsmouth, NH: Boyton, 1991.

9 Rhetoric of the "Contact Zone": Composition on the Front Lines

Terry Craig, Leslie Harris, and Richard Smith

In "The Rhetoric of Technology and the Electronic Writing Class," Gail Hawisher and Cynthia Selfe decry the uncritical rhetoric that champions the introduction of computers into the writing classroom without examining possible problems that such an innovation can pose. As they observe, "Our objections lie not in the use of computer technology and on-line conferences but rather in the uncritical enthusiasm that frequently characterizes the reports of those of us who advocate and support electronic writing classes" (56). They continue:

> In this paper, we have suggested that the current professional conversation about computer use in writing classes, as evidenced in published accounts, is incomplete in at least one essential and important way. While containing valuable accounts of electronic classes, this conversation fails to provide us with a critical perspective on the problematic aspects of computer use and thus with a full understanding of how the use of technology can affect the social, political, and educational environments within which we teach. (64)

By discussing our spring 1995 English Composition classes, in which we incorporated both synchronous and asynchronous computer conferencing, we hope to provide the "critical perspective" that Hawisher and Selfe advocate. In the course of a semester-long experiment, we discovered the exciting possibilities and the bewildering perils of computer-mediated communication, especially when we used the Internet to bring together regionally and socioeconomically diverse students. By linking students in this way, computer-mediated communication (CMC) allows multiple perspectives to emerge. However, in allowing students to express themselves more openly, CMC can also lead not to the kind of harmonious discourse community that proponents cite in discussing the advantages of computer use but to an instantiation and a rhetoric of the "contact zone" (see Pratt; Bizzell 166), in which divergent perspectives and communities clash as they confront and negotiate their differences.

The uncritical enthusiasm expressed by some many proponents of CMC focuses on its ability to foster an idealized community among class members. For example, in "Pedagogy in the Computer-Networked Classroom," Janet Eldred claims that "electronic bulletin boards . . . provide a forum for groups of users: all members of a group can read the posted messages. The bulletin board also fosters a sense of community, gives the individuals a stronger sense of their place in a group. Again, the sense of writing as a social, communal act is heightened" (50). Eldred continues (citing a corollary claim about the benefits of CMC), "Almost everyone who has worked with the technology notes that networking's main advantage is the egalitarian quality of the participants' discourse, the dissolving of certain inequities—produced by gender, class, ethnicity, and personality differences—that exist in normal classroom discussions" (53). Delores Schriner and William Rice provide the most glowing assessment of the success of electronic conferencing in fostering close ties among their students. They describe a project in which students exchanged messages using a system for asynchronous CMC called CONFER. Schriner and Rice observed a "great warmth, respect, and intellectual kinship that developed in classes using CONFER." They report that:

> All the instructors in the pilot project reported never having seen a group of first-year students, thrown randomly together by the registrar's computer, become as close as their students had. Students set up meetings in the library and in campus computer labs, came early to class and stayed late, made plans together for the next semester, and exchanged addresses. The computer, far from making the class more impersonal, fostered a strikingly close community in one of the nation's largest universities [the University of Michigan].
>
> (476)

According to these authors, then, asynchronous computer-mediated class discussions foster "a strikingly close community" among students, one filled with "great warmth, respect, and intellectual kinship." Computer bulletin boards foster a "sense of community" (although we don't know that nature of that community: harmonious? boisterous?), one especially marked by "egalitarian" participation. It all sounds like a brave new world, what Lester Faigley calls (in a chapter title) "The Achieved Utopia of the Networked Classroom" (163 ff.).

Faigley actually provides an alternative to the glowing praise of CMC and its ability to foster friendly communities. In his discussion of Daedalus Interchange, he argues, "This equality of participation [in which marginalized students participate more freely and the authority of the instructor is decentered], however, does not necessarily lead to 'community building' as some teachers have theorized, following Kenneth Bruffee's model of collaborative learning, where conversation leads to cooperation. . . . Indeed, Lyotard theorizes just the opposite, that conversation is inherently agonistic and to speak is to fight" (185). Faigley's final claim—that "electronic written discussions create dissensus because they give voice to diversity" (180)—is crucial to understanding CMC as a rhetoric of the "contact zone." Although CMC can give rise to the kind of intimacy of interaction and community-building that Schriner and Rice discuss, it can also promote dissensus and conflict. By freeing students from some of the constrictions of polite, face-to-face conversation, CMC allows a less socially constrained self to emerge. In a discursive environment in which students from diverse backgrounds meet to discuss controversial issues, this honesty of communication may reveal the differences that we frequently ignore, in the hope that they are insignificant and will eventually disappear. These differences, however, can be profoundly significant and inevitably reappear. The bad faith of polite conversation, in which we try not to say anything controversial for fear of conflict or of exposing our own prejudices and limitations, leads to a suppression of dialogue and honest exchange. Beliefs—and the ignorance or prejudice that underlie those beliefs—remain hidden, still secretly influencing behavior. By promoting a rhetoric of the "contact zone," CMC allows beliefs to be exposed, examined, and (perhaps) modified, especially through the clash of divergent opinions. Although potentially conflictual and dangerous, Internet-based CMC can foster the "pedagogical arts of the contact zone" (Pratt 40) that Pratt and Bizzell advocate, creating an environment where students educate one another in active, engaged discussion.

Background

Environments for CMC offer unique opportunities for educational community building. Students from across the country and across the world can now meet, exploring difference and finding commonality in real-time conversation, learning about others and expressing themselves to new audiences. In order to provide such an audience for our students, we paired our composition classes with regionally distinct partners. A first-semester composition class at Susquehanna University was paired with a second-semester composition class at George Washington University. An honors composition class at West Virginia Northern Community College was paired with a different second-semester composition class at George Washington University. These four classes included Internet-based discussions as an integral part of the classroom experience.

The three schools involved in this project are very different. Susquehanna University is a small, private, liberal arts university in rural Pennsylvania. Its student body is 95 percent white, and it is situated in a county (Snyder) that is 99 percent white. Many of its students come from small, sparsely populated areas of the state, others from small, affluent towns in New Jersey. The students are almost exclusively "traditional" in that they have graduated from high school and have moved directly on to undergraduate study. West Virginia Northern Community College is also in a rural setting; the college has students from considerably less privileged backgrounds than Susquehanna's, however, as well as many continuing and nontraditional students. But despite such differences, the students still come from relatively homogeneous racial and socioeconomic backgrounds. George Washington University is a large, urban private university. The student population is geographically diverse: the school's location in Washington, D.C., attracts students from throughout the United States, and the school also has a substantial foreign student enrollment. Just over 20 percent of the students are from minority backgrounds.

As a reflection of the pairing of regionally and socioeconomically diverse classes, the course readings focused on the theme of families across cultures. Using the anthology *Rereading America: Cultural Contexts for Critical Thinking and Writing*, along with James Baldwin's *Notes of a Native Son*, Sandra Cisneros's *Woman Hollering Creek and Other Stories*, Harvey Fierstein's film *The Torch Song Trilogy*, and Amy Tan's *The Joy Luck Club*, we explored the family and cultural identities of mainstream, African-American, Hispanic, Native-American, homosexual, and Asian-American communities. We shared syllabi for the course, ensuring that the students were exploring similar readings as the course progressed. Four times during the semester, the classes convened on Diversity University MOO to discuss shared readings, meeting in a virtual classroom and then in smaller discussion rooms, each containing a blackboard with specific discussion questions. Students were responsible for discussing the topic, reaching a group consensus (if possible), and then summarizing their findings and presenting to the class as a whole. They therefore engaged small-group discussions, but within a text-based environment, composing their ideas at a keyboard and expressing those ideas to a synchronously present audience.

These MOO sessions were complemented by an online journal, which maintained an asynchronous connection among the students, who were linked as a collective group by an electronic discussion list (or listserv). Messages sent to the class journal were received by all members of the paired classes. In order to foster a continuing dialogue, each student was responsible for posting one discussion question to the journal during the semester and a minimum response of one journal entry per week.

The purpose of the MOO sessions and the class journal was to create a writing community between the paired classes. The journal provided a continuing forum for discussions of course material, and the MOO sessions provided a synchronous responsive audience. No longer simply writing essays to be graded by their instructors, students were expressing their ideas to their peers— and doing so frequently. The interaction of the classes therefore inevitably reinforced the multicultural focus of the class syllabus. Students from very different socioeconomic, regional, and ethnic backgrounds came together as a writing community, exploring their similarities and negotiating differences as they read and discussed not only differing representations of family across cultural communities in the course readings but also their own differing responses to those readings. An early politeness of discourse gave way to the increasing "dissensus" that Faigley describes, as differences between the classes became more apparent. Students thus learned the "rhetoric of the contact zone," in which assertions must be carefully supported in order to be persuasive and to forestall potentially hostile responses from other students who may not share their views.

The Contact Zone: Early Politeness

The initial sessions—MOO and journal—were characterized by a tentative politeness, a self-conscious effort to behave properly and, more important, not to offend. The first MOO session between GW and WV was a model of courtesy. As the students gathered in the virtual LaraGrove Auditorium (before dispersing to various discussion rooms), they greeted one another, discussed a recent basketball game, and chatted politely. Typical was the apparently cheerful "hello to all that have entered this wonderful realm called cyberspace" from Steve-gw (February 6, 1995).

The group discussions for the first MOO session were also polite. Students were exceptionally patient with one another, teaching each other how to read the electronic blackboard, check online descriptions, and execute other MOO commands. For example, after extensive introductions between the SU and GWU students and then some confusion about how to determine the topic of discussion, one GW student politely urged his fellow students: "everyone, please read the dry-erase board" (Phil-gw, February 6, 1995). During the first GW-WV session, the GW students were careful to include the WV students in the discussion. In Group 3, Kelly-wv (a shy nineteen-year-old) had dropped out of the conversation, and there were several "Where's Kelly? Did Kelly go away?" questions from Sharon-gw and Richard-gw. There was only one flurry of temper in that group, namely, when Vicki-wv (a slow typist and a rather insecure student), made what seemed to be a harmless (and again politely phrased) request: "could you please write exactly to one person unless it is to everyone thank you." Steve's response seemed to trigger her insecurities:

STEVE–GW [to Vicki]: I'm telling everyone, is that all right?
VICKI–VW: It's really confusing for Sarah and me. We're completely at a loss these days.
STEVE–GW: Is that okay?
[TO VICKI]: I'm telling everyone, is that all right?
VICKI-WV: it is really confusing for sarah and i. Is that okay STEVE!!!!!!!!!!!!!!!

Despite the disagreement, the students were obviously being cautious. Vicki's capital letters and exclamation points (considered shouting online) prompted Steve to apologize—"so sorry, VICKI, okay?"—his irritation (indicated by the mocking use of all capital letters for her name) buried beneath the otherwise polite discourse.

We saw a similar initial politeness in another of the GWU-WV MOO groups. Relations among the students were harmonious but superficial, with one GW student commenting, "i think we need to be more real while mooing, but all are afraid to offend the other school" (Brent-gw, March 2, 1995). This early facile harmony contrasts sharply with a later MOO session:

LISA–WV: I pick Jack [as spokesperson]
GINA–GW: We already have a spokesperson
STEVE–GW: Allison is it
LISA–WV: Who is it?
STEVE–GW: coke is it
James–GW arrives from nowhere.

JACK–WV: Then who the hell is it. I've ask once already
SHERRY–GW: I have to be—at least I have to do the post
JACK–WV: fine as long as someone lets us know
STEVE–GW: it was predetermined by the professors already jack chill out
JACK–WV: sorry Steve just asking since nobody acknowledges us so you chill
STEVE–GW: first of all join in and we'll acknowledge you
GINA–GW: Jack could you please try to stick to the question?
JACK–WV: listen all I asked a simple question and all I get is flack
STEVE–GW: alright jack lets forget it cool?

The topic of conversation is trivial, yet the underlying tension is apparent. Jack's "Then who the hell is it" reveals his obvious frustration, inspired partly by Steve-gw's flippant joke ("coke is it") and primarily by his sense that his audience is ignoring him and his fellow West Virginians ("just asking since nobody acknowledges us"). Gina-gw expresses a different kind of impatience, wanting Jack-wv to return to the topic. Steve-gw defuses the conflict, allowing the discussion to continue. By the time of this later MOO session (March 27, 1995), the dissensus between the two groups has become apparent.

Email journal entries displayed a similar movement from empty politeness to conflict. For example, initial journal entries from the WV group sounded like self-introductions at a party: polite and innocuous, almost hopeful. Ironically, those same introductions almost certainly helped to establish a contrast between the rural WV students and the urban GW class. Lisa's introduction is typical:

> Howdy, everyone, my name is Lisa. . . . My hobbies include spending time with my friends, going to the races, and just being a bum. My favorite NASCAR driver is Jeff Gordon. I think he is gorgeous. . . . I hope to go to Bristol Tennessee this year for my first race.   (Lisa–WV 8 February 1995)

Two students actively tried to counter the West Virginia stereotype and encourage online conversation. Gary, seventeen, introduced himself as a "private detective" who enjoyed "intellectual pursuits (somewhat intellectual)." He continued:

> I am presently living in a small town in West Virginia, New Martinsville, but I have lived in NJ and traveled abroad, so at least I think that I know the world. Maybe. I will enjoy our ensuing controversy and camaraderie. Bye for now.
> (Gary–WV 8 February 1995)

Jack, at twenty-six, is one of the oldest students in the class and certainly the most outspoken; he challenged the WV stereotype immediately but still offered an invitation to talk:

Hi all. And now for the mandatory introductions. I'm known as STEEL [a.k.a. Jack]. . . . I'm from the WV class but i have lived in major cities before, so don't think i'm some red-neck hick :) ha, ha. I like life in the fast lane and the slow lane. I used to sing in a band but now i just hang out and write. Feel free to email anytime, i'm always up for a lively discussion.

(Jack–WV 8 February 1995)

Like the early MOO sessions, the initial journal entries were characterized by careful courtesy and fear of offending. WV students were particularly concerned about their audience, a GW class composed of students of ethnic and racial backgrounds very different from their own. During one posting session, the WV students frequently asked the instructor to review posts because they didn't want to offend anyone. Similarly, there were questions about proper forms of address: "Is 'Black' capitalized?" one student wondered, while another asked about the "correct" term: *African-American* or *Black*. Students at this point were much less concerned with content than they were with the feelings of their audience.

In their journal postings, the students themselves displayed an awareness of this ineffectual, empty politeness. Crissie wrote

I would like to start off with the little war that is occuring between Eduard, Barb, and any others that were surprised at their outrage. Barto, you seem to be a decent person . . . but, come on, it is time to get out of the boy scouts.[1] According to the stupid article in Rereading America on pages 1 through 15, the editor writes on how we are suppose to challenge cultural myths. This is what Eduard is doing. To challenge (according to that great guy, Webster) is to test, question, or object to something proposed. Basically, this email thing is going (if it hasn't already) to get REALLY boring if we just accept everything said.

OK . . . not only that, but this email thing will get even worse if SU continues to talk to themselves (Hey, try class, that's what it's for)! GW proposed some indepth questions, better than "Yeah, Boyz in the Hood was good," but they didn't seem to be noticed. We aren't waiting for an invitation, we are just waiting for something interesting! BY THE WAY, IF YOU HAVEN'T REALIZED, SINCE EDUARD's SHOCKING STATEMENT . . . SU AND GW ARE TALKING TO EACH OTHER (What a concept!)

(Crissie–GW, 24 February 95)

With her "it's time to get out of the boy scouts," Crissie suggests that false politeness isn't very productive, especially in an email forum that is intended to produce an exchange of views. She feels sufficient authoritative power to criticize one of the readings for the class ("the stupid article in Rereading America on pages 1 through 15"), yet she recognizes the validity of its basic point: that we need to "challenge cultural myths." She also defines "challenge" for us, indicating her source. Her final (shouted) comment shows her awareness of the effect of the conflict: a dialogue has begun, fostered by an honest—and passionate—exchange of ideas.

A True Contact Zone

Many of the students advocated such productive, healthy conflict. For example, DeShawn-gw commented, "Maybe the status quo is not such a bad thing for many of you. I, however, realize that there is a major problem called racism, and I have a big problem with it. Now healthy debate is what is needed and if we choose to ignore the issue things will never change for the better" (March 5, 1995). Eduard agrees, criticizing what Faigley has called "bourgeois standards of politeness" (190):

> I'm responding to Aaron Summer's entry about using euphemisms to hide one's racism or to merely use the right words to hide rascist remarks. This DOES NOT solve anything. Just because something is said in a nicer way, it doesn't mean that the malice that is intended is not there anymore. From what I understood in your message, it's okay to be rascist so long as you do not use crude or vulgar words. In effect, would you approve of comments such as "Minorities' mental abilities are hindered by a chromosomal aberration in the 22nd chromosome" as opposed to "Minorities are stupid" ? Would you probably approve, then, of what Rutgers University president, Francis L. Lawrence, said in November 1994 about S.A.T.'s being unfair to that "disadvantaged population that doesn't have the genetic, hereditary background to have a higher [test] average" ? (Did I get that right, DeShawn?)
>
> This is actually how most rascist organizations operate. They subtly use just the right words and employ propaganda to spread out their messages.
>
> This is not meant as an attack on you. . . . It is an open forum and I am merely asking you to clarify your position.   (Eduard–GW, 7 March 1995)

In characterizing the electronic discussion as "an open forum," Eduard is calling for engaged, honest debate, in which the strong expression of one's opinion is viewed not as an "attack" but as a challenge, a request to "clarify your position" so that the writer can convey it more effectively and so that a frank, productive exchange of ideas can occur.

Students in the WV-GW pairing also recognized the need for open, honest exchange. One student asserted:

As Ricardo pointed out in his post, for some reason racial tension continues. My response to this would be that a lack of understanding by all groups in America has caused the continuing hatred. . . . I just wanted to throw out the idea that honesty may be the solution. Possibly confronting racial problems without fear of offending anyone may remove certain political correctness and other issues not discussed outside a close circle of friends. Everyone agreed in their email messages that individuals should not hold a grudge, but is it any different to remain silenced by political correctness, allowing our true opinions to form a deeper hatred?   (Rachel–GW, 14 March 1995)

Other students agreed. With the provocative subject header "Can you handle the truth?" Ricardo asked:

How honest are you when responding to a posting? Are you expressing your true beliefs or are you expressing the most socially acceptable answers to the issues raised? . . . Let's be honest for once, tell the truth. Because if you don't you are actually making things worse by lying than if you actually told the truth. . . . Can we as a society handle the truth that we are all a bunch of liars? Or has it become so ingrained in our heads, just like racism, to say not what we are actually thinking, but what we have been taught to say?

(Ricardo–GW, 16 March 1995)

In his comment, Ricardo makes a fascinating connection between lying (or false politeness) and racism, with both reflecting "ingrained" beliefs that need to be challenged through open, honest exchange. By using the medium of computer-mediated communication to create a contact zone among our students, we can perhaps foster such honest exchange. Students sense a greater freedom to express their ideas, and they must defend their beliefs in front of others and even abandon or modify those beliefs when they no longer prove tenable.

The benefits of this conflictual model are demonstrated in a later entry by Bernouli. Less than a month after the earlier, polite entries, Bernouli began to fire off much more impassioned postings, directly addressing the comments made by his fellow students:

Hello everyone!
     Yesterday I was watching T.V. and while glancing at a few talk shows I begin to have this feeling build up in side of me. In one of my earlier discussions I said I thought T.V. was glamourized. Well I strongly stand by this fact, so I have to disagree with Barb's statement. The people on the talk shows are being displayed, like animals in a zoo. The producers are clearly looking for high ratings and cheezy topics.

In response to Crissies statement. I come from a city in which racisim is prevelant. White toward Hispanic, Hispanic toward White, and so on. There is constant tension! People begin to be scared off from the city. Stereotypes begin to amass. A snowball effect occurs. Racisim seems to begin then become greater because of the snowball effect. The U.S. is not under one race, language, religion. My Grandparents were born in Italy, so was my father. How could I as the first Generation American be racist towards other people!!! But people should not say racisim is caused by radical groups like the Klan, Skinheads, Black Panthers, etc. It is true that there is a little bit of racisim in everyone. The reason these groups attack their opposition so hard, is because they need someone to displace their anger on. Most of the members of these groups went through some sort of hardship. They might have been abused as children, runaways, poverty stricken and so on. These groups are ignorant.

In my highschool we had several skinheads. They would walk around with their boots, white t-shirts, red suspenders, and jeans, mocking the minorities, ranting and raving about Hitler, a white nations AND SOME OTHER BULL-SHIT!!! But the truth of the matter is, they do not even know what the real skinheads in Germany stand for. The original skinheads were children of blue collar families after world war II. They were angered because of the lack of jobs in Germany, and they were pissed off because the Turks were taking all the German Jobs. SO they began to make a political statement. Thier outfits became representations of the working class. The fact is, the skinheads in my high school were looking only for attention, and some way to displace their internal anger.

I really think there will never be an end to racisim. I truly believe this!!!!
(Bernouli–SU 3 March 1995)

The passion behind this journal entry is obvious. The statements of strong opinion, the personal revelations, and the "shouting" and exclamations clearly convey the intensity of the student's feelings and his engagement with the topic. Despite another student's objection, he reasserted his earlier opinion about television's being "glamourized," responded to a GW student's comment—without, however, giving the specific reference—and agreed with an earlier journal statement, once again without identifying its source.[2] He then moves onto an area in which he feels he has special expertise—skinheads—relying in his comment on his personal experience and on knowledge of the history of the movement.

The length of Bernouli's posting is significant and fairly typical of this stage of the journal. Students were not rewarded for the length of their entries, although they were given a grade at the end of the semester based on the frequency of their contributions. Bernouli chose to respond at such length because he *cared* about what he was saying. He *wanted* to contribute to the debate, to reinforce his earlier comments, and to prove his point. Writing persuasively because he was confronting a diverse audience who had already disagreed with his claims and could very easily disagree with this comment as well, he relies substantially on personal knowledge, although he attempts to support his claims with other information.

Bernouli's comments stirred other students. Crissie questioned whether he truly understood the skinheads' motivation:

> I have a question for Paul from SU . . .
>
> Recently you metioned the skinheads at your school, and you so quickly described them as standing up for bullshit. However, you spent a great deal of time telling all of us what most of us already know . . . and that was about the original skinheads. Now I am sure you are intelligent and you know your history . . . but did you ever ask those skinheads in your school, what they stood for? Did you ever take 10 seconds away from reading about history, to see the present? Why I ask all of these questions is because if you did ask them, I'm sure you would have found out that skinheads today do not stand up for the same thing they did in Germany years ago. So, I'll be happy to wait for your response.   (Crissie–GW 3 March 1995)

Though Crissie is impressed by Bernouli's knowledge of the early history of the skinhead movement, she challenges his quick dismissal of contemporary skinheads, prompting him for further information. In a subsequent email entry, Bernouli took up the challenge:

> This message is in response to [Crissie], Yes, I do understand the difference between skinheads of today and skinheads of the past. If you look at most of today's skinheads you find that they are troubled "children." And I quote *children* because that is how they act. I do not know if you saw what I am about to describe but I am going to describe it anyway. A year ago HBO presented a Documentary called "Skinheads, soldiers of the white race." The documentary showed a group of runaways, abused, and troubled kids being taken in by an ex-convict. Yes, these kids became skinheads because they were pissed and had no where to turn but on the minorities. This Ex-con took them into his house and brainwashed them. Well, to summarize. The Ex-con was arrested for weapons charges and the skinheads in the end declared it was time to become militant.
>
> What does this prove? becoming militant! nothing! It causes innocent people's lives to be taken away. . . .   (Bernouli–SU 6 March 1995)

Bernouli is attempting to support in more detail his psychological reading of the skinhead movement: that is, that skinheads are needy youths who "were looking only for attention, and some way to displace their internal anger." He now cites the source for his information: an HBO documentary about the skinhead movement. He also tries to reinforce his basic point: that the original skinheads were "representati[ve]s of the working class" attempting to make a political statement, whereas today's skinheads are troubled youths displacing their anger and aggression onto innocent scapegoats.

Not to be outdone, Crissie responds to Bernouli's clarification, questioning the appropriateness of his source:

> Bernouli,
>   Have you based your opion on what you saw on HBO? I mean if you have, then we have a bigger problem on our hands. . . . I know skinheads that have come from wealthy, happy families. I know skinheads that are not all racists. The point I'm trying to make is that society constantly stereotypes different groups of people. Skinheads are subjected to this continually. Not all skinheads are the same—not all of them believe in the same thing—and until you know everyone of them in the world, don't be so quick to judge. I mean, do you immediately think all hispanics belong to a gang? I hope not.
>   (Crissie–GW 8 March 1995)

Crissie criticizes Bernouli for overgeneralizing based on stereotypes, as well as for insufficient research (relying on a single documentary). She is trying to combat what she believes is prejudice and ignorance, using her own knowledge to enlighten others.

As this exchange reveals, the effective use of evidence becomes more and more crucial to a rhetoric of the contact zone, as participants defend their points of view in the presence of critical peers. As one GWU student perceptively asserted, "I don't know of any other way to have lively discussion other than arguing and supporting points. Can't you just come right back and give better support for your arguements?" (Bill-gw, April 10, 1995). The level of evidence in postings became much more substantial over the course of the semester.

The students themselves acknowledged the productiveness of the discussions. One student commented on the educational effect of the interclass dialogue:

> The journal gave us an open forum to discuss what we know and think, and to learn from what others know and think. Using our prior knowledge learned through entries, we formed opinions. Those opinions were then questioned in order for others to form their own or for the individual to re-

evaluate theirs. This project has made me confront many issues and problems, such as my religion. The experience has also made me realize many
things about myself as well as about others around me.

(Sterling–SU, e-mail portfolio cover letter, 5 May 1995)

In confronting other students through the views they express, students reevaluat-
ed their own beliefs. In the process, they learned about themselves and about others. Also importantly, they learned to be better writers. As one student observed:

> [The email journal] gave me a sense of writing to an audience, and not just to
> my professor, as is the case with term papers. Because the audience was var-
> ied in their backgrounds, experiences, and beliefs, the journal also helped me
> to express my ideas more clearly, and to support those ideas. When your opin-
> ions and ideas are under the scrutiny of about 30 other people, you have to
> make sure that your opinions are supported and that your beliefs are based
> on some tangible evidence, not stereotypical information, prejudice, or unfair
> bias. As a result of this email journal, I think that my formal writing has also
> improved, and I can more clearly express my ideas and support them in a for-
> mal term paper.   (Zweig–SU, e-mail portfolio cover letter, 9 May 95)

Despite the effectiveness of the contact zone as a space for student writing,
however, the clash of disparate students and ideas can also lead to unproductive
conflict, as student groups define their identity in relation to a demonized
Other. For example, one GW student remarked: "I have been reading some of
the email entries and unfortunately, I am getting the impression that this experiment is turning into a GW vs. Susquehana type of format and this should
not be happening. We are the generation that has to work together and try to
bring about change in our society. We should identify problems and attempt to
bring about solutions to eradicate injustices. Hopefully, we will all come out
more enlightened and understand one another better" (DeShawn-gw, February
28, 95). The "GW vs. Susquehana type of format" refers to a series of postings
in which one Susquehanna student responded to James Baldwin's "Notes of a
Native Son" essay, in which Baldwin describes being refused service at a diner
because of his race. The student admitted that "when I read things about whites
discriminating [against] other people simply because of race I am somewhat
embarresed to be white" (Hinman-su, February 21, 1995). A GW student challenged her posting, using an email reply function to respond directly to her
comment. Other students jumped into the fray, defending their classmates,
starting what Crissie called "the little war that is occuring between Eduard,
Barb, and any others" (February 24, 1995).

Although that conflict was ultimately productive (it began the dialogue between the two classes), the tendency to form communities against an Other is
a dangerous one, because it can lead to excessively and unnecessarily hostile exchanges. Several students expressed dissatisfaction with the journal and MOO
sessions because of this conflict. On an anonymous end-of-semester journal
survey form, one Susquehanna student wrote, "I thought the students at GW
were rude and obnoxious. They tried to find conflict, and tried to exploit it. They
would purposely point out a specific person's beliefs and bash them. Not very
fun." A WVU student commented, "The MOO sessions sometimes became virtually violent, but mostly they remained fun." Another Susquehanna student
observed: "I think the immature name-calling and condescending attitudes
made it less effective than it could have been, but it made me think about how
hard it is in the real world. If our classes couldn't even get along, and we have a
lot more in common than many other possible groups, it goes to show why society is so screwed up." Although a classroom is a more controlled environment
than urban streets, it too can virtually explode, especially when students discuss
controversial issues.

We saw such an explosion in the final GW-SU MOO session, in which students were primed for conflict by the recent discussions in the journal. A
journal entry by Maria-gw on the subject of religion and homosexuality had
provoked a heated email exchange. Evidently, students entered LaraGrove Auditorium with conflict in mind, as evidenced by these preliminary exchanges:

> Winter-su exclaims, "yo check the flow mo jo we got a little brawlin to do!"
> Paulie-su says, "hells yeah"
> Bechard-su says, "let's brawl"
> Sterling-su says, "SUers, you've got to calm down."
> Barr-su exclaims, "Listen Sterling there's some pride to be restored here!!"
> Bechard-su says, "I agree with Barr we need to fix a few things up"
> . . . .
> Tarneisha-gw says, "what's up, Maria!"
> Maria-gw says, "not much girl. Got picked on By SU"
> Tarneisha-gw says, "I know. They're so stupid! I read it yesterday."
> Paulie-su says, "right back at cha"
> Muller-su says, "we're stupid? Whatever"   (24 April 1995)[3]

Conflict quickly developed in the discussion room where Maria-gw was situated. A very reasonable debate about the issues raised by the movie *Torch Song
Trilogy* quickly disintegrated when religion was reintroduced into the discus-

sion.[4] The bitterness of the email interaction was reactivated in the virtual setting:

> Bernouli-su says, "I am very sorry but i have problems feeling comfortable with Homosexuality"
>
> Bernouli-su says, "the bible clearly states that homosexuality is wrong"
>
> Jill-gw says, "Why do you, Bernouli, have to feel comfortable with homo-sexulaity, are you wondering about yours?"
>
> Maria-gw says, "why are you uncomfortable with homosexuality?"
>
> Bernouli-su says, "no I am very comfortable with women thank you"
>
> Paulie-su says, "well, it is not your decision, it's your siblings decision, and you should support them and what they believe." "Paul, i don't think you're gay! ha ha ha"
>
> Maria-su [to Bernouli]: "so you are basing your feeling on homosexuality on what your religion says?"
>
> Bernouli-su says, "yes I am"
>
> Muller-su says, "Maria what is your problem with religion????"
>
> Maria-gw says, "prove there is a god"
>
> Bernouli-su says, "read the bible dammit"
>
> Bartkowsk-su says, "Prove there isn't"
>
> Winter arrives from nowhere.
>
> Maria-gw says, "how petty you are becoming, Bernouli"
>
> Bartkowsk-su says, "Why do you question God's existence?"
>
> Maria-gw says, "why not"
>
> Winter-su says, "I got your back PAUL!"
>
> Winter-su says, "yo erica why dont you open a big fat can of liquid reality?"
>
> Maria-gw says, "why are you all so upset bout what I wrote about religion. Is this the first time you have had to defend your views and beliefs"
>
> Paulie-su says, "i think that these people are simply looking for a fight . . . . . . get a clue, people."
>
> Bechard arrives from nowhere.
>
> Winter-su suddenly disappears.
>
> Maria-gw says, "hey Bechard"
>
> Muller-su says, "Maria, have you read your email today?"
>
> Muller-su says, "I tried to explain nicely why that entry was offensive, but you make it hard for me to remain calm"
>
> Maria-gw says, "is little old me causing conflict?"
>
> Bechard-su says, "Yes I think so . . ."
>
> Maria-gw says, "what a shame"
>
> Bechard-su says, "what's up your ass that you have to be so nasty?"
>
> (24 April 1995)[5]

This exchange indicates the perils of the contact zone, especially if classes become polarized by false identifications: a temporarily unified "us" against a demonized "them." In such an explosive environment, provocative and highly sensitive issues can lead to angry, unproductive disputes. Winter-su and Bechard-su actually join the discussion from other MOO rooms, with the obvious intention of provoking a fight. For the only time in the course, one of the instructors had to intervene in order to diffuse what became a virtually violent conflict:

> Paulie-su says, "but you're just f-ing picking fights andit's getting old real fast. GO STEVE!"
> Maria-gw says, "don't make me tell your mothers about the horrid language you are using"
> Winter-su arrives from nowhere.
> Maria-gw says, "i thought church going folk did not use such language"
> Paulie-su says, "i'll say it then, stop being a BITCH!"
> Jill-gw says, "Go girl!"
> Paulie-su says, "RIGHT BACK AT CHA. . . . .CHILDREN!!!!!!!!!!!!!"
> Winter-su says, "yo Jill go play with fire or in traffic or something . . . .with a blind fold!"
> Muller-su says, "This is so pointless. Can't we just agree to disagree???"
> Bernouli-su says, "I have my own beliefs so If you do not like them well then take off"
> Jill-gw fires a arrow at Winter. In mid air, the arrow bursts into flames, and grazes the top of Winter's head, lighting it on fire! It burns until all Winter's hair is black, and then burns out.
> Maria-gw gives the babies at SU pacifiers
> Jill-gw says, "suck away SU"
> Bartkowsk-su says, "You started it"
> Winter-su says, "Aaron gives them a boot to the skull!"
> Bernouli PUNCHES MARIA IN THE FACE
> Leslie arrives from nowhere.
> Leslie says, "Hi, folks. Having fun?"
> Bernouli-su says, "THANK YOU LESLIE"
> Muller-su says, "TONS"
> Paulie-su says, "hell yeah leslie. . . . ."
> Maria-gw says, "hey leslie"
> Leslie shakes his head. "Um—what were you discussing?"
> Maria-gw says, "homosexuality and religion"   (24 April 1995)[5]

By this point, the conversation had degenerated, and participants were resorting to swearing and virtual violence. Maria-gw's comment, "i thought church going folk did not use such language," and her labelling of the Susquehanna students as "children" reveal what became the overall GW opionion of the SU partners: immature, provincial, religiously conservative. Winter-su's sign about being "ready to rumble" and his shouted exhortation "SU STICK TOGETHER WE CAN TAKE THEM" reveal not only the immaturity that the GW students complained about but also the bitter polarization that had occurred: "we" were now fighting against "them." Those creating contact zones in their courses need to be prepared for such fireworks, and they need to try to prevent polarizations that can hamper productive exchange.

The Contact Zone(s): Analysis and Limitations

Over the course of our semester-long experiment, we discovered (or, perhaps more precisely, uncovered) three different contact zones, three quite distinct "social spaces where cultures meet, clash, and grapple with each other, often in contexts of highly asymmetrical relations of power" (Pratt 34). The creation of the first contact zone was intentional and in fact encouraged by both the course structure and the selection of readings. After the gradual dissipation of the excessive politeness that characterized the early interactions, the discussion of controversial issues produced impassioned, sometimes angry, and often disputatious discourse. On occasion, student email exchanges bordered on "flaming." More often, though, the interactions exemplified a startling emotional honesty that was usually an asset in discussion rather than a deterrent. The exchange of opinions between students from a range of racial and socioeconomic backgrounds produced marvelously provocative (and provoking) reactions. Indeed, Charles Moran's somewhat utopian notion that such cyberspace interactions could become "forums for our emerging cultural democracy" and "a site that will encourage an emancipating discourse . . . in which status is less than it now is a function of race, gender and class" (21) often seemed a decided possibility, a suddenly realizable goal.

But along with this usefully dialogic space we witnessed the emergence of two other related contact zones, conflictual domains whose effects we, as teachers, were unprepared for and, in retrospect, unable on first acquaintance to manage constructively. In time, the separate classes, although composed of groups of diverse individuals, came to form unique communities whose group subjectivity was constructed in relation to an identifiable Other. Gradually, the desire to interact with or reason with that Other decreased, despite the increased frequency of the journal entries: "they" were just too different, "they" were not like "us." Identification thus becomes a detour through the Other that defines a self: "Identification is from the beginning, a question of relation, of self to other, subject to object, inside to outside" (Fuss 388). The development of an increasingly conflictual relation and the subsequent creation of an unresponsive Other proved rather convenient for the construction of an identity for the individual classroom communities. *Intraclass* hostility, of which we saw a great deal earlier in the semester, was retargeted as *interclass* hostility and thus served as a safety valve of sorts. Attacking the opinion of a student at the other institution proved much easier than directly confronting an individual in the same classroom who may have actually shared the disputed opinion. Targeting members of the other community typically served as an exercise in internal civility, a means of maintaining equilibrium and order within the face-to-face debate of the host classroom.

The interclass contact zone was permeated by unfortunate stereotypes. End-of-semester exit surveys reveal that the students from the two smaller schools had come to view many of their urban peers as arrogant, condescending, and privileged. Similarly, the George Washington class came to view the Susquehanna and West Virginia classes as perpetuators of small-town values: religiously doctrinaire and blue collar. In retrospect, excessive stereotyping was exacerbated by the course structure itself and, in particular, by the two different, perhaps mutually exclusive definitions of *community* that came to undergird our syllabus. In fact, the creation of the contact zone between classes may have been the result of a well-intentioned error: we unthinkingly conflated two quite distinct communities. Our course was very much concerned with the notion of community in the context of an ongoing debate about American multiculturalism. The selections from *Rereading America* frequently reiterated that the United States is a very special kind of community experience: a community made up of communities. But while our classes discussed the problematics of identity politics and witnessed the continual reinforcement of the idea that ethnic communities are unique and therefore challenge the hegemonic ideology of the American melting pot, we were, as teachers, simultaneously engaged in another different community project. The second community was in cyberspace, a meeting of equals within an interactive discursive domain where reasonable discussion and reasoned argument might hold sway. These two different ideas of community were themselves in conflict. The message promulgated by class readings was the intrinsic value of small-community resistance and rebellion. This, of course, directly contradicted the structural arrangement of the experiment, which said to the students: "The small classroom community you know is good, but a larger classroom community is even better." Formal structure contradicted thematic concern and, as the course developed, the students became highly resistant to the apparent ambiguity.

Interestingly, the more general resistance of the students, expressed in a variety of ways, provided a striking third contact zone of asymmetrical power relationships: an emerging, although often muffled, conflict between the students and their teachers. As the semester progressed, students increasingly engaged in a critical reflection on the experiment itself, questioning the course goals, their roles as guinea pigs, and the motives of the instructors. We had anticipated that, aside from demonstrating the social construction of knowledge and providing a forum for articulating and negotiating difference, the process would also decenter the authority of the teacher. We failed to consider, however, the extent to which we would ourselves be implicated in the rhetoric of the contact zone and how thoroughly unsettling such implications would prove to our own pedagogic identities. At times, we regretted the fact that we lost control during MOO sessions and couldn't intervene the instant an inappropriate message was sent. Supposed practitioners of liberatory pedagogies, we did not especially enjoy relinquishing local control, especially when discovering an unfortunate or hurtful remark that would never have been uttered in the somatic proximity of a conventional classroom. But as the students were themselves only too aware, our abdication of pedagogical authority was essentially illusory. From reading the logs and perusing the email, we in fact knew everything they did. Hawisher has suggested that "instructors sometimes use networks to keep tabs on students and inadvertently, perhaps, end up creating as oppressive a learning space as might occur in traditional classrooms" (93). Confronting the paradox of how to examine empirically (and record for study) the value of computer sessions without creating an overtly dictatorial regime, we may in fact have inadvertently re-created Foucault's panopticon by creating a medium in which everything could be seen by the eyes of the instructor (see chapter 8).

In this context, the emergence of the third contact zone was revelatory. In fact continual student objections to the focus of the class manifested themselves in emerging self-reflexive discussions about the honesty of the participants in the interaction and, in turn, evolved into pointed discussion about the course structure and requirements (in other words, about the honesty of the teachers themselves). For example:

Well, this entry is in response to the question about altering what you say so as not to offend anyone. Well, I think that if you can say something and still get your point across without offending anyone, than you should try to do it. As someone already said, you have to be able to think before you speak. Sometimes an off-hand comment can be taken in a way that was completely opposite of what it was meant to be. This is one problem with this email journal, and with anything that is written. You can't see the person and be able to "know" what he means by the way he says it, and the way he looks when he says it, that's something that can't be done over email and problems can arise because of it. . . . I think that courtesy should be the general rule when talking with anyone. (Zweig–SU 7 March 1995)

Maria–GW further links this silencing political correctness to the course structure itself, when she inquires:

Why are hispanics the forgotten minority? We concentrated on blacks for a month and half. Then we spend a week and a half on hispanics. We barely discussed the book. We hardly scratched the surface when talking about the hispanic culture. Moving right along to the next minority. But why? Why did we breeze through the hispanic culture? For the black culture we read several different selections from different authors. For the hispanic culture we only read one book. I feel that we should have read different selections from different authors with different nationalities. Latin Americans tend to be lumped together into one group. They simply assume all hispanics are alike and they relate hispanics with Mexicans. Just like the people who set up our syllabus. . . . Upon reading the entries on Cisneros, I've noticed that there is hardly any reference to her ethnicity. Why? If the girl in the story about the red sweater had been black instead of hispanic, do you think you would have read the story differently? The teacher in the story was blatantly mean to her. The teacher forced the little girl to put on the sweater. Maybe the teacher doesn't like hispanics? (Maria–GW 12 March 1995)

These critical assertions insinuate that the presence of teachers can inhibit genuine debate and honesty, especially when the actual agenda of those teachers is itself questionable. What if, for example, other teachers, rather closer to home, "don't like Hispanics?" either? What our students continually advocated was in fact more conflict and a further opening-up of the third contact zone. Indeed, no matter how frayed the relationships between our classes became, students demonstrated that a community could be founded on hostile reaction to the hegemonic authority of teachers and their politically correct ideas. This unexpected contact zone evidenced our classes' engaging the lessons of community, oppression, and resistance that permeated the reading selections for the course. The creation of the third contact zone proved that our students had indeed become critical thinkers. Perhaps the most startling manifestation of this was that, at significant argumentative cruxes, the students began sending emails directly to one another, thus circumventing mechanisms of surveillance and challenging instructor authority.

Underlying a pedagogy of the contact zone is the view that conflict can be productive in exposing hidden beliefs, in fostering honesty of expression, and in promoting dialogue and a healthy exchange of ideas. In "Community, Conflict, and Ways of Knowing," Parker J. Palmer similarly praises the effectiveness of what he calls "creative conflict" (25). He asserts:

> It troubles me when we frame the issue as community vs. competition, because too often we link competition with conflict, as if conflict were what needed to be eliminated. But there is no knowing without conflict.
>
> Our ability to confront each other critically and honestly over alleged facts, imputed meanings, or personal biases and prejudices—*that* is the ability impaired by the absence of community. . . . Competitive individualism squelches the kind of conflict I am trying to name. Conflict is open, public, and often very noisy. Competition is a secret, zero-sum game played by individuals for private gain. *Communal conflict* is a public encounter in which the whole group can win by growing.   (25)

According to Palmer, if we stress the independent, individual learner, we create an unhealthy competition among the students, reducing the possibility of productive conflict and true intellectual growth. If we foster a community among our students in which conflict is valued and embraced, we can expand the knowledge of each individual, allowing the whole group to win by growing. We create what Vygotsky would call a "zone of proximal development," in which the development of the individual is enhanced by collaboration with capable peers (86).

Despite the productiveness of such communal conflict, we must be wary of the kinds of communities that form in our classes. It is true, as Palmer claims, that a "healthy community . . . includes conflict at its very heart" (25). We must therefore make sure that we create and maintain such a healthy community in and among our classes, especially when we foster the potentially explosive arena of a contact zone. We can experience what Pratt and her students felt: "Along with rage, incomprehension, and pain, there were exhilarating moments of wonder and revelation, mutual understanding, and new wisdom—the joys of the contact zone" (39). However, we must also be sure we teach our students to respect those who hold opposing views, so that disagreement can lead to productive exchange, rather than to a destructive silencing. If we learn to manage the conflicts that result, our students can become not only more forceful, persuasive writers but also more powerful critical thinkers, courageous enough to challenge oppression and open to disparate ideas and value systems.

Notes

1. Crissie is responding to the following posting by Barto, in which he calls for calmer discussions:

> Eduard, Barb
> The first thing the two of you have to do is calm down. . . . One shouldn't get caught up in his or her emotions; when this happens, many times, immature comments are the result.   (Barto, 2/24/95)

2. In the Susquehanna-GWU and WVNCC-GWU journals, Susquehanna and WVNCC students tended to respond more generally to ongoing threads, whereas the GWU students took advantage of the "Reply" feature in the Pine email program to respond very specifically to what other students had said, with the earlier posting incorporated into the message, preceded by ">" characters. The West Virginia students didn't have a "Reply" option, and Susquehanna students couldn't use it (because the software would misread the external email addresses and misdirect the responses). These software differences had a rhetorical effect. GWU students had the means (as well as the analytical ability) to dissect other students' prose and fire it back—amended—at them, including relevant comments and reactions. Susquehanna and WVNCC students were forced to take responsibility for their utterances, since those utterances could be so easily reflected back to them—and challenged. GMU students could also use the same "Reply" feature when commenting on their fellow students' postings.

3. In order to make the exchange more coherent, we have edited out some of the irrelevant intervening dialogue. On MOO spaces, threads of conversation are frequently interwoven, with various dialogues taking place simultaneously.

4. The tension behind these discussions arises in part because of the sensitive nature of the subject, especially for Susquehanna students. Susquehanna is historically affiliated with the Lutheran church, a church whose official position condemns homosexuality as sinful behavior. Most Susquehanna students are highly uncomfortable with the subject of homosexuality. For most, the movie *Torch Song Trilogy* was their first experience of gay sexuality, an experience that made them extremely uncomfortable.

5. We have once again edited out some of the intervening dialogue to improve the coherence of the passage.

Works Cited

Bizzell, Patricia. " 'Contact Zones' and English Studies." *College English* 56, no. 2 (Feb. 1994):163–70.

Eldred, Janet. "Pedagogy in the Computer-Networked Classroom." *Computers and Composition* 8, no. 2 (Apr. 1991):47–61.

Faigley, Lester. *Fragments of Rationality: Postmodernity and the Subject of Composition.* Pittsburgh, PA: University of Pittsburgh Press, 1992.

Fuss, Diana. "Look Who's Talking; or, If Looks Could Kill." *Critical Inquiry* 22 (Winter 1996):383–92.

Hawisher, Gail. "Electronic Meetings of the Minds: Research, Electronic Conferences, and Composition Studies." In *Re-Imagining Computers and Composition: Teaching and Research in the Virtual Age.* Ed. Gail Hawisher and Paul LeBlanc. Portsmouth, NH: Boynton/Cook, 1992. 81–101.

Hawisher, Gail E., and Cynthia L. Selfe. "The Rhetoric of Technology and the Electronic Writing Class." *College Composition and Communication* 42 (Feb. 1991):55–65.

Moran, Charles. "Computers and the Writing Classroom: A Look to the Future." In *Re-Imagining Computers and Composition: Teaching and Research in the Virtual Age.* Ed. Gail Hawisher and Paul LeBlanc. Portsmouth, NH: Boynton/Cook, 1992. 7–23.

Palmer, Parker J. "Community, Conflict, and Ways of Knowing: Ways to Deepen Our Educational Agenda." *Change* 19, no. 5 (Sep./Oct. 1987):20–25.

Pratt, Mary Louise. "Arts of the Contact Zone." In *Profession 91.* New York: Modern Language Association of American, 1991.

Schriner, Delores K., and William C. Rice. "Computer Conferencing and Collaborative Learning: A Discourse Community at Work." *College Composition and Communication* 40 (Dec. 1989):472–78.

Vygotsky, L. S. *Mind in Society: The Development of Higher Psychological Processes.* Ed. Michael Cole, Vera John-Steiner, Sylvia Scribner, and Ellen Souberman. Cambridge: Harvard University Press, 1978.

IO Reading the Networks of Power: Rethinking "Critical Thinking" in Computerized Classrooms

Tim Mayers and Kevin Swafford

As the initial wave of enthusiasm for computers in the writing classroom, along with its attendant celebratory rhetoric, has subsided, many scholars have launched brilliant, at times scathing critiques of various educational uses of electronic technology. Valuable as these critiques are, few of them offer any suggestions for how thoughtful, engaged teachers might incorporate such critical awareness into their pedagogical practices. For while an entirely utopian rhetoric of technology is certainly dangerous, a critique of computer use as an act with social, political, and economic implications is problematic if it leaves no room for the possibility that the hegemonic tendencies supported by computers might be at least partially resisted without giving up computers entirely. Computers simply are not going to go away. The primary challenge for teachers and students, as we see it, is to discover ways in which computers might be used in the classroom to increase critical awareness of the ideologies bound up with technology and, when possible, to subvert those ideologies. To put it another way, we want to discover ways in which computers might be used against those ideologies.

To do so, we will first outline, and cite examples of, both the celebratory and the critical rhetorics of technology. Next we will question whether certain aspects of these rhetorics ought not be dismissed out of hand, and then we will present a concrete example of how the valuable insights of past scholarship on computers and writing might be put to use in a classroom practice that aims to promote critical awareness of, and resistance to, the ideologies of technology without inculcating mere technophobia. Such a classroom practice would aim to provide students with both the skills required of them in a technological world and the ability to discern the designs such a world might have on them.

Networked writing instruction, we hope to demonstrate, is an enterprise shot through with ironies and contradictions. One of these ironies is that in some ways networked classrooms provide fruitful space for critiquing the very ideologies that allow them to exist, of which such classrooms are palpable, visible signs. Yet while the computerized classroom provides a space where critique is possible, it by no means guarantees that such critique will actually happen. It is equally possible, perhaps even more possible, that such an environment can work to *prevent* critical awareness. Critical thinking and writing, we will argue, do not simply happen as a result of the technology, nor merely from savvy pedagogical uses of the technology, but rather from a specific type of pedagogical practice in relation to the technology.

Computers and Writing Scholarship: Celebration and Critique

In order to mark the terrain that may allow for the realization of critical thinking and writing in electronic environments, we will rehearse some of the typical positions regarding computer technology in the writing classroom. We certainly do not claim to provide a thorough overview of computers and writing scholarship, but we do find two rather distinct rhetorical strands in that scholarship, and the examples we present here, we believe, are representative of those strands.

Within much of the early scholarship on computers and writing (and some of the most recent scholarship as well), there is an enthusiasm marked by a utopian rhetoric of radical change and possibility. The networked classroom is often lauded as a site of democracy, pluralism, and heightened critical engagement where traditional classroom dynamics of authority and control are erased. In the new, decentered environment, debate, negotiation, and consensus shape the knowledge that is produced. Perhaps one of the best-known examples of this celebratory rhetoric is the sixth chapter of Lester Faigley's *Fragments of Rationality*. Despite Faigley's hedging retreats from his boldest pronouncements, and despite the fact that he includes a compelling example of how online class discussions can go wrong, this chapter is entitled "The Achieved Utopia of the Networked Classroom." Here, Faigley claims that the nonsequential dialogue and writing produced in the networked classroom (with the help of software programs like Daedalus InterChange) allow for the realization of a student-centered classroom or, to quote Faigley directly, "the utopian dream of an equitable sharing of classroom authority" (167). According to Faigley, the online classroom, almost magically as a result of the presence of the technology, invites student participation while seriously limiting the teacher's ability to control the direction of discussions. It also allows students to achieve a different sense of textuality, textual meaning, and textual production. Faigley writes: "Just as the authority of the teacher is decentered, the authority of the text is also decentered in electronic written discussions, demonstrating Lyotard's claim that truth is local and contingent. Students are often shocked to find that other students arrive at different interpretations from theirs, even from readings of seemingly transparent, commonplace texts. Thus they are forced to confront different ways of constituting meaning from experience and to negotiate those meanings with other students" (185). Ultimately, for Faigley, the online writing class allows students and instructors to investigate and address problems of race, sexism, and economic prejudice and determination in ways not wholly possible under traditional classroom conditions.

Edmund Farrel sounds a similar note in his foreword to the 1990 NCTE collection of essays entitled *Evolving Perspectives on Computers and Composition Studies.* Farrel writes, "Present technology—desktop publishing and the use of hypertext/hypermedia and other electronic writing systems—now threatens traditional relationships in discourse: between writers and the 'ownership' of their written 'properties'; between writers and their editors, layout designers, and publishers; between writers and their audiences; between teachers of writing and their students" (xi). This, according to Farrel, threatens to disrupt the repressive system of discursive production that has been most explicit within traditional college writing classrooms. With the development and implementation of computer technology and its linkage with international networks such as the Internet, the old models of discourse are seemingly blown apart and discarded, leaving a realm of discursive freedom and the potential for unhindered imagination.

Enthusiastic reports such as Faigley's and Farrel's, we believe, serve an important purpose: to make teachers aware of the possibilities for critical, liberatory pedagogy opened up by networked classrooms. But there is something missing in these accounts, as Gail Hawisher and Cynthia Selfe pointed out in 1991: "The current professional conversation about computer use in writing classes, as evidenced in published accounts, is incomplete in at least one essential and important way. While containing valuable accounts of electronic classes, this conversation fails to provide us with a critical perspective on the problematic aspects of computer use and thus with a full understanding of how the use of technology can affect the social, political, and educational environments within which we teach" (64).

A trace of what is missing in Faigley and Farrel might be found in places such as Robert Muffoletto and Nancy Nelson Knupfer's collection entitled *Computers in Education*. Written by educational theorists, the densely argued, theoretically sophisticated essays in this book demonstrate persuasively how computers in classrooms always participate, in some fashion, rhetorically and economically, in ideologies of technology and education that will prove harmful to many students. Howard Besser, for example, notes that when Apple donated thousands of computers to public schools during the 1980s, any losses the company may have incurred were more than offset by tax breaks and the probability that students would become predisposed to Apple computers and thus purchase them instead of other brands (57). In another essay, Robert Muffoletto argues that discourse on educational technology tends to cover over social hierarchies that protect certain types of knowledge as the domain of experts (91–102). But these essays and the others in the collection, insightful as they are, seem to offer no suggestions for what teachers who are critically aware of technology might do (short of refusing to use computers altogether) in order to incorporate such critical awareness into their pedagogies.

In this regard, Cynthia and Richard Selfe's "Politics of the Interface" takes an important extra step. Selfe and Selfe begin with a critique of their own, arguing that computer technology, and computer interfaces in particular, "order[s] the virtual world according to a certain set of historical and social values" that predominately reify "monoculturalism, capitalism, and phallologic thinking" (486). Though the main focus of their critique is that computer interfaces represent a largely white middle-class cultural perspective that needs to be problematized and corrected, the most powerful point within the essay is Selfe and Selfe's reminder of the relationship between computer technology and the information commodity culture of late capitalism. The development of computer technology and its introduction into the educational system (as many of the authors in Muffoletto and Knupfer's collection demonstrate) is bound up in a general process of commodification of information through technology. Selfe and Selfe emphasize this point when they write:

> Electronic spaces . . . are becoming more expensive, more rigidly aligned along the related axes of class privilege and capitalism. The refinement and use of packet charging technologies, for example, and the increasing exploitation of large-scale commercial networks that appeal to the public will continue to support such an alignment. Recent figures published in a recent *New York Times* article indicate that commercial public networks such as

Prodigy and Compuserve charge approximately $50 for starter kits on their systems, between $8 and $15 for basic use each month, and some additional per-message or per-minute charges as well. The capital stake that commercial groups have in promoting these electronic systems to citizens is not a small one: Information-as-commodity is a big business—approximately 3.4 million people subscribe to commercial networks at the rates we have mentioned.

(487–88)

We would argue that the association of computer technology with business and the commodification of information has always been in place and that the primary problem with computer technology in the writing classroom relates to obviating this relationship and exposing not only how the technology orders the virtual world but how ideologies of technology order the "real" world in the service of various types of social and cultural control. Selfe and Selfe, admirably, suggest ways in which this might be done, one of which is to train teachers of composition to become "technology critics as well as technology users" (496–97).[1] They are not, however, as specific in outlining this task as they are in presenting their critique. In the rest of this essay, we plan to offer more specific ways in which the powerful critiques of technology may be put to use along with more optimistic visions of technology in a networked first-year college composition classroom.

Situating Ourselves as Teachers With(in) Technology

Before we begin to put critiques of technology to work in our own classrooms, however, we must situate ourselves within the complex social field created and sustained by technology. And because so few of us are formally trained or encouraged to do so (Selfe and Selfe 497), this is no easy task. We are immediately faced with a problem: the unexamined assumptions regarding technology and the dominant ideologies of technology that many instructors and students share. If we are to use technology to foster critical thinkers and writers, then we must not approach it as an isolated, value-free mechanism or tool but as a crucial signifier residing within a highly complex cultural, historical, and economic continuum.

Our first task is to recognize that technology is not neutral nor are there any neutral uses of it, at least not within our contemporary society. Furthermore, we must recognize that despite whatever immediately practical use or function computer technology may have within the writing classroom, it always already signifies something more than its mere use or function. Indeed, computer technology represents a culturally complex signifying economy whose ultimate power and signification is perhaps found in the unspoken and thus unexamined social pressures and controls placed on ourselves and our students. As important as the task of exposing ways in which ideologies of technology order experiences and notions of reality is the attempt to situate and understand social pressures and mechanisms of control through technology. In a writing class, this is easy enough to do, for on some level, students are always aware of the social and economic meanings and significance of computer technology; they know they are now expected to be computer literate if they are to be considered educated and competitive. Indeed, because they are so anxiously conscious of the world of work and careers, students are deeply aware of the social pressures placed on them in relation to technology long before they enter the networked classroom. This type of experiential cultural knowledge is a treasure chest of possibility. It is our responsibility to have students use and reflect on their experiences in order to rethink and problematize technology within a larger social and cultural totality. For the most part, we have found, students are predisposed not to think critically about technology and its functions within our society. Rather, they are under the anxious spell of a social imperative that says, "Learn and consume the technology or suffer the consequences." The consequences, of course, are assumed to be ignorance and, ultimately, lower socioeconomic status.

Of course, it is not students alone who are pressured to be technologically up to date. There is also an enormous pressure on schools to appropriate and utilize computer technology for instruction. In different ways, the pressures placed on schools are as great as those placed on students and teachers to learn computer skills. As Ellen Barton and Ruth Ray point out in their essay "Technology and Authority," media-hyped social pressures have exhorted U.S. schools to produce trained workers for our information and computer society, and the schools are often criticized publicly for not meeting the challenge. The near-hysterical and apocalyptic pronouncements that appear recurrently in various public forums over the lack of computer skills among high school and college graduates have led to many calls, from divergent places in our society, for major changes in the U.S. educational system. Time after time we hear or read that students must acquire technology skills. Implicit within this argument is the idea that schools have a responsibility to produce workers who can use technology in ways that will help U.S. capitalists compete in the global economy. In 1986 the Carnegie Commission wrote the following:

Advancing technology and the changing terms of international trade are remolding the basic structure of international economic competition. . . . In the future, the high-wage-level societies will be those whose economies are based on the use of a wide scale of very highly skilled workers, backed up by the most advanced technologies available. . . . We do not believe the educational system needs repairing; we believe it must be rebuilt to match the drastic changes needed in our economy if we are to prepare our children for productive lives in the 21st century.   (qtd. in Barton and Ray 280)

The idea that education is, or ought to be, merely a tool that appeases the demands of the economy runs deep in the United States. Gauging from the responses of our first-year composition students to questions about what they imagine the purpose and function of their educations to be, most students believe that education is merely a preparation for the so-called real world of careers and business, their primary task being to acquire necessary skills. Part of our challenge, as we see it, is to interrogate and broaden the notion of what might constitute such skills. For if critical thinking is to be considered a skill (or a set of skills), then it is certainly more than just "the mere manipulation of tools" (Heidegger 23).[2] If, then, students are to be more than merely paranoid and anxious consumers of technology who feel absolutely pressured to develop the prescribed technology skills dictated by our economy, then they must develop a *critical awareness* of computer technology. They must be in a position to question the authority ceded to technology by the economy and to raise and explore issues of technological learning and access. They must also have the opportunity to explore the potential for various types of resistance to the controlling ideologies of technology. Ironically, these tasks are perhaps nowhere more possible than in the networked writing classroom itself, for the very presence of the technology, coupled with the discursive capabilities it allows and the students' immediate access to it, is conducive to an invested group discussion and reflection on technology. But successful discussions (which we define here as those that problematize, at least to a degree, the dominant ideologies of technology) do not simply happen because the topic of technology is presented for consideration. A teacher's task is to contextualize the discussion carefully so that these ideologies may be wrested from the domain of common sense.

If, as so many composition theorists and critics have argued, it is part of our responsibility as writing instructors to introduce public discourse into the classroom, with a belief in the possibility of rational critique despite the complexities generated by capitalism, then we must not only foster and develop an environment in which we can investigate how mass culture is produced, circulated, and consumed; we must also allow and develop a critical dialogue regarding computer technology. Otherwise, any perceived "liberating" moments may turn out to be merely ways of making ourselves feel good about a seductive and expensive apparatus. Furthermore, in our pedagogical practices in the online writing course, we must avoid an overly optimistic approach to computers, their utilitarian function, and their latent social and political significance. Such an optimism may lead to a potentially dangerous blindness to how the computerized writing classroom may implicitly reinscribe and forward the interests of the computer-information-commodity industry or, to put it more directly, the interests of the mechanisms of capital itself. Whatever charge we receive from working with advanced computer technology should be coupled with an instructional practice that allows the relationship between technology and capital to surface. This relationship is primary and should not be forgotten or put aside. To the extent that economic and ideological problems regarding computers in the writing classroom are not addressed, it seems to us that instructors are in a type of collusion with consumer capitalists, encouraging students who learn to use computers to become consumers who buy computers, without facing the larger issues related to technology. To counteract this, our enthusiasm for the technology should be tempered, critical, and reflective, for such an approach helps to neutralize, perhaps, some of the contradictions that emerge within the hopeful perspectives on the technology. If the liberatory aspects of the technology are to be achieved even remotely, it is our responsibility to rethink the technology along the axes of its larger social, economic, and political implications. Indeed, those of us who would seek to realize the utopian potential of computer technology must not forget Adorno and Horkheimer's shrewd reminder in *Dialectic of Enlightenement* that technology is only "as democratic as the economic system with which it is bound up" (4).

What Should We Do? How Might We Do It?

As Selfe and Selfe have pointed out, teachers who use technology in their classrooms should be technology critics as well. But as we have already noted, they do not provide any specific guidelines for how technology criticism might be incorporated into a complex cultural-social nexus such as the required first-year college writing course. Toward that end, we will outline an assignment we have used.

We do not offer this assignment as the way to integrate technology criticism into a networked composition pedagogy. Rather, we want to demonstrate that technology criticism must be carefully integrated into a writing course, not presented in an isolated, out-of-context fashion. It must somehow be congruent with the stated aims of the course, and it must be carefully prepared for. For those reasons, it is important to note that the following assignment is the last in a sequence of five. The previous assignments require students to write semiotic analyses of popular cultural signs and self-reflexive analyses of their own language practices. These assignments serve both to introduce students to thinking and writing strategies they will need to use in later academic courses and to make possible a critical dialogue about popular culture and technology. Having spent the semester engaged in semiotic and self-reflexive interpretive practices, students are asked to write a critical semiotic analysis of the networked classroom in which they have spent a semester. They are offered several options. They may "read" the classroom as a network of signs, considering their social, political, and economic significance. They may address the question of why the university requires them all to take a first-year composition course, and/or they may question what the existence of such a classroom (considering the fact it was originally financed by grant money, not the university's regular budget) suggests about the priorities and aims of the university.

While the product of this assignment is a critical essay, the manner in which it is prepared for bears some consideration. We begin with a range of readings dealing with computers and education. These include advertisements for computers (which often urge parents to buy computers for their children—or else), an editorial from the school newspaper that exhorts students to acquire computer skills lest they find themselves unemployable, brochures produced by business-writing students who use the networked classroom,[3] and writings critical of the enterprise of composition instruction and the educational uses of electronic technology. In the last category, we find Fan Shen's "The Classroom and the Wider Culture: Identity as a Key to Learning English Composition" and Selfe and Selfe's "The Politics of the Interface" quite helpful. Such articles may be difficult (and sometimes painful) for first-year students to read, but we supplement these readings with online class discussions in which students consider the entire range of readings. The question guiding these discussions is not so much "Whose side are you on?" as "How do we negotiate our ways through all these competing perspectives?" The discussions may be pseudonymous, an option that often allows competing ideologies to confront each other more directly. Pseudonymous networked discussions can even encourage students to compose ideologically charged sound bites, because terse, punchy messages often draw more responses than longer, deliberative ones (Mayers; Van Dyke). Not all students are seduced into exchanging slogans, however; some wait patiently for their chance to critique other messages. Once they are completed, discussions may be saved as (electronic and/or printed) texts that are then available for students to reread and even cite as they draft their essays. We have found it useful to require students to reread and reconsider online discussions, because this practice helps reinforce the course's emphasis on self-reflexivity.

It is important to note here that we do not see this assignment as designed to cultivate antitechnological attitudes in students.[4] Indeed, most of our students remain optimistic and excited about computers even while they are aware of some of the more sinister designs computer manufacturers may have on them. A few of our students have expressed discomfort over being drawn into the IBM versus Apple computer wars, struggles in which the students stand to gain little and perhaps lose much.[5] Others have expressed concern that emerging technologies may work to split the middle class into a small technological elite that can afford to keep up continually and a much larger group that is effectively left behind, unable to afford personal access to the Internet, where most business, including job interviews and hiring, may be conducted.

Writing instruction in networked classrooms is, as we have mentioned, an endeavor shot through with contradictions. Those of us who engage in it may feel, at times, that we are working simultaneously toward both the liberation and the oppression of our students. And while we need to be aware of this contradiction, we should not let it paralyze us; nor should we allow ourselves to be seduced either by the notion that electronic technology has at last allowed us to realize our utopian dreams or that oppressive ideologies are so deeply entrenched in our world that we cannot possibly do anything about them. Further (and we have found this a difficult task ourselves), we should strive to avoid the complacent feeling that we are successfully navigating between extremes, that we have found a proper middle road. For it is either/or thinking, we believe, that characterizes one of the most oppressive assumptions prevalent in our society (and our classrooms) today: the assumption that political positions and perspectives can all be located along a (decidedly linear) spectrum. Working toward agreement or disagreement—between individuals or within groups—is always a more complex affair than it may initially seem. And it is in this spirit—the recognition of contradiction and complexity—that we have offered this critique and these suggestions. We hope they will provide a way in (or at least a place to start) for technologically-minded teachers and intellectuals committed to practicing a truly critical pedagogy.

Notes

1. Another strategy suggested by Selfe and Selfe is for teachers to become actively involved in the writing of pedagogical software. Paul LeBlanc also makes this suggestion in *Writing Teachers Writing Software* (NCTE, 1993).

2. Heidegger's critique of technology locates the "danger" of technology not in

the products of technology but rather in "the essence of technology," or the increasing tendency for human beings to think in purely instrumental terms.

3. One of these brochures tells the hypothetical, melodramatic story of two university graduates who differ only in that one took the required first-year writing course in the computerized classroom while the other took the course in a traditional classroom. Ten years after graduation, the former is enjoying a successful business career, while the latter is flipping hamburgers.

4. In fact, we are currently considering using parts of the Unabomber manifesto in future classes as an example of the dangers of certain types of radical antitechnological thinking.

5. Some students have also noticed how easy it is to be drawn into corporate loyalties from which they really have nothing to gain. The "choices" between Coke and Pepsi, McDonald's and Burger King, Democrat and Republican, we believe, always involve something more than mere personal preference.

Works Cited

Adorno, Theodor W., and Max Horkheimer. *Dialectic of Enlightenment.* Trans. John Cumming. New York: Continuum, 1994.

Barton, Ellen, and Ruth Ray. "Technology and Authority." In *Evolving Perspectives on Computers and Composition Studies: Questions for the 1990s.* Ed. Gail E. Hawisher and Cynthia L. Selfe. Urbana, IL: NCTE Press, 1991. 279–99.

Besser, Howard. "Education as Marketplace." In *Computers in Education: Social, Political, and Historical Perspectives.* Ed. Robert Muffoletto and Nancy Nelson Knupfer. Cresskill, NJ: Hampton, 1993. 37–69.

Faigley, Lester. *Fragments of Rationality: Postmodernity and the Subject of Composition.* Pittsburgh: University of Pittsburgh Press, 1992.

Farrel, Edmund. Foreword to *Evolving Perspectives on Computers and Composition Studies: Questions for the 1990s.* Ed. Gail E. Hawisher and Cynthia L. Selfe. Urbana, IL: NCTE Press, 1991. ix–xii.

Hawisher, Gail E., and Cynthia L. Selfe. "The Rhetoric of Technology and the Electronic Writing Class." *College Composition and Communication* 42 (1991):55–65.

Heidegger, Martin. *What is Called Thinking?* Trans. J. Glenn Gray. New York: Harper and Row, 1968.

LeBlanc, Paul J. *Writing Teachers Writing Software: Creating Our Place in the Electronic Age.* Urbana, IL: NCTE Press, 1993.

Mayers, Tim. "(Inter)Changing Names: Pseudonymous Networked Discussions and Critical Pedagogy." Paper presented at Computers and Writing Conference, University of Texas at El Paso, 20 May 1995.

Muffoletto, Robert, and Nancy Nelson Knupfer, eds. *Computers in Education: Social, Political, and Historical Perspectives.* Cresskill, NJ: Hampton, 1993.

Muffoletto, Robert. "The Expert Teaching Machine: Unpacking the Mask." In *Computers in Education: Social, Political, and Historical Perspectives*. Ed. Robert Muffoletto and Nancy Nelson Knupfer. Cresskill, NJ: Hampton, 1993. 91–103.

Selfe, Cynthia L., and Richard J. Selfe, Jr. "The Politics of the Interface: Power and Its Exercise in Electronic Contact Zones." *College Composition and Communication* 45 (December 1994):480–504.

Shen, Fan. "The Classroom and the Wider Culture: Identity as a Key to Learning English Composition." *Signs of Life in the USA: Readings on Popular Culture for Writers*. Ed. Sonia Maasik and Jack Solomon. Boston: St. Martin's Press, Bedford Books, 1994. 485–94.

Van Dyke, Richard. "Sound Bites and Scrambled Eggs: Media(ted) Authority in the Networked Classroom." Paper presented at Conference on College Composition and Communication, Washington, DC, 25 Mar. 1995.

11 Writing Teachers, Schools, Access, and Change

Patricia Fitzsimmons-Hunter and Charles Moran

It is clear that access to emerging technologies is a function of wealth, which is itself a function of the situation into which you happen to be born: your country, class, race, and gender. The more resources at your disposal, the more likely you are to have a desk and technology on or near that desk.

In the U.S. literature of technology studies, however, the issue of access is treated in two different and unproductive ways: it is ignored, or it becomes the occasion for a diatribe against the unequal distribution of wealth in this country. For us, the literature that ignores the fact of differential access falls into the category established by Hawisher and Selfe (57) as the "rhetoric of technology." Hawisher and Selfe critique this literature for its assumption that technological change will produce hoped-for benefits. We want to critique this literature for its companion assumption: that the unequal distribution of technology is not important, or if it is important it will somehow take care of itself. For examples of this rhetoric in relatively pure form, see the September 1995 issue of *Scientific American*, titled "Key Technologies for the 21st Century," in which it is assumed throughout that everyone will have equal access to, and benefits from, the technological revolutions that are now in progress. For examples of this rhetoric in the field of computers and writing, see, for example, Bolter, Landow, Moran, and Tuman.

The literature that focuses on the fact of differential access—and there is not much of it—embodies the rhetoric of social revolution. This strand of the literature deals with the problem at the macro level: social change is both the end and the means. We are thinking here of C. Paul Olson's "Who Computes?" Richard Ohmann's "Literacy, Technology, and Monopoly Capital," and, to a lesser degree, Helen Schwartz's "Ethical Considerations of Educational Computer Use." In this strand of the literature, the fact that access to hardware/software is a function of wealth permits only one solution: a massive redistribution of wealth. Until such redistribution occurs, this literature implies, there is nothing we, as teachers or school administrators, can do. The problem must be solved at the macro level; in our daily work-lives, we can only wait.

The difficulty with both of these approaches is that they overlook and thereby disable the human beings involved. Both have in them more than a suspicion of technological determinism: the rhetoric of technology assumes that somehow technology will itself solve the problem of its own distribution, and the rhetoric of social revolution assumes that without the redistribution of wealth/technology across our society the technologically rich will vault still further beyond the technologically poor and there is nothing that anyone can do to halt this process except actively call for the revolution.

As teachers ourselves and as people engaged in kindergarten through college staff development, we are driven to suggest an alternative to these two approaches, one that accounts for the ability of human beings to shape their own lives and to cope on their own with the inequities they find in their particular situations. With more than a slight debt to the vision of Paulo Freire, we call our approach "the rhetoric of enablement-through-technology." In this approach we begin with these assumptions: that instead of starting with technology, we start with people; and that we consider as our goal the integration of low-end, relatively affordable technology into the lives and work of those who are, or see themselves as being, left behind by the pace of technological change: "roadkill," to use a popular contemporary metaphor, on the information highway.

We do not want to be misunderstood. We are not at all trying to discover a via media, a compromise or middle way between two unproductive positions. And we are not suggesting for a moment that we accept as inevitable the widening gap between this country's rich and its poor (as Faigley discusses in chapter 1). What we are suggesting is that if given the most modest of opportunities, students and teachers can themselves be agents of change: by initiating change in their own situations, they can begin the work of institutional change in their own classrooms. Their example will provide other teachers with models and school administrators with functioning programs to support. As teachers become able to articulate clearly what they need in the way of technology to attain their goals for their students' learning, they will present their schools and school systems with concrete plans and programs to fund and support, not simply the abstract goal of a "computer in every pot" but specific educational programs that require the use of technology for their full implementation.

In the sections that follow, we report on a collaborative staff-development project in which two technology-poor institutions, the Springfield Public Schools and the University of Massachusetts at Amherst, together permitted a group of students and teachers to empower themselves through technology.

Embedded in our report is a new definition of the term *access*. Institutions and organizations most often define access as the ratio between people/users and computers. Seen in this way, both of us teach in institutions that could be seen as technologically disadvantaged: relative to our counterparts in wealthier institutions in our region, our students have, per capita, fewer computers and more difficult Internet access. Yet the issue of access, we will argue, cannot be fully or even appropriately defined by numbers of computers per student or computers per classroom. We therefore expand our definition of access to include these factors:

1. Numbers of computers available to students and to teachers;
2. Teachers' and students' perceptions of their access to technology;
3. Teachers' and students' understanding of the ways in which appropriate technology can help them achieve their goals for their own teaching and learning;
4. Teachers' and students' willingness to exploit the technologies available to them; and
5. Teachers' and students' willingness to fight for the technologies that they need to pursue their goals for their own teaching and learning.

In the three staff-development projects we describe below, we made a minimal investment in item one to achieve substantial gains in items two through five. Now, at the end of the projects, we feel convinced that we have, without great expense, dramatically increased the access of Springfield students and teachers to emerging technologies. We have done this by altering teachers' and students' perceptions of their access to technology and by enlarging their understanding of the ways in which technology can help them achieve their teaching and learning goals. Teachers who were, before these projects, inexperienced in the use of emerging technologies have now become advocates for, and exemplars of, the use of these technologies in the curriculum. Similarly, students, as well as their families and caregivers, have become advocates for the use of these technologies. What might have been a technological underclass has become something altogether different: a set of teachers, students, and parents who are more knowledgeable about technology and more able and willing to make compelling arguments to achieve their fair share. In addition, teachers and students together have discovered innovative and effective ways of making the equipment they have go further through innovative ways of sharing and leveraging the equipment that they do have. They have also demanded and achieved access to facilities previously closed to them.

In fiscal year 1996, the Massachusetts Department of Education allocated the Western Massachusetts Writing Project substantial funding to improve the teaching of writing throughout western Massachusetts. We, project codirectors, chose to commit a portion of that funding to exploring the impact of technology on teaching and learning in the Springfield Public Schools. We designed three staff-development projects that would engage teachers in the development of writing curricula that would include technology, specifically, low-end word processors that we made available in small numbers. We wanted to test our new definition of *access*. How would teachers and students react? How would teachers use the time, support, and minimal equipment that we provided? We were stepping into the unknown. How, we asked, would this program affect the integration of technology into teaching and learning in the teachers' classes? What difference would the program make in the ways teachers and students used technology? What classroom management issues would we all face? How much equipment is necessary to promote change? With these questions and others in mind, we invited Springfield teachers to help us develop prototypes of effective technology integration into the curriculum. Several different projects emerged.

We made a minimal investment in equipment, buying thirty AlphaSmart Pro Boards, one of a number of commercially available, simple, inexpensive, portable word processors. We purchased the rechargeable battery packs and traveling cases that allowed teachers and students freedom from electrical outlets and computer carrels: the SmartBoards could be transported from classroom to classroom, from school to home. We bought two Macintosh computers and two printers to serve as the downloading and uploading print stations necessary for formatting and printing. This equipment was housed in Springfield for the 1995–1996 school year. The total investment in hardware and software for the projects came to $11,000: $7,000 for the SmartBoards and $4,000 for the computers and printers. We budgeted another $40,000 to compensate the participating teachers for the time required to familiarize themselves with the equipment, to plan curriculum units that used this and other equipment available to them, to share and refine these plans collectively, and to reflect together on their own and their students' experiences in the curricula they had designed.

The ratio of money spent on teacher's time and support to money spent on equipment was thus just under 5 to 1. Forty-one teachers, nineteen schools, and 775 students were directly impacted by the projects.

Writing for Publication Seminar

In our first project, the Writing for Publication Seminar, we invited thirty Springfield K–12 teachers from nineteen Springfield schools to participate in a venture that would support the integration of technology into daily classroom practice. Each teacher was challenged to design and execute a ten-week, collaborative classroom project, one that incorporated effective writing-process instruction, included successful use of appropriate computer technology, and would result in a published end product. The teachers were exemplary classroom teachers, not computer experts: several had never used computers before, and although a few had access to labs on a limited basis and several had one to five computers in their classrooms, the majority had no access to computer technology up to this point. Even so, interested in the potential of technology as a tool for teaching and learning, the teachers enthusiastically elected to participate.

The seminar provided thirty teacher-participants with one SmartBoard each, signed out to them for the duration of the project. The participants used their SmartBoard differently. Some pooled their resources and rotated, taking six or seven SmartBoards to their students at a time (teachers met at gas stations, restaurants, or homes to facilitate the sharing); others set up an input station in their classrooms (individual students would step out from classroom activities to enter their writing); still others signed the SmartBoards out to their students to take home; other used the boards themselves to enter student data. The creativity and flexibility of the teacher-participants and their students maximized the impact of one word processor per teacher.

The seminar provided time for the teachers to plan their projects, design project components, set timelines, and meet every two weeks to share news of progress and receive the necessary training. Involvement in the seminar motivated teachers to work hard to improve access to technology in their schools, creatively and cunningly gathering allies in campaigns to gain greater access to more sophisticated and larger numbers of computers. School administrators and other teachers supported the efforts of our participants. A final celebration drew some six hundred people, including the thirty teachers, their students, parents, and community members.

Many of the teacher-participants who reluctantly returned their Smart-Boards at the end of the project have since capitalized on their success and persuaded school administrators to give them computers for their classrooms. Three principals and their school councils have ordered sets of SmartBoards for their schools. Other teacher-participants, thanks to the recognition of the project's impact on regular classroom instruction, have more access to existing computer labs. In addition, student enthusiasm has fostered greater parental involvement. When students employ technology—with enthusiasm—as a tool for learning, parents demand that such technologies become readily available.

We conclude from this project that a well-designed in-service staff-development program can increase teachers' and students' access to technology, not necessarily through the purchase of expensive, high-end equipment, and not necessarily through technology-based teacher-training, but through giving teachers resources in the form of planning time, collegial support, and a challenge. The teachers themselves become a resource for us here: as more exemplary teachers enact the integration of technology with curriculum, school systems will build their knowledge base and thus the basis for effective uses of and clearly articulated arguments for the increased availability of technology in schools and classrooms.

Forest Park Project

The Forest Park Project differed from the Writing for Publication Seminar in an important way: In the seminar we gave teachers an assignment: to develop a project that would be published. In the Forest Park Project, we asked the teacher-participants to become our coresearchers, helping us conduct an investigation into the ways in which teachers and their students could use technology to advance students' learning. We gave these teachers no specific assignment, as in the seminar, but we did give them time for planning and reflection, and we did give them access to the SmartBoards and two print-station computers.

Two interdisciplinary teams of eighth-grade teachers in one middle school committed themselves to a semester-long investigation of ways to integrate writing effectively into core-curriculum courses. They agreed to participate in the project on the understanding that they would use writing-as-learning strategies with their students, incorporate writing-process strategies in their assignments, and work as a team to provide consistent expectations and classroom management techniques. The teachers—none of whom was experienced in using computers—would also explore the impact of having twenty Smart-Boards in the new writing-as-learning program. In addition to the Smart-Boards, which the teachers received at the end of January (after the Writing for Publication Seminar concluded), each team was given one Macintosh computer with CD-ROM and a printer. The teacher teams attended biweekly meetings with Patricia Fitzsimmons-Hunter to discuss writing-as-learning activities and also to receive technology training.

The low cost of the SmartBoards permitted teachers to have many computers in the same classroom. This altered the way in which the technology was used by the students. In a classroom with two or three expensive and powerful computers, students typically compose with pen and paper and then use a computer to input, format, and print their final drafts. In the Forest Park classrooms, each student had a SmartBoard on his or her desk. Students sometimes composed free-written reflections, first-draft responses, or journal entries. Instead of using the computer to print out the finished product, students used the SmartBoards to record their thoughts and reflections in a way that they had not in the past. Access to low-cost word-processors thus engaged students in writing in ways that pen and paper had not. During the project only one student among the one hundred sixty student-participants preferred pen and paper to the SmartBoard.

Furthermore, as one teacher observed, the apparent limitations of the Smart-Boards were in some ways an advantage: their lack of sophisticated bells and whistles forced students to concentrate on composing, focusing on content, rather than format. Many of the teachers noticed that some students became distracted on more powerful, high-tech computers, playing with fonts, graphics, and formatting before they had composed and revised their early drafts. With the SmartBoards, composing was foregrounded because sophisticated formatting was not possible.

Teacher-participants also found that the cross-disciplinary use of the Smart-Boards fostered important synergies. Because students had access to the Smart-Boards in all their courses, they did not need to be trained to use different technology in each class. Teachers could thus plan to use the SmartBoards with confidence. Likewise, students, knowing that they had access to the Smart-Boards in all their classes, began to see writing, particularly writing with computers, as an important interdisciplinary activity. As students invented ways of using the technology to facilitate their own learning, teachers, meeting regularly to discuss their work, could pass along to one another the new ways technology helped support the writing-as-learning program.

There were some negative dimensions to such use of technology. For example, teachers reported bottlenecks when printing became necessary. Yet the teachers and students worked to mitigate these, coming to school early and using the print stations before class, staying after school, or using the print stations during lunch. Together, students and teachers developed housekeeping systems for uploading writing onto the print stations and for printing out drafts. They also established a technology folder system in which each student had a folder, containing both paper and diskette, that traveled with them from class to class.

Overall, however, the benefits far outweighed the drawbacks. Teachers became less threatened by their students' expertise on computers. Some who had been reluctant to use existing computer labs in their schools came to delight in and fully exploit their students' technological backgrounds. Teachers created teams of students, each team having one designated *techie* as a leader. Responsibility for computer knowledge was thus decentralized; students and teachers together became learners, pooling and sharing their different expertise. We suspect that because the participating teachers came to value their students' knowledge of computers, they grew more willing to push even further their exploration of technology as a tool for teaching and learning. Students and teachers alike developed a deeper understanding of the potential value of technology for their teaching and learning. The teachers claim to look at their lesson plans differently now, seeing them as sites for the use of emerging technologies. Students look at writing differently, seeing it as an essential interdisciplinary activity that can be enabled and extended by emerging technologies.

The teachers were understandably frustrated at having to return the Smart-Boards and printing stations at the end of the year. Yet they are not complaining; they are acting, aggressively exploring other avenues for access to the technology they need. One teacher has already received a grant that will furnish her classroom with three computers in 1998. Others are generating proposals to purchase more technology for their classrooms. In the course of the project, teachers worked their way into a formerly closed lab, and it seems likely that their new approaches to access will continue in the future. It is clear to us, as observers and evaluators of the project, that these teachers are now powerful and already successful advocates for the effective integration of technology with their own curricula.

Lending Project

The Lending Project moved even further toward teacher autonomy. While in the Writing for Publication Seminar we required a finished project and in the Forest Park Project we required research, in the Lending Project we simply created a pool of eight SmartBoards that alumnae of the Writing for Publication project could sign out for a limited time. Unlike the first two projects, the Lending Project gave participating teachers no paid planning or preparation time and no substantial technical support. We were testing the hypothesis that given their initial training in the Writing for Publication Seminar, the teachers would themselves find exceptionally creative uses for admittedly low-tech equipment.

One teacher used the SmartBoards for a community service learning project at a local nursing home, in which students used the boards to transcribe interviews. Another teacher used the SmartBoards in conjunction with a parent-teacher group to generate promotional brochures and pamphlets celebrating black history month. Another teacher borrowed the SmartBoards to support a pen-pal partnership between ninth and second graders in separate district schools. The SmartBoards have also been lent out for record keeping and grant writing. We conclude from the Lending Project that staff-development programs such as the Writing for Publication project can have long-term effects if followed up by additional opportunities to build on earlier experiences.

Train the Trainers: Technology Share Fair

Based on the success of the Writing for Publication Seminar, the Western Massachusetts Writing Project and the Springfield Public Schools applied to the Massachusetts Department of Education for funds to support a "Train the Trainers" program, one designed to disseminate the Writing for Publication Seminar throughout the state as an exemplary staff-development program. Funding was granted, and the Train the Trainers program became a reality. We chose as participants eighteen teachers from the Writing for Publication project. The work began in April 1996 and was completed in June.

The Train the Trainers project was much like the Writing for Publication project in that the participants had a task to accomplish: in this case, the development of in-service workshops for teachers in Springfield and other western Massachusetts schools. As in the Writing for Publication project, the grant included funds for release, so that teachers could work to develop their projects alone or in teams and share their work with others. The grant also included funds for minimal technology: eighteen SmartBoards, one for each participant. The ratio of money spent on time to monies spent on equipment was 4 to 1, slightly lower than the first three projects but still substantially weighted in favor of investing in teacher training.

In the workshop sessions, the teachers were challenged to reexamine, revise, and refine the projects they had developed for the Writing for Publication program, using them as the basis for a formal presentation that they would shape into a ninety-minute in-service workshop. This time the SmartBoards were used exclusively for creating handouts and overheads for the workshops they were shaping. None of the participating teachers owned a laptop; one teacher-participant said as she received her SmartBoard, "Great! Now I can work all the time!"

At the end of this program the eighteen teachers presented their workshops in abbreviated form at a "Technology Share Fair" that was attended by teachers and administrators from other area school districts. Each teacher had twenty minutes to demonstrate what he or she had prepared, using handouts and overheads composed on the SmartBoards and formatted on more sophisticated computers. The teachers used scanned-in pictures, clip-art graphics, and graphics of their own design in extremely professional presentations. These teachers, most of whom had used technology sparingly before their work with us, were now the creators and originators of spin-off projects integrating technology with curriculum. They are now being invited to conduct technology workshops across western Massachusetts.

Lessons Learned

The staff-development programs described above have, in different degrees and ways, accomplished two related goals: the integration of technology into the curriculum and the increase of teachers' and students' access to technology. The teachers have become agents in this integration, not simply victims left to cope with the fallout from the introduction of computers into their classrooms. Other projects in the same school system involved placing computers in classrooms and labs, often through corporate sponsorship, without project-based training programs such as ours, apparently in the hope that if the equipment were available, teachers would automatically use it. The results of these types of projects have been universally unsatisfactory: equipment-rich classrooms in which the technology was not integrated with the teachers' and students' needs and where, in some cases, the equipment was not used at all.

Training-oriented projects such as ours have also clearly helped teachers become powerful advocates for the installation of technology in their schools and classrooms. For example, during the Writing for Publication program, one teacher brought her home computer to school so that she could help her students more effectively complete a number of projects. The teacher reported this to the principal and reminded him often that her home computer could do things that the computer she had at school could not. She noted that after a while the principal began to feel ashamed; the result: the school is buying her a more powerful computer for her classroom. Other teachers in our project requested SmartBoards for their own use, and administration has responded by ordering one hundred of them for a lending-program modeled on the one we completed. In both of these cases, teachers approached administrators with particular projects that required specific technology. Such requests seem to be powerful, much more powerful than the abstract complaint that without technology the students will fall behind.

We believe that some principles can be distilled from our experience and used to guide other educational institutions as they confront rapid technological change.

First, we focused on teachers and not on hardware. Our projects, with the exception of the Lending Project, principally bought time for teachers to work together to plan and to reflect. The ratio of funds expended on release time to equipment was 5 to 1 in three of the projects and 4 to 1 in the fourth (in fact, we believe that practically any school system could fund similar projects through staff-development and equipment budgets). The lesson: Teachers are the most effective agents of change.

A second lesson is that successful introduction of technology into a curriculum is best done not in the abstract (e.g., a workshop on *Excel* or *Claris Works*) but in the context of a particular project, ideally one that can be published to an audience beyond an individual, isolated classroom. A third lesson is that relatively inexpensive, low-end technology may be a good place to begin. From an institutional perspective, buying enough up-to-date PCs and printers for all users is often simply not possible; even if it were, schools cannot typically afford to replace equipment every four years or so. Beginning with low-end technology may also be best in terms of staff development. It is much less time-consuming and expensive to train teachers to use SmartBoards as compared to full-fledged personal computers. SmartBoards provide a transition to more complex machines, permitting teachers to develop their skills gradually instead of facing a steep learning curve. Much of the activity of writing simply does not require high-end technology. It thus seems that much of the activity of writing, and perhaps of other activities as well, can be accomplished using low-end, inexpensive, specialized technology.

Much has been written about how technology will revolutionize education. Our experience suggests that technology will indeed revolutionize education but that the principal agents of change will and should be teachers, as long as they are given effective programs for development and support. Such programs help teachers increase access to technology, both for themselves and their students.

Works Cited

Bolter, Jay D. *Writing Space: The Computer, Hypertext, and the History of Writing.* Hillsdale, NJ: Erlbaum, 1991.

Hawisher, Gail E., and Cynthia L. Selfe. "The Rhetoric of Technology and the Electronic Writing Class." *College Composition and Communication* 42 (1991):55–65.

Landow, George. *Hypertext: The Convergence of Contemporary Critical Theory and Technology.* Baltimore: Johns Hopkins University Press, 1992.

Lanham, Richard. *The Electronic Word: Democracy, Technology, and the Arts.* Chicago: University of Chicago Press, 1993.

Moran, Charles. "Computers and the Writing Classroom: A Look to the Future." In *Re-Imagining Computers and Composition.* Ed. Gail E. Hawisher and Paul LeBlanc. Portsmouth, NH: Boynton/Cook-Heinemann, 1992. 7–23.

Ohmann, Richard. "Literacy, Technology, and Monopoly Capital." *College English* 47 (1985):675–89.

Olson, C. Paul. "Who Computes?" *Critical Pedagogy and Cultural Power.* Ed. David W. Livingstone and contributors. Granby, MA: Bergin and Garvey, 1987. 179–204.

Schwartz, Helen J. "Ethical Considerations of Educational Computer Use." In *Computers and Writing: Theory, Research, Practice.* Ed. Deborah H. Holdstein and Cynthia L. Selfe. New York: MLA, 1990. 18–30.

Tiffin, John. "Telecommunications and the Trade in Teaching." *Education and Training Technology International* 27, no. 3 (1990): 240–44.

Tuman, Myron C., ed. *Literacy Online: The Promise (and Peril) of Reading and Writing With Computers.* Pittsburgh: University of Pittsburgh Press, 1992.

Contributors

Don Byrd
State University of New York–Albany

William A. Covino
Florida Atlantic University

Terry Craig
West Virginia Northern Community College

Lester Faigley
University of Texas at Austin

Patricia Fitzsimmons-Hunter
Massachusetts Public Schools and University of Massachusetts–Amherst

Leslie D. Harris
State University of New York–Plattsburgh

Cynthia Haynes
University of Texas at Dallas

Johndan Johnson-Eilola
Purdue University

Beth Kolko
University of Texas at Arlington

Tim Mayers
University of Rhode Island

Derek Owens
St. John's University

Raul Sanchez
University of Utah

Robert Smith
Knox College, Galesburg, Illinois

Kevin R. Swafford
James Madison University

Todd Taylor
University of North Carolina–Chapel Hill

Gregory L. Ulmer
University of Florida

Irene Ward
Kansas State University

Index

TIME   : Mon Apr 07 2003 08:09AM

TERMINAL : 300

TITLE   : Literacy theory in the age of the Internet / edited by Todd Taylo

CALL NUMBER : LC 149.5 .L49 1998 clgii

BARCODE : 3983500581813

STATUS   : IN TRANSIT

PICKUP AT : SLCC-FP Circulation Desk

Received. Item has hold to be picked up at SLCC-FP Circulation Desk

When it arrives at SLCC-FP Circulation Desk, please check-in item to activate hold.